Co-Designing Economies in Transition

Vincenzo Mario Bruno Giorgino
Zack Walsh
Editors

Co-Designing Economies in Transition

Radical Approaches in Dialogue with Contemplative Social Sciences

palgrave
macmillan

Editors
Vincenzo Mario Bruno Giorgino
Department of Economic and Social Sciences
University of Turin
Turin, Italy

Zack Walsh
Claremont School of Theology
Claremont, CA, USA

ISBN 978-3-319-66591-7 ISBN 978-3-319-66592-4 (eBook)
https://doi.org/10.1007/978-3-319-66592-4

Library of Congress Control Number: 2017963222

Cover illustration: Romas_ph / Alamy Stock Photo

Printed on acid-free paper

This Palgrave Macmillan imprint is published by Springer Nature
The registered company is Springer International Publishing AG
The registered company address is: Gewerbestrasse 11, 6330 Cham, Switzerland

Foreword

Environmentally, time is running out for the world as we know it. As we find ourselves in what Paul Crutzen termed the Anthropocene epoch, the earth could be up to seven degrees hotter by the end of the century. But perhaps a name even more apt for our epoch is what in this volume Zack Walsh refers to in his chapter as the Capitalocene, for much of what is currently disruptive environmentally can be traced to the normal functioning of the now worldwide capitalist economic system. From externalized costs to air and water quality that result from ever fiercer capitalist competition to the proliferation of ever more commodities to satisfy a culture of consumption, the capitalist system has become as out of control as, per *The Communist Manifesto*, the conjurings of the sorcerer's apprentice.

Even apart from the environment, things are not well. World capitalism struggles, both north and south, to generate the number of good jobs that could accord everyone a middle-class income. With the newest advances in artificial intelligence, automation will make good job generation even more difficult. And as things stand, the world's richest eight people now enjoy the same wealth as the world's poorest 50%, with executives—at least in the USA—making now hundreds of times the income of average workers.

The effects go beyond the economic to the political and spiritual. Often the jobs that are produced are alienating, done exclusively for extrinsic reward rather than for intrinsic fulfillment. As in a game of musical chairs, each job-holder comes to be in permanent competition with many other job-seekers, making job insecurity an ever-present anxiety. It is hardly surprising therefore that among the economically insecure, suspicions arise across ethnic divides over any special treatments, regardless of the previous disadvantages for which those treatments are supposed to compensate. It is unsurprising as well that those economically insecure would begrudge immigrants and even refugees, whom they judge as threats. Thus, even professed religious values are displaced by perceived threats to economic interests.

In such milieu, it is also unsurprising to find parents regarding higher education principally as a way to enhance their children's employability. While in a market economy self-marketability is an ever-necessary concern that certainly needs to be addressed, too often the students too, sometimes grudgingly but more often with enthusiasm, come to regard their entire being as commodities to be bought and sold on the market, eschewing therefore coursework in the arts or humanities that will not somehow eventuate in cash. The students forget—and are encouraged to forget—to feed also their souls as well as their future coffers. They forget and are encouraged to forget that we are meant to be more than just factory products and our education more than just cultural capital inputs to our employability. We are also called and need to learn how to be good citizens, not just of our own countries but of the world. And beyond good citizens, good people. But our institutions of higher learning, themselves increasingly under competitive pressure, increasingly regarding their students as customers, are themselves losing devotion to their greater call.

If ever there were a time calling for good citizenship and good personhood, it is now. Across Europe and the USA, we witness the rise of a mean-spirited—and in the USA certainly a vulgar—populism, motored by resentment, fear and disrespect. Before now it would have been hard to imagine a movement and a presidency that was intent on building a literal wall across a national border to keep neighbors out. It is a movement, unfortunately, that begets its opposing mirror image: a corresponding resentment, a corresponding fear and a corresponding contempt. The resulting polarization, perhaps most acute in the USA but apparent elsewhere as well is something from which we all need redress.

Especially in the USA, which paradoxically presents itself as the bastion of democracy, economic inequality distorts both the political process and national cultural consciousness. Against the specter of big money that always threatens to run more conservative candidates against them, US Republican Congress people have been pulled so far to the right that they fear even to acknowledge the human contribution to climate change. It is an alienation as it were from the world and from truth, and it legitimates and encourages similar alienation culturally. Republican constituencies, looking to their leaders, find legitimacy for untenably extreme views. To win votes, even the oppositional Democratic party is likewise obliged to concede ground to politically induced idiocy and move rightward itself. Thus, the land most committed to the freedom of free enterprise must also struggle to find cultural support for the universal health care that is taken for granted in most other advanced industrial societies.

Suffice it to say that the night is dark and we are far from home. And the social sciences have not always been guiding stars. As professions, economics and political science have often served instead to justify the current world order. Just think, as mentioned in this book, of the *homo economicus* that dominates professional economics, a model of the human actor as what philosopher Harry Frankfurt once termed a *wanton*, that is, a creature who can only want without moral reflection or prioritization among felt wants. Sociology often has been more critical, but with the exception of anthropology, the whole of the social sciences have generally been tied to a positivist philosophy of science that holds, among other things, to a rigid split between facts and values. The social sciences have accordingly been ambivalent about addressing moral facts that carry an ineluctable value component.

Even more have the social sciences been at pains to distance themselves from anything that smacks of spirituality. Understood perhaps as personal religion sans the organization, even spirituality can seem too otherworldly to fall under the examination of empirical social science. That sentiment too is a legacy of positivism, which sees values as purely subjective rather than anything objective and all matters of an ontological nature as meaningless metaphysics.

But if the social sciences refuse to move from facts to values or toward addressing ontology, then they cannot address, as the chapters in this book do, what the title of Margunn Bjornholt's chapter explicitly refers to as "what really matters". What matters is clearly a question of values, but if we ask what as a matter of fact does happen to matter to people, our question remains entirely empirical, entirely factual, and not particularly evaluative in itself. Conventional sociology thus has no problem with such questions. In different ways, it asks them all the time.

But if we ask what should matter or what matters ultimately, then we are no longer asking empirically what others think matters but as analysts making value judgments ourselves about what ought to matter. It is here that positivistically inclined social sciences would demur, denying that what should matter is a properly scientific question.

Positivistic social sciences are certainly correct that what ought to matter is not strictly or at least not entirely an empirical question. It is a question about values. But the collapse of the fact/value distinction goes both ways. In other words, just as many facts are theory and value laden, so are values theory and fact laden.

The theory- and fact-laden nature of values is what distinguishes values from brute tastes, like a preference for vanilla over chocolate, about which there is nothing to argue. In contrast, when it comes to values, there is much over which we can argue. One once common argument, for example, to value capitalism over socialism was that capitalism aligns better with human nature, held to be selfish, aggressive and greedy. That capitalism does align better with human nature is a theory and whether human nature is as described is a matter of fact to be determined empirically. Were humans shown to be more altruistic and social in nature, that determination would undermine at least this particular rationale for valuing capitalism over socialism and hence call the value itself into rational question.

An evaluative preference for capitalism over socialism could be saved by alternate reasoning, but that is the very point here. The point is that unlike brute tastes, rationally held values depend on some sort of rational reasoning that is in part theoretical and factual. Thus, arguments about theories and facts should affect the values we hold and, if we operate in good faith, lead us to values that are more rationally tenable.

Not to entertain such value-laden questions is to leave important areas of our social life unaddressed. In fact, it is to leave unaddressed what really matters or most matters.

When we ask specifically about what most matters, we are driven to fundamental ontology. Who are we and what are we about? What is most conducive to our collective flourishing?

These questions have a spiritual dimension but they are accessible to reason. Even Karl Marx, the historical materialist, trod in this direction when he spoke of species being. And, indeed, it would be difficult for Marx to speak of alienation without any specification of that which we are alienated from.

The contemplative traditions are likewise a call in this direction, an inspiration to be mindful of who we really are and are meant to be. It is especially welcome therefore to have a book such as this that seeks to reimagine a new economics from a mindful, contemplative perspective. Not only transdisciplinary, the volume is also transnational in character. With both theoretical expositions and practical exemplars of alternative economic forms, the book offers an important opportunity to think through our way ahead.

Doug Porpora

Foreword: Toward Contemplative Social Science

The current crisis in the economy could teach us to look beyond material value and unrealistic expectations of limitless growth. When things go seriously wrong such as in the financial crisis, it is often because a new reality is still being viewed with outdated concepts, and this is certainly also the case in the domain of the economy today. (The Dalai Lama)

As this quote, expressed by the Dalai Lama in 2009 after the eruption of the financial crises (Tideman, 2016), indicates, the changing economic reality calls for a fundamentally different way of thinking and seeing. Philosopher Thomas Kuhn (1962) defined this as a shift in paradigm, meaning a fundamental change in the mode of perception, frames of reference and underlying beliefs and assumptions. French novelist Marcel Proust (1923) described this shift in vivid terms: "The real act of discovery consists not in finding new land but in seeing with new eyes".

The current book testifies that an increasing number of scholars recognize the need for such shift in perspective. They seem to agree with my view that the economic crisis has been created (and persists), because our political and economic leadership employs flawed and increasingly outdated frames of reference, based on limited assumptions about the current economic reality and the multifaceted drivers of human behavior.

These assumptions of classical economics were mainly derived from Newtonian physics and Darwinian biology. In this worldview, the economy and environment are seen as separate spheres of life, and humans—the 'fittest' among competing species—are supposed to hold dominion over all natural (and human) resources. This privileged role gives humans the power to extract value from all resources, against as low as possible cost, and utilize it for our human agendas (or, for that matter, to liquidate it to maximize GDP or quarterly profit margins). In this worldview, individuals and companies regard themselves as autonomous, individual agents who make their own rational choices—the image of *homo clausus* or *homo economicus*—in a relatively static and predictable context. Economist Milton Friedman (1970) expressed this worldview in the business context in a famous quote: "the only business of business is business".

This way of thinking was the cornerstone of the industrial age when both natural and human resources seemed abundant and inexpensive. Its underlying worldview, however, is no longer fit for purpose. In fact, this rather simplistic ideology of economic activity is increasingly recognized as the prime driver behind the emerging "tragedy of the commons", in which producers, consumers and financiers hold each other in a "prisoners' dilemma": a race to the bottom of over-production/consumption/borrowing and consequential ecological overshoot and social inequality. Given the fact that we have finite common resources for a rapidly growing population, by continuing to focus primarily on our own short-term business interests, we collectively end up as losers.

Fortunately, thanks to discoveries in many scientific disciplines, most notably in social psychology and neuroscience, there is a new worldview emerging that is more suitable to the modern context. It is a view in which people, business, economy, environment and society are no longer separate worlds that meet tangentially, but are deeply interconnected and mutually interdependent. This matches with the view of sociologist Norbert Elias (2000) who said that humanity should see itself as *homines aperti*, in which people are in open connection with each other and their environment, being formed by and dependent on others and nature.

For example, Daniel Kahneman (1979), who received the 2003 Nobel Prize in Economics for his studies on intuitive judgment and decision-making, has explored the intersection of neuro-science, psychology and real economic behavior. The significance of this work lies in its ability—for the first time in the history of economics—to describe the neurobiological basis of economic behavior. This work is bridging the heretofore distinct disciplines of psychology and economics.

These insights are revelatory because they provide empirical evidence derived from a physical-biological basis for the notion that human nature is *not* driven by greed, materialism, extrinsic motivation and egoism alone; at least equally important are pro-social motives, such as inclination to cooperation, moral fairness, altruism and psychological well-being. This not only uproots the classical model of *homo economicus* but also challenges the deep-felt belief that only external gratification through money and consumption can meet our needs.

The financial crisis that erupted in 2008 and the increasing impact of social technology has made it clear that this interconnected worldview is not merely academic: it best describes the reality of global society, business and finance, which functions as a tightly interwoven web of human relationships and interaction. This web extends into our global climate and ecosystems, which has been recently recognized by the global community as evidenced by UN Global Sustainable Development Goals. They are built on the scientifically determined notion that in order for our economies to function and societies to survive, we need to respect planetary boundaries and ecological laws (Rockstrom et al., 2009). In the new reality "business as usual" or "politics as usual" is no longer an option from a long-term survival viewpoint. Indeed, leading companies have recognized the new reality—which is generally labeled as "sustainability"—as the next business "Megatrend", just like IT, Globalization and the Internet did earlier, determining their long-term viability. Or in the words of management scholar, Frank Horwitz (2010): "The only business of business is *sustainable business*".

The shift toward sustainability implies a departure from the simplistic three-pronged production-consumption financing model in which money is abundantly made available by banks, to a more holistic and realistic life-based model in which constraints in financial, natural and ecological resources are recognized as natural and consumers are recognized as real people. It is a shift from the speculative debt/growth economy to the real economy, not only in a macroeconomic sense but also in terms of understanding the *real* drivers of economical value and sustainable performance.

Matching real needs and resources entails a focus on *the way we think* and *relate to each other*. Given the central role of human thinking and interacting in the new economic paradigm, we should shift our perception of markets as anonymous transactional trading places to a community operating in an interdependent economical and ecological context. The members of the community are all interrelated stakeholders who are engaged in a continuous complex inter-dependent process of co-creation of value, while fulfilling needs, both short and long term. These needs go beyond merely material economic needs, but also include emotional, social and ecological needs. Therefore, the rules of the new economic game should no longer be to maximize return on invested capital, but to create optimum resilience of the system by enhancing well-being, shared value creation and performance of all participants within the system. This presents a major shift in economic thinking indeed!

The leading management thinker Gary Hamel (2007) described this shift as follows:

> The biggest barrier to the transformation of capitalism cannot be found within the observable realm of org charts, strategic plans and quarterly reports, but rather *within the human mind itself* [.....]. The true enemy of our times is a matrix of deeply held beliefs about what business [and economics] is actually for, who it serves and how it creates value.

The reinstatement of the mind as a prime driver in economic value creation and the revolutionary insights into the mind's pro-social nature are giving rise to a new economic science. It is here that one can find the exciting intersection with *contemplative science*. This field, first postulated by Francesco Varela (1992), gained popularity through the research conducted by medical researcher Jon Kabat-Zinn (1990) whose program called Mindfulness Based Stress Reduction (MBSR) turned out to diminish the suffering experienced by people with chronic pain, and neuroscientist Richard Davidson, who has shown that contemplative practices such as meditation and other forms of mind-training, can be observed in measurable change patterns in the brain (Davidson & Begley, 2012). Since then, multiple research studies have shown that this process of contemplation results in positive effects on one's mental and physical health and well-being. Most interesting is the fact that, when these practices are complemented with other educational methods, they become more than tools for people's sense of well-being: they help people to expand their awareness of one self and one's environment—in other words, they expand our frames of reference. MIT researcher Otto Scharmer (2013) describes this shift as a transition from ego-system consciousness to eco-system consciousness.

Continued research in this field shows that contemplation is not merely an internally oriented process: it is both embodied and interpersonal, which means that it is shared in and through relationships and with the world (Siegel, 2016). The process of contemplation, over time, is set to evoke the discovery of one's natural interconnectedness with the world around oneself. Such recognition will inevitably lead to a shift in the perception of one's role in the world, ultimately to the point of recognizing one's interdependence with the world around oneself, which typically results in an adjusted sense of purpose. At that point, one can no longer see oneself as a disconnected isolated *homo economicus*, but rather as a full co-creative member of the human family and the sacred natural world.

While this mind-state has been recognized as a possibility for individuals, the question is if it can be applied to the field of economic policy. For example, when people become overly greedy/fearful when confronted by the ups and downs of markets, can policies be envisioned that help people to make more balanced choices by not giving in to the 'primal' fight-flight-freeze response? Can governments design economic policies that discourage mindless consumption, and instead empower consumers to make sustainable purchasing choices? Currently, many policies achieve the opposite: they reinforce a vicious cycle of desire and fear, with countless negative impacts on nature and society.

Thus, the crucial question is as follows: Can the groundbreaking insights of the emerging contemplative science be translated to the level of policy making? Can we learn to develop policies that help people to transform negative mental states into constructive and compassionate action, replacing negative economic incentives into more positive ones that stimulate sustainable economic behavior of individuals *and* institutions? These are excellent questions to ask in this new field of science, which we can call *contemplative social science.*

In conclusion, while there are many initiatives addressing the crisis in capitalism directed at changing political-economic systems from the 'outside'—such as ecological footprint reduction, the circular economy, green product innovation, sustainable investing, new governance and accounting systems—this book makes the argument that equally important is changing the 'inside' realm of the mind-sets and worldviews underlying the outer economic systems. Contemplative science has ascertained that these mind-sets can be developed through education and mind training (they are available to us because they are integral to our human nature). This argument is not just theoretical: it may be the most important work that we need to do in order to sustain human life on this planet. *Contemplative social science* can now take this further by exploring how to develop the mind-sets, beliefs, assumptions and mental models that can help us create sustainable economic systems that are in line with actual human nature and respect planetary boundaries.

Winterhur, Switzerland Sander Tideman

Bibliography

Davidson, R. J., & Begley, S. (2012). *The emotional life of the brain, how its unique patterns affect the way you think, feel, and live-and how you can change.* New York, NY: Hudson Street Press.

Elias, N. (2000). *The civilizing process. Sociogenetic and psychogenetic investigations.* Oxford, UK: Basil Blackwell.

Friedman, M. (1970, September 13). The social responsibility of business is to increase its profits. *New York Times*, p. SM17.

Hamel, G., & Breen, B. (2007). *The future of management.* Cambridge, MA: Harvard Business School Publishing.

Horwitz, F. M., & Grayson, D. (2010). Putting sustainability into practice in a business school. *Global Focus, 4*(2), 26–29.

Kabat-Zinn, J. (1990). *Full catastrophe living: Using the wisdom of your body and mind to face stress, pain, and illness.* New York, NY: Bantam Books.

Kahneman, D. (1979). Prospect theory: An analysis of decision under risk. *Econometrica, 47*, 263–291.
Kuhn, T. S. (1962). *The structure of scientific revolutions*. Chicago: University of Chicago Press.
Proust's. (1923). *Remembrance of things past* (Vol. 5—The Prisoner—Originally published in French, C. K. Moncrief, Trans.).
Rockström, J., et al. (2009, September 24). A safe operating space for humanity. *Nature, 461*, 472–475.
Sharmer, C. O. (2013). *Leading from the emerging future: From ego-system to eco-system economies*. San Francisco, CA: Berrett-Koehler.
Siegel, D. (2017). *Mind: A journey to the heart of being human*. New York: WW Norton & Company.
Tideman, S. G. (2016). *Business as instrument for societal change—In conversation with the Dalai Lama*. Sheffied, UK: Greenleaf Publishing.
UN Sustainable Development Goals. Retrieved from https://sustainabledevelopment.un.org
Varela, F., Thompson, E. T., & Rosch, E. (1992). *The embodied mind: Cognitive science and human experience*. Boston, MA: MIT Press.

Contents

List of Figures

List of Tables

1

Introduction

Vincenzo Mario Bruno Giorgino and Zack Walsh

Life as we know it is changing rapidly and dramatically. We have entered what scientists now call the Anthropocene—a new geological epoch underscored by large-scale social and ecological changes. The truth is humanity has become a geophysical force—one whose actions profoundly shape Earth systems and increasingly determine the conditions of life for its many inhabitants. By 2050, for example, the UNDP and the International Organization for Migration say there will be an exodus of about 250 million people due to drought (Brown, 2007; Pinto-Dobernig, 2008). It is high time we asked how we will meet the great challenges of the twenty-first century, including climate change, technological unemployment, and widening social inequalities.

V.M.B. Giorgino (✉)
Department of Economic and Social Sciences, Mathematics and Statistics, University of Torino, Torino, Italy

Z. Walsh
Institute for the Postmodern Development of China, Claremont, CA, USA

Toward Ecological Civilization (EcoCiv), Claremont, CA, USA

Institute for Advanced Sustainability Studies, Potsdam, Germany

V.M.B. Giorgino, Z. Walsh (eds.), *Co-Designing Economies in Transition*,
https://doi.org/10.1007/978-3-319-66592-4_1

Some have suggested that we can make a Great Transition to a socially just and sustainable future. But fundamentally, this would require a cultural transition aligned with a new economic system. All of us can easily recognize that the continuous changes we deal with exert an enormous pressure on us, our relationships, and our existing institutions. Few of these changes do not affect our economic interactions. By overcoming the presumed independence and a-historicity of economics, we may more accurately understand economic interactions in relation to society and as part of a broader set of human interactions. Most scholars agree that we are embedded in various systems of economic relationships, some of which are market-based, state-based, voluntary or non-profit-based, and household-based. What needs to be better understood, however, is the quality of these relationships—the texture of the different binds that they create. This is why sociologist Viviana Zelizer (2012) prefers to define the economy as *relational work*.

It is difficult to understand the immense challenges of our everyday lives in such exciting and complicated times, since the changes we experience often appear new, confusing, and incapable of being easily encapsulated in established conceptual frameworks. The anxiety to classify our experiences under a known umbrella is quite strong, motivated especially by academics' never-ending battles for theoretical dominance, rather than their desire to transcend paradigms. As a result, there is a clear cultural need to develop tools and methods able to reduce our strong tendency toward divided thinking. When we attempt to go beyond the principles and values of our field and observe processes as they appear, then new interactional patterns will likely emerge. This, however, requires a return to the basics—a return to the elementary condition of our humanity, considering all our relationships, so that no one and nothing is left out for lack of attention or empathy.

Contemplative social sciences place these processes at the core of their inquiry. Their specific contribution is to help us become aware of our pre-judgments and find a way to a more open-minded approach to understanding very different phenomena within a participatory, but not pre-classificatory, scheme. They establish wise and pragmatic methodologies to develop and nurture fresh approaches to social interactions. At the core, they are based on systematic efforts to integrate the wisdom traditions with the social sciences. This implies that the understanding of contemplative knowledge transcends the religious contexts in which they are typically born and cultivated. It also means that we are taking the first steps in uncharted territory, in which wisdom traditions and social sciences are invited to dismiss their respective dogmas and be open to unexpected solutions. Approximately 50 years ago, Michael Polanyi (2015) wrote that the production of knowledge is a personal enterprise that is neither subjective nor objective; rather, it is a personal commitment characterized by *dwelling in*.

John Dewey said rationality and reflective thought does not ground us (D'Agnese, 2016). Rather, we are all groundless, situated knowers. Our personhood and our capacity for knowledge are both processes. We are all events. With this understanding, we may use embodied, embedded, extended, and enactive (4E) approaches to cognition to provide us new ways of understanding how minds and bodies are co-produced in interaction with environments (Hutchins, 2010; Thompson, 2007). These innovative approaches help researchers better understand the role of cognition in social and ecological systems, affording them new ways to more consciously and sustainably design structures and systems to support ethical values. This can help us not only become aware of people's subjective (cognitive and affective) processes, but also become aware of the social and ecological conditions underlying our existence and the possibilities for transforming perception and behavior "intra-actively" with material transformations (Barad, 2007).

This book creates dialogue between radical knowledge-practices and contemplative social science to create these connections more clearly. It seeks to transgress disciplinary boundaries, imagine, and implement new visions of reality—in short, to co-design economies in transition. What that specifically entails varies dramatically depending on a variety of factors, including one's scope of interests, expertise, and social and geographical location. The chapters in this volume thus do not all agree with one another, nor should they. Showcasing their differences is productive of grasping the interconnections between fields and disciplines, and including such difference is part of the task of mapping the Great Transition. In this sense, this book is more akin to a proposition, than a statement. Its chapters are intended to have an un-disciplining effect, decentering our habitual ways of thinking about challenges exclusively in terms of technical problems with technical solutions. They are intended instead to provoke thought and conceive possibilities, which exist but remain largely unseen. This is clearly tangible, for instance, if we pay attention to the newly distributed technologies and the efforts underway to implement a collaborative commons at the urban level. These changes are intended to forever modify our landscapes, and we can play a fundamental role in directing them toward collective well-being.

At the same time, despite such differences between its individual authors, this book presents a transdisciplinary vision pragmatically oriented toward social transformation, able to create islands of change chiefly concerned with disintermediate and dehierarchized social and economic ties. The languages and competencies of each author remain separate, but in our opinion, there is a thread that connects each of the following chapters. That thread is the awareness that we are entering an era characterized by new social and economic forms beyond our understanding.

Part I

In Part I, we examine the "Transdisciplinary Foundations for Contemporary Social and Economic Transformation." Vincenzo M. B. Giorgino leads off the discussion in the first part of Chap. 2 by specifically addressing the disruptive potential of distributed ledger technologies toward our social and economic relationships. Some of these technologies' possible architectures can enhance our lives, while others may cause many challenges and enact certain prejudices in their support of collective well-being. Along these lines, the tokenization of nonmaterial values is the most intriguing area for its unexplored potentialities. In the second part of his chapter, Giorgino maintains that it is important to pay attention to the forms of divisive thinking with which we interpret social relations and orient our social action so as to allow that kind of urban co-design that favors the joy of living and purposive action. He concludes, in the third part, by emphasizing the centrality of an enactive approach to ground our efforts.

Then in Chap. 3, Zack Walsh continues the discussion by mapping the conditions under which a socially just and sustainable global future could emerge from large-scale structural transformations to contemporary society. First, he considers how the global political economy is undergoing world-historical changes, in response to the pressures of mounting inequality, climate crisis, and the growing illegitimacy of neoliberal capitalism. Then, he examines how current political, economic, social, and technological changes could positively and negatively shape the construction of a new world system beyond capitalism. And, finally, he outlines possible avenues for exploring these world-historical changes by developing new fields of inquiry in the emerging transdisciplinary field of contemplative social sciences.

After the editor's introductory chapters, Ugo Mattei and Michel Bauwens propose values frameworks for commons-based economics. In Chap. 4, Ugo Mattei approaches the positivistic distinction between subjects and objects as derived from Cartesianism and as historically developed and currently applied in private law. From early modern times, the institution of property has been constructed as the relationship between a free subject and a legal "object." Progressively abstracting from primitive relationships of material possession, private law has served as the main pillar in the foundations of capitalist extraction within current financial forms. Rethinking property as "being in common," thus, constitutes the foundation of building a "generative" legal system.

In Chap. 5, Michel Bauwens offers an ethical evaluation of the emerging mode of commons-based peer production, and its associated governance and property regimes, in order to see how it stacks up as an implicit or explicit expression of a number of ethical values. In particular, he examines whether the peer to peer logic represents an opportunity for a more complete realization of the aims of the social doctrine of the Catholic Church, which shares the vision of the centrality of civil society, with the market and the state function having a service orientation toward civil society. He concludes that there is a correspondence between the two value systems.

Chapters 6 and 7 present two different perspectives on Buddhist economics. In Chap. 6, Laszlo Zsolnai argues that wisdom traditions of humankind require self-transcendence of the person to achieve a meaningful and ethical life. His chapter uses the example of Buddhism to show how "going beyond the self" can be realized in economic and social contexts. It is argued that Buddhist economics represents a strategy which helps Buddhist and non-Buddhist people alike to reduce the suffering of human and non-human beings by practicing non-violence, caring, and generosity.

Whereas Laszlo compares the major tenets of Buddhist and Western economics as two opposing frameworks, Julie Nelson argues in Chap. 7 that capitalism has no essential nature and that we should take a more pragmatic, less ideological approach to economics grounded in our own experience. Her agnostic view invites us to consider the adage "If you meet the Buddha kill him." Nelson challenges the reader to consider the question "What is a market?" as a koan—an invitation for investigation. Many advocates for social justice, including many followers of wisdom traditions, call for an economy that is defined in opposition to what is assumed to be the essence of our current economic system. Believing that current economies are based on competition and globalization, for example, critics claim that the alternative must be defined by cooperation and local initiatives. But are these beliefs correct? Opening up to a recognition of the interdependent co-arising of economic relations reveals new avenues for advocating social justice.

Chapters 8 and 9 both give overviews of feminist economics. Feminist economics broadly refers to the application of a feminist lens to both the discipline and subject of economics. It is explicitly interdisciplinary and encompasses debates about the narrow range of mainstream economic methods and researched areas, including questions on how economics values the reproductive sector and examinations of economic epistemology and methodology. In Chap. 8, Zofia Łapniewska provides a brief overview of how feminist economics critiques established theory, methodology, and policy approaches and how it aims to produce gender aware theory, especially in defining economic activity. She argues for a reality check on how people actually live their lives as relational, vulnerable, and interdependent beings and emphasizes the urgency of rethinking mainstream economic approaches.

Then, in Chap. 9, Margunn Bjørnholt delves deeper into the development of feminist economics. She offers a reflection on 25 years of feminist economics providing illustrative examples of how feminist academic critique, within and outside of academia, in combination with civil engagement, has evolved, promoting change toward better economics, better policies, and well-being for all. Mirroring the widening scope over time of feminist economics, Bjørnholt discusses the following: the exclusion of care and other life-sustaining, unpaid work from systems of national accounts and efforts to make them count; efforts to achieve gender justice through gender responsive budgeting; the effort to bring society's attention to the extent of domestic violence and its consequences; and understanding economics as social provisioning, which considers the responsibility to care for everything, including human rights and our shared living space (Earth), when assessing the consequences of macroeconomic policy.

Finally, Xabier Renteria-Uriarte concludes part I by outlining the foundations of contemplative economics. He examines the economy and economics from the perspective of contemplative knowledge. He argues that the economy is a manifestation of deep consciousness, and economic agents choose between alternatives by connecting or disconnecting their consciousness from it—that is, acting ignorantly as *homo economicus*, with more awareness as *homo socioeconomicus* and *eticoeconomicus*, or with full realization as *homo deepeconomicus*. Contemplation helps agents act according to *wu-wei*, *karmayogi*, and *appamada* actions, and in "flow" or "optimal experience"—states which cultivate absorption in tasks and remove the ego and its related rational cost–benefit analysis. This allows them to know the economy as it really is: a space of abundance without the illusion of scarcity, where self-realization, rewarding work, and constructive human relationships arise, accompanied by simplified consumption, equitable incomes, and stable prices.

Part II

In Part II, we examine "Collective Awareness, the Self, and Digital Technologies." The first three chapters focus on how the application of technology in cities and communities affects social and economic transformation. In Chap. 11, Igor Calzada illustrates that the same technical innovations developed in smart systems can be used to enhance democracy or technocracy. He examines the ways in which the hegemonic approach to the "smart city" is evolving into a new intervention category, called the "experimental city." While this evolution presents some innovations, mainly regarding how smart citizens will be increasingly considered more as decision makers than data providers, likewise, some underlying issues arise, concerning the hidden side and ethical implications of the techno-politics of data and the urban commons. These issues engage with multi-stakeholders, particularly with the specific Penta Helix framework that brings together private sector, public sector, academia, civic society, and entrepreneurs. These innovations in urban life and its governance will inevitably bring us into debate about new potential models of business and society, concerning, for instance, the particular urban co-operative scheme employed.

Chapter 12 is coauthored by Alessia Calafiore, Alessio Antonini, Guido Boella, and Vincenzo M.B. Giorgino. It shows how social network and Web-sharing sites represent a novel and ever-growing source of information that usually contains geographical information. They first present FirstLife, which is a specific social platform that has been recently awarded a prize from the national-level competition in the "Smart Cities and Social Communities" context. FirstLife aims to foster co-production (in the sense articulated by Nobel Prize winner Elinor Ostrom) and Do It Yourself initiatives, providing a virtual place connected via maps to concrete reality. Thus, the platform by itself is intended to involve different actors in developing new services, from institutions to associations, from citizens to enterprises. In conclusion, the authors propose a set of methodologies to face such complexity in terms of data management, integration, and smart functionalities, as well as social innovations that develop soft skills and life skills in workshops designed to ground smart Information Communication Technologies (ICTs) on a wiser approach to human interactions with living beings and things.

Then, in Chap. 13, Panayotis Antoniadis describes the dual potential for corporate versus autonomous control in new ICT infrastructure. Popular Internet platforms that currently mediate our everyday communications become more and more efficient in managing vast amounts of information, rendering their users more and more addicted and dependent on them. Alternative, more organic options like community networks do exist and they can empower citizens to build their own local networks from the bottom-up. This chapter explores such technological options together with the adoption of a healthier Internet diet in the context of a wider vision of sustainable living in an energy-limited world.

The final two chapters articulate ethical and philosophical issues in the development of technology and digital devices in a post-human era. In Chap. 14, Philip Butler explores potential realities of technocratic automation at the intersection of criminal sentencing, artificial intelligence, and race. The chapter begins with a synopsis of the role automation plays in technocratic electronic governance. It then moves to demonstrate how the implementation of automation has adversely affected Black communities. Butler then illustrates how artificial intelligence is currently outpacing human performance, implying that soon, in the realm of criminal sentencing, artificially intelligent judges will emerge, outperforming and eventually replacing human judges. Next, he applies the lens of race to outline how current concepts of artificial cognitive architectures merely reiterate oppressive racial biases. The chapter concludes by imagining how contemplative overlays might be applied to artificial cognitive architectures to allow for more mindful and just sentencing.

Finally, in Chap. 15, David Casacuberta discusses the potential outcomes of designing technologies with respect to the mind–body relation. He argues that key functions of digital apps are based on the disembodied nature of our selves, which is not compatible with our human nature. The solution is not just to redesign those digital apps—a proposal that blindly accepts the premises of technological determinism—but to reconsider the whole concept of what it means to be human. He concludes by giving a brief sketch of the practical philosophy and metaphysics of the thirteenth-century Japanese philosopher Eihei Dōgen to present another view of what it means to be human, in order to conceptualize a reembodied self in the World Wide Web.

Taken as a whole, this book is a call for repurposing structures, technologies, and fragments, not of the past, but of possible futures—futures characterized by resiliency, hope, and flourishing. We think that the time is ripe for a systematic dialogue between the radical perspectives, which this book provides. Furthermore, we expect that this book will be a step forward in our understanding of social suffering and in our pursuit of individual and collective well-being. Alfred North Whitehead (1968) said the job of philosophy is "to maintain an active novelty of fundamental ideas illuminating the social system" (p. 174), and it is our hope that this book provides new ideas for envisioning a socially just and ecologically sustainable system. We hope you agree that the dialogue between a contemplative approach to social sciences and radical knowledge-practices has great potential, and we sincerely hope that the ideas we sketch may inspire a broader community of researchers to develop this field in a richer, more substantive way. Toward this end, we have created an online community as a home for continuing this work together, and we invite you to join us:

https://www.loomio.org/g/oVUOrcTq/contemplative-commons
http://wiseandsmartcities.eu/en/

References

Barad, K. (2007). *Meeting the universe halfway: Quakntum physics and the entanglement of matter and meaning*. Durham, NC: Duke University Press Books.

Brown, O. (2007). Climate change and forced migration: Observations, projections and implications. *Occasional Paper*, Human Development Report Office, UNDP, Geneva.

D'Agnese, V. (2016). Undergoing, mystery, and half-knowledge: John Dewey's disquieting side. *Studies in Philosophy and Education, 35*, 195–214.

Hutchins, E. (2010, October 1). Cognitive ecology. *Topics in Cognitive Science, 2*(4), 705–715. https://doi.org/10.1111/j.1756-8765.2010.01089

Pinto-Dobernig, I. (2008). *Migration and climate change*. Geneva: International Organization for Migration (IOM).

Polanyi, M. (2015). *Personal knowledge towards a post-critical philosophy*. Chicago, IL: University of Chicago Press. (Original publishing 1958).

Thompson, E. (2007). *Mind in life: Biology, phenomenology, and the sciences of mind*. Cambridge, MA: Harvard University Press.

Whitehead, A. N. (1968). *Modes of thought*. New York, NY: Simon and Schuster.

Zelizer, V. (2012). How I became a relational economic sociologist and what does that mean? *Politics & Society, 40*, 145–174.

Vincenzo Mario Bruno Giorgino (PhD in sociology) is an aggregate professor at the Department of Economic and Social Sciences, Mathematics and Statistics, University of Torino, Torino, Italy. Since 1998, he has been primarily devoted to the integration of contemplative knowledge and sociology in action-research and higher education, with a focus on transformative methodologies. In 2016, he co-edited with Valerie Malhotra Bentz the book *Contemplative Social Research: Caring for Self, Being, and Lifeworld* (Fielding University Press).

Zack Walsh (Claremont School of Theology, USA) is a research specialist at Toward Ecological Civilization, the Institute for the Postmodern Development of China, and the Institute for Advanced Sustainability Studies in Potsdam, Germany. His research is transdisciplinary, exploring process-relational, contemplative, and engaged Buddhist approaches to political economy, sustainability, and China.

Part I

Transdisciplinary Foundations for Contemporary Social and Economic Transformation

2

In Search of a New Compass in the *Great Transition*: Toward Co-designing the Urban Space We Care About

Vincenzo Mario Bruno Giorgino

Introduction

The increasing pervasiveness of digital networked society and the apparent state of economic, social and cultural impasse in which Western countries seem to be stranded raise increasing questions about the real possibilities of technologies to improve by themselves individual and collective lives, once it is agreed that *improvement* means not only a more rational use of resources, but also greater democratic participation in decisions that affect us. Some basic processes of technological innovation undermine the belief in a recovery of sustainable economic development as we knew it. On the contrary, an increasing number of separate data and events seem to fuel the belief that we are experiencing a *Great Transition* toward a social and economic configuration whose details are as yet unknown.

V.M.B. Giorgino (✉)
Department of Economic and Social Sciences, Mathematics and Statistics, University of Torino, Torino, Italy

V.M.B. Giorgino, Z. Walsh (eds.), *Co-Designing Economies in Transition*,
https://doi.org/10.1007/978-3-319-66592-4_2

Mainframe	PC	Internet	Social networks and Smart phones	Blockchain
70s	80s	90s	2000s	10s

Fig. 2.1 Major steps in technological change after World War II

There is a long list of social problems that are shaping the world we live in, such as climatic change, gender inequality, social injustice, forced migration, higher unemployment rates, job precariousness—many of which concern the authors in this volume. Though we each prioritize these problems differently, in my case, I choose to discuss a specific technology, called distributed ledger technologies, in terms of the role it plays in general and the disruptive reach it can have in the social and economic domain. I will use this chapter to support the conviction that it is credited as the next revolution after the Internet (Andreessen, 2014). Figure 2.1 recaps the major technological changes after World War II that gave rise to the so-called Network Society (Castells, 1996/2010; Swan, 2015), and if it is proved true, the blockchain will play a key role in shaping the previously mentioned social issues.

The Blockchains as a Challenge. What They Are and How They Work

Blockchains, also known as digital ledger technologies (DLTs), developed out of a long period of study in the field of cryptography in combination with peer-to-peer networks, distributed data storage and decentralized consensus mechanisms (Wright & De Filippi, 2015). They made their debut as the infrastructure on which the most famous cryptocurrency was created: the bitcoin (BTC). BTC's basic concept dates to the 1980s and was subsequently followed by contributions by Nick Szabo (in 1997 he published a paper on peer-to-peer transactions without an intermediate party as a trusted authority: Szabo, 1997) and Satoshi Nakamoto

(2008)—a pseudonym of the author of the paper on which BTC was born in 2009 (Dodd, 2014, pp. 362–365). The basic ideological underpinnings on which it is built value decentralization and pseudonymity in order to disintermediate transactions from the intervention of the state and market, as stated by its designer, Satoshi Nakamoto in 2008:

> A purely peer-to-peer version of electronic cash which would allow online payments to be sent directly from one party to another without going through a financial institution.
>
> A "database that is shared by all network nodes, updated by miners, monitored by everyone, and owned and controlled by no one".

It was championed by both free-market libertarians and anarchists. Public opinion associated BTC with the dark Internet and illegal markets, attributing to this cryptocurrency and to similar tools a label of high risk, despite the fact that the most important criminal events that have occurred, pertaining to the Silk Road (Bearman & Hanuka, 2015) and Mt. Gox (Mcmillan, 2014), are not linked to the DLT itself but to external elements (Maurer, 2017, p. 226).

A distributed ledger technology is a database that permits the tracking and recording of assets and transactions by storing a list of transactions without a central server acting as a central authority. A set of transactions are stored in a block, and each node (each computer in the network) has complete information about the block. All members of the network get access to information on all transactions ("public visibility but private inspection": Mougayar, 2015) and once entered, information can never be erased. In the case of the BTC blockchain, data validation of each block, or *proof of work*, is pursued through the attribution of a hash code.[1] This process requires an algorithm, which makes it expensive—in terms of required energy—to enable a node to add blocks. The hash of a block is stored in the next block, making it resistant to tampering. So far, each node independently validates the prior blocks, and before the block is added to the chain it is confirmed by a majority (51%) of nodes (Cognizant, 2017). The energy costs required of such a process create incentives. In the case of the BTC blockchain, validators are called *miners*, and they receive X BTCs as incentive for each set of transactions that is blocked in a node, which happens around every 10 minutes.[2] In the end, the proof of work (PoW) is a very expensive system that costs $600 M per year to manage (Mougayar, 2015). In general, it is fair to say that decentralization is not free—somebody has to pay for it.

"Competition between miners allows the creation of blocks of transactions and their validation is subsequently given by a mechanism of consensus… between nodes to get the incentive and distributed consensus to confirm the block. As competition is not on a fair ground, depending on the computational power available" (Dodd, 2015, 2017).[3] The reader can find at work here two principles, competition and consensus, which is clearly not what we intend by a democratic process.

This is how the permissionless or public blockchain works. The cryptographic proof algorithm varies by blockchain framework. In the case of a permissioned ledger under the control of a private or state agency, the rules of functioning could be simpler as vertical organization come to shape it (see Lewis, 2015a): control is in the hands of those with ownership according to a traditional vertical model, while the social innovation characterized by a peer-to-peer distributed network is lost.

The BTC blockchain is just one design possibility of a cryptocurrency. Some intentional features and some unexpected consequences of the BTC design, which include the unequal distribution of BTC, the possibility of hoarding and the creation of monopolist mining, have enhanced creativity in the field, generating multiple alternatives to develop, as the following examples will testify.

FreiCoin, linked to the Frei Foundation of the Occupy Wall Street movement, is designed to solve the hoarding problem with a demurrage impeding the accumulation of currency via the introduction of a $5 annual fee to promote currency circulation and encourage sustainable investments (Dodd, 2014: http://freico.in/).

Duniter is a coin based on a sort of rotation mechanism between members in writing the blockchain to ensure trust and lower energy costs with respect to the PoW. Moreover, since there is no provision of money as an incentive, subscribers won't be much interested in competing to write the next block (more details on https://duniter.org/en/theoretical/#a-free-economy).

FairCoin (König & Duran, 2016) has remarkable differences regarding mining and governance. The second version issued in 2016 is no longer based on mining and minting in order to avoid inequality and accumulation. It relies on proof of cooperation, which does not allow anyone to receive any reward for block creation. The concept at the basis of this cooperative effort by the anarchist Cooperativa Integral Catalana could be better grasped reading "Building a New Economy" (Cooperativa Integral Catalana, 2014). In terms of governance, FairCoin chain administrators execute decisions taken by the General Assembly, introducing in the process an element that their founders consider to be democratic, but which may be considered hierarchical from the perspective of a peer-to-peer model.

Ether is the cryptocurrency created by the Ethereum infrastructure—the platform enabling the most complex operations envisioned by Satoshi Nakamoto in his seminal 2008 paper. Ethereum is a "general purpose platform that can run any coin, script, or cryptocurrency project" (Swan, 2015). It is not a blockchain, as it can run all blockchains and protocols (for a short introduction, see also Lewis, 2015b). Ether is transacted using the *proof of stake*, which differentiates itself from the BTC blockchain PoW because it's less expensive ".... and minimizes or excludes the risk of forking[4]" (Swan, 2015).

Although the first wave of blockchain has been characterized by its link with the BTC, financial transactions are only one category of possible functions deployed by DLTs. Whatever the results achieved by the BTC, decentralization is a contemporary trend in every field of our society (Mougayar, 2015, p. 2). In spite of the incoherence between the ideals of equality and the real processes implemented, which critics underline (see Dodd, 2014), as we have briefly seen in the case of cryptocurrencies, there also exists incessant experimentation. Mougayar underlines that the separation of consensus logic from the application itself is the lever that generates what is truly innovative: "Applications can be written to be organically decentralized... and this is a spark for a variety of system-changing innovations in the software architecture of applications, whether they are money or non-money related" (Mougayar, 2015).

Following Swan (2015), the key point is that the term *currency* could mean:

> … different things in the cryptoeconomy context, especially much more than in the basic *money* sense of serving as a payment mechanism for goods and services. A second important sense of the word *currency* in the cryptoeconomy context is emerging as "something of value that can be usefully deployed in some situation," or, as described previously, "a unit of value that can be earned and used in a certain economic system." There is the general idea of a token, currency, or appcoin allowing access to certain features of an economic system.
>
> … Considering currency more broadly in these ways starts to widen its applicability to many other situations. A currency is a token of value that can be earned and deployed. A currency stores value and is transmissible. This generalized definition supports the claim that there can be many nonmonetary currencies that are conceived in the same structure. For example, reputation is a unit of value that can be earned and deployed in certain situations; it is a nonmonetary currency in the sense that it is a proxy for status or some kinds of tasks that a person can do. Likewise, health is a commodity of value that may be earned and can be deployed in specific situations. This broader notion of currency as an earnable and deployable commodity extends to many other nonmonetary currencies beyond reputation and health, such as intention, attention, time, ideas, and creativity.
>
> A blockchain is quite literally like a giant spreadsheet for registering all assets, and an accounting system for transacting them on a global scale that can include all forms of assets held by all parties worldwide…. (Swan, 2015, p. xi)

This stage of development finds a key tool in *smart contracts* (Swan, 2015, see also Wright and De Filippi (2015), and for a short introduction, see Lewis, 2016), which are functions automatically executing an agreement in a distributed network. This could allow the decentralized transaction ledger function of the blockchain to be used to register, confirm and transfer all manner of contracts and property (Swan, 2015, p. 10).

Finally, the creation of organizations such as DAOs makes a further step towards establishing a self-sustaining networked system[5] (Wright & De Filippi, 2015, p. 17), DApps and so forth (Swan, 2015, also Mougayar,

2015, p. 8). Considering the list by Swan (2015) of task operations that DLTs can perform, I will only introduce one belonging to the general type—the escrow platforms. The DApp Counterparty is a good example of the development of blockchains of greatest interest. It provides a case of appraising value by an affinity group that bets on the outcome of a future event.

> … Each player puts his or her money into an escrow account that is sealed prior to the race. After the results are registered, the DApp autonomously transfers the money from the combined account to the winner. Now imagine 500 bettors putting their money into the escrow account prior to the contract event. Upon completion of the event, the money is automatically assigned by algorithm to the winners in pre-assigned proportions. It does not take too much imagination to see this as an insurance product…
>
> … marathon runners can pool health insurance more towards sprains and falls, and less toward heart disease. Mini-van moms can pool auto insurance for number of passengers rather than miles driven. Professionals can pool E&O insurance by peer review. In fact, any affinity group can accurately price the perils that they are also most capable to manage. DApps are massively scalable; one application can serve infinite users.
>
> The market size of binary betting (sports, insurance, coin toss, etc.) combined with complex betting (contracts for difference, hedging, options, etc.) is in the trillions of dollars. So while Counterparty has only one use case, the use case is massive. Now imagine 100,000 DApps operating autonomously, combining and integrating into complex relationships—not unlike building a jigsaw puzzle. (Robles, 2014)

As the ECSA team points out clearly in their presentation of a "multiverse economic space":

> … Do we really need to pay experts to do actuarial underwriting and to process claims? …Furthermore, we can invest our premiums and pay dividends each year to ourselves as policy holders. It's decentralized, globally hedged captive insurance for the 99%. (ECSA, 2017)

This apparently unstoppable development has found the first critical node in 2016 with Ether (see above), but with wider effects in the "blockchain" culture. I am referring to the accident occurring in July 2016 (Vigna, 2016), in which a hacker stole $60 M (one-third of the whole fund) by taking advantage of a bug in the software. The majority of users decided to rewrite the software in order to cancel the theft. Once the transactions were erased, the money returned. A minority of people chose the "non-forked" version due to its commitment to the inalterability of the transactions by human intervention, which forms the basis for operating without third-party control. This happened a few weeks after the creation of the Ethereum DAO in June 2016. So far, two identical versions of Ethereum exist ("New" and "Classic") (Vigna, 2016). In a study on this episode, DuPont (2017) sustains that this event testifies to the current failure of the DAO, as the solution to the problem has been found in coming back to the traditional forms of hierarchical governance. Or, more pragmatically, it could mean that some ideological underpinnings on which these technologies are designed must be carefully reviewed.

Another example of a DAO comes from Bitnation (https://bitnation.co/)—a decentralized, open-source movement, in which support is provided to refugees and migrants without state intervention. It suggests, in my view, the disintermediation of constitutional rights from the state.

In this *tokenization* of our interactions, there is a growing interest in attention skills. There are those who interpret the next step as a way to capitalize on what has not yet been valued. Some platforms allow individuals to be rewarded for their "digital labor and be paid for our attention" (a newborn in the field is BAT, an Ethereum-based digital advertising platform (BAT, 2017)). Micropayments present the possibility of large-scale transactions exchanged on the basis of a massive development of "self-entrepreneurialism" (Hampshire, 2017a, 2017b). One implication is that such wide diffusion of micropayments will include users without the basic skills to manage these transactions, and this will open the window to those third-party intermediaries who were already eliminated by the development of these platforms.

Ruppert (2017), in an intriguing speculative mapping of the future of decentralization, sustains that we could see a shift from the data economy to the attention economy. It's just a matter of time: it depends on the development of infrastructure that allows the implementation of sovereignty of personal data.

On the other side, the main concern of critical social scientists seems to be the commodification of attention, as discussed in a recent seminar (Alcock, 2015). The 2012 special issue of *Culture Machine* deals with this topic in a similar framework (Crogan & Kinsley, 2012). Contributors seem to stay close to a definition of experience that is language-based (as in Marazzi's use of Derrida's concept of grammarization), while others extend the critical approach to neuroplasticity. Peter Doran (2013) introduces a novel argument about mindfulness in what seems to be a deterministic vision of the capitalist system:

> Whether we realize it or not, our minds and culture are being colonized by markets—through advertising and data-mining, entertainment media and social networking. The hidden political and economic struggle of our times is focused on shaping our inner lives.

In this gloomy picture, he nevertheless sustains that people are able to create self-organized commons in the area of care and self-care. According to his view, the mindfulness revolution can be of great help, but its commodification—*vis-à-vis* McMindfulness—is a tendency that can nullify its emancipatory potential.

In my view, it is of the utmost importance to reflect on the frameworks we follow in looking at society and the economy in order to find a feasible pathway forward. Digital technologies have the "potential of reconfiguring all human activity" (Swan, 2015) and may allow us to overcome the idea of money as we know it. They may also promote eco-friendly economic interactions via different forms of reciprocal or gift-giving exchange. Nevertheless, these cannot be effective if our lenses are not clear. The possibility of tokenization in a "multiverse economic space" enables the network to co-design relational elements such as reputation, attention, gratitude and calls for a careful review of the toolkit available. In the next part of this essay, I will argue that we should reconsider the current perspective.

The Risks of Divisive Thinking: "Alternative Something" is the Illness, Not the Remedy.

There is no doubt that critical and radical thinkers, practitioners, social activists and hackers manifest a growing attention to the personal dimension, not only because it is increasingly involved in the production of data which digital technologies collect in more and more granular and global formats, but also due to the limits of the *progressive* narrative, including the way it is narrated in the social sciences. After all, the expectation to overcome or reduce intermediaries of all kinds and pursue a non-hierarchical society is part of the *progressive* technological dream. What seems to find a way through a somewhat static mode of thinking typical of this perspective is the need for an "inner transformation" in which attention is not uniquely oriented to the *outside* world—"the structures"—that must be conquered and changed from the top.

One of the most interesting contemporary authors, J.K. Gibson-Graham, carries out research-action with forms of co-design beyond a hierarchical approach, grounding her proposal on an epistemological model focusing on the need for an internal transformation of the social actor. She says a new paradigm is more than a new intellectual achievement (as in T.S. Kuhn), "but the enactment of a revolution in a performative sense (Gibson-Graham, 2014, p. 14)… to imagine and enact 'other' economies is no small feat. A significant barrier resides in ourselves, in the very way we understand 'the economy'" (Gibson-Graham & Roelvink, 2011, p. 2).

In her well-known book *The End of Capitalism As We Know It* (1996), she recalls the social experiments presented at the World Social Forum and specifically the Zapatista movement in Chiapas (Mexico) with

> their ongoing ethical project of self-transformation, their continual search for ways to exercise power, and their freedom to act, which arises from practices of autonomy and self-determination. Focusing on the *here* and *now* as the place and time of transformative action, the Zapatistas have energized others around the world… (viii).

And in Chap. 7 of a more recent book (Gibson-Graham, 2007, p. 127), significantly entitled *Cultivating subjects for a community economy*, she says, "we have ultimately found ourselves engaged in what might be called 'a politics of the subject' …. If to change ourselves is to change our worlds, and the relation is reciprocal, then the project of history making is never a distant one but always right here, on the borders of our sensing, thinking, feeling, moving bodies".

The increasing social experimentations and literature about the commons exhibit a similar pathway forward. Two of the most influential thinkers in this area, David Bollier and Silke Helfrich (2015), conduct their work in the wake of the *Institutional Analysis and Development* (IAD) program set up by the Nobel Prize Laureate Elinor Ostrom. The main difference represented by their work comprises the introduction of "subjectivity and intersubjectivity as central elements of commoning" (ib., p. 9): the commons must be seen from the inside

> through the experiences, feelings, histories and cultures of every participant ... the commons calls into question the idea that discrete individuals and objects are self-evident, privileged categories of analysis. (ib., p. 11)

In the introduction to a book focused on designing effective self-governance after the advent of the DLTs, Clippinger and Bollier (2014) sustain a similar view about the role individuals should play in building an effective and fair *New Ecology of Data*. In particular, Clippinger's personal contribution in the volume (Clippinger, 2014) is of utmost interest as explicated by its title "Why Self-Sovereignity Matters". To defend what he calls "contextual identities" or *personas* (understood as the multiple identities qualifying individuals), he suggests preserving the current compartmentalization of data since they are essential for both personal and social freedoms.

It appears to me that aforementioned aspirations maintain contradictory assumptions about how the system works and about the configuration of the social and economic forms within which technologies can perform. They are frequently characterized by a pre-defined dichotomy.

To succinctly recall Gibson-Graham's framework, I reproduce a figure from her work (Fig. 2.2).

In my view, this framework does not seem clear in terms of its understanding of the market. An implicit dualism distinguishes between interpretations at the expense of clarity, and although opposite, they both share a reductionist reading. In reality, the economic landscape is hybrid, based on open-ended categories, and internally differentiated. For example, the category of the non-capitalist firm includes both exploitative slave-based and feudal enterprises and non-exploitative independent (self-employed) producers and worker-owned cooperatives that appro-

Transactions	Labour	Enterprise
Market	Paid	Capitalist
Alternative market	Alternative Paid	Alternative capitalist
Non-market	Unpaid	Non-capitalist

Fig. 2.2 A diverse economy framing (Source: Gibson-Graham, 2006, p. 71). Note (from Gibson-Graham): The figure must be read only along the columns, not along the rows

priate and distribute the surplus they produce. Heterogeneous non-capitalist economic activities coexist with capitalist firms "interacting in ways that must be investigated rather than presumed (103). The presence of non-capitalist, non-market activity in the household does not presume that such activity is non exploitative..." (104).

To me, the definition of the cooperative is as "a non-capitalist enterprise in which workers appropriate and distribute the surplus ... that they jointly produce. It is thus a democratic and non-exploitative type of enterprise, unlike a capitalist form in which the surplus is appropriated and distributed by an individual capitalist or board of directors ..." (114) This seems pretty problematic, because it's one thing to define an economic organization on its principles and another to take care of its effective internal functioning as well as its relationships with other stakeholders in the community (consumers, public institutions, the for-profit sphere) and the environment (for a more realistic description within a view sympathetic to cooperativism, see Bauwens & Kostakis, 2014).

In general, Gibson-Graham's argumentation is of great help in disentangling Marxism from the shallows in which it ended up, as it helps to recognize the plurality of economies that cannot be identified with capitalism. However, in my opinion, she fails to find an analytic tool appropriate to this task. Moreover, it is easy to agree with the aims she attributes to social sciences and with the great honesty pervading her project; nevertheless, the pitfalls in her proposed classification (Gibson-Graham, 2006, Fig. 1.1. in, xiii), in my opinion, derive from her need to leave open the door to one main Marxist dogma: the dichotomy between capitalism and other forms of production.

So far, the openness and flexibility of Gibson-Graham's ontology is highly appreciable (Gibson-Graham, 2014), but the bricks used in its construction raise some doubts. My attention is drawn to the heterogeneity within the same form. It is not the result of empirical investigation, but of a presupposition about the specific profit-oriented nature of the capitalist economy. Once that form has been defined in terms of its general principles of functioning rather than on its observed functioning, the rest of the world becomes an oppositional entity excluded *a priori*. A similar ambiguity emerges in David Graeber's distinction (2011) between the human economy and capitalist economy. For him, capitalism is, per definition, a non-human economy, while slavery is classified as part of the human economy. My point is that the conceptual umbrellas under which economic forms are collected need to pay more attention to details that cannot be discovered without the abandonment of an *a priori* classification. A framework anchored to the opposition capitalism vs. anti-capitalism undermines any declared aspiration to an open scheme.

In the technological field of the P2P commons, three authors try to imagine what could be the near future of ICT at the urban level. They identify four scenarios represented in a four-quadrant scheme. One axis concerns the polarity between centralized vs. distributed control of infrastructure, while the second axis concerns the polarity between the accumulation of capital vs. the accumulation of the commons.

Netarchical Capitalism (Kostakis, Bauwens, & Niaros, 2015) is identified at the crossroads of centralized control and the accumulation of capital (upper left). *Distributed Capitalism* describes distributed control and the accumulation of capital (bottom left). *Resilient Communities* describes distributed control and the accumulation of the commons (bottom right). *Global Commons* (upper right) describes centralized control and the accumulation of the commons (upper left).

The discussion raised by this configuration is of great interest; but in this, as in other cases, there is little room for the *meanings* attributed by actors involved in these processes, and the capitalist process is shaped in a way similar to what Karl Marx did at his time. Even in the visionary and inspiring framework offered by Bauwens (2005), in spite of the redefinition of the old and new forms of the economy, the market is still described within the traditional neo-classical view (see the paragraph P2P and the Market). In addition, Simone Cicero remarks that there is a need to distinguish with more precision the various functions played by the different components of the process: Bawens et al. identify infrastructures and platforms, whereas Cicero argues about the failed distinction between interfaces and infrastructures. This leads them to hasty conclusions about the process of ubiquitous commodification. Of equal relevance are his observations on distributed capitalism and, most importantly, on the underestimation of the capacity of capital and talent to combine, transform and distribute "elements of innovation to a larger audience"—a fact that limits the attribution of exploitation to the netarchical form (Cicero, 2015).

In general, it seems we still have to free ourselves from the success of selling a narrative of the market that seduces both its advocates and its detractors. Callon (1998) has highlighted the performative value of mainstream economic theory. The separation of economic theory from real markets is not simply its limit. It's the way economists developed theory in order to set up their construction of the market. It appears that it worked quite well. If market opponents agreed on definition of the economy and constructed new lands for the dispossessed based on humanity, solidarity and social relations, then they could claim that those properties were not characteristics of *homo oeconomicus* and should be replaced by a new society.

The feminist economist Julie A. Nelson provides a very convincing argument to support the view that markets are depicted by a pre-classificatory scheme:

> A very old definition of economics says that it is about the provisioning of goods and services to meet our material needs. That is, economics is about the way we manage our time and money so we can obtain groceries and shelter and thus "keep body and soul together."
>
> In many discussions of economics, however, it seems that body and soul grow even-farther apart. A particular belief about commerce and its relation to ethics is implicit in many contemporary discussions, both academic and popular. This is the belief that money, profits, markets, and corporations are parts of an "economic machine." This machine operates in an

automatic fashion, following inexorable and amoral "laws." While the machine organizes provisioning for our bodies, it is itself soulless and inhuman, according to this belief. Ethical questions, on the other hand, concern the appropriate respect and care for other creatures that we—as living, social, and soulful beings—should demonstrate. Since machines are incapable of morality, thinking about economies as machines puts commerce firmly outside the ethical realm. If this belief is true, then there is no point in worrying about the ethical implications of how we work and spend within contemporary capitalist or market-oriented economies.

Sometimes this belief takes a decidedly promarket form... Sometimes this belief about the amoral economic machine comes with a decidedly antimarket or antibusiness slant...

Contemporary economic life is systematically driven by greed and rampant materialism, such market critics say, and so is utterly opposed to the attainment of an ethical, meaningful social life. People with a "critical," "alternative," or leftist view of society often believe that "business ethics" is an oxymoron—a contradiction in terms like "personal computer" (how personal can a computer be?) or "jumbo shrimp." They consider discussing ethical issues as they arise *within* the structure of capitalism to be largely a waste of time.

- The idea that economic systems are inanimate machines operating according to amoral laws is a *belief*, not a fact.
- This belief has harmful effects—for life on the planet, for human society and for you in particular.
- Understanding that economies are vital, living, human-made and shaped by our ethical choices can help to improve our decisions—both individually and as a society.

Possibly, you have listened to some of the "alternative" economics voices but find it confusing when different people each identify a different "structure" or "mechanism" as being the one that is in dire need of fixing. Or you may be turned off when such discussions seem unrelentingly pessimistic or propose only utopian-sounding solutions. (Nelson, 2006)

Divisive interpretive schemes distort our interactions and distract committed actors from channeling their energy into positive transformation for all. In practice, it is noteworthy that when you try to define empirically "alternative" practices, you get stuck, as recognized in a recent empirical study carried out in Barcelona by a research group led by Manuel Castells (Conhill et al., 2015).

Almost all the aforementioned authors forgot to take into account the individualization process. In industrial society, according to sociologists Ulrich Beck and Elisabeth Beck-Gernsheim (2002), the individual is constituted by a series of roles in a variety of institutions (see also Giddens, 1999). In the post-industrial stage of society, individuals transform their identity as "given" to form many "commitments". Consequently, although this change can be considered a systemic requirement, actually the new situation means that the change is produced internally (Giorgino, 2013). They are open systems: they do not simply reproduce themselves, but are able to change themselves. This has profound implications in understanding social transformation.

For example, the fact that we notice an increase in social inequality does not mean that classes have a decisive influence, but rather that inequalities are activated by separate biographies. This is the collective experience that the reference to classes hides (Beck & Beck-Gernsheim, 2002, p. XXIV). This experience involves a process of uprooting (dis-embedding) from traditional social ties. An indicator of this is the increase in the number of households consisting of a single person. In 1999, London and Monaco already had more than 50% of the population living in this condition. In Turin, a former industrial city, it is now higher than 40%. At the same time, we see a pluralization of lifestyles. In the 1980s and 1990s, between 30 and 40% of the German population were involved in experimental forms of life. Individualization also involves a process of gradual separation from social affiliations as a source of personal identity, which leads to political self-organization rather than participation.

These examples comprise the main reasons why I have proposed an extended version of Zelizer's approach to economic interaction as relational work (Giorgino 2014a, 2014b). In brief, Zelizer's framework implies four elements: social ties, transactions, media for transactions and meanings (Zelizer, 2012). Whereas Zelizer confines her model to group interactions, I suggest looking also at single individuals as inner networks of interactions (for an initial discussion, see: Giorgino, 2014a, 2014b). Individuals are more than society. This extension is related to the current debate about the self, nurtured by different radical lines of thinking, like second-wave feminism. My main aim is to identify and sustain the already existing archipelago of social transformation at the urban level. What these heterogeneous areas of action have in common is the aspiration to reduce the social space for "intermediating" actors and institutions—an element, as I have already written earlier, that characterizes the emerging social movements (Hawken, 2008).

An enactive model must be based on the absence of any alternative form. The word *alternative* itself should be dropped. If we do not leave room for the unexpected, we cannot find anything that we did not know already. The cultivation of *an alternative to something* can be a hindrance when the original, rejected model is depicted in unrealistic terms. We could define what is positive for us and what is not in the here and now of our social and economic interactions, and later scrutinize the consequences of our choices, leaving room for opportunities to change our course of action.

The systematic downgrading of our theoretical ambition, as in grounded theory (Glaser), and the open discussion of scientific generalization are complementary to this framework. Or, as Gibson-Graham says, "A politics of the subject (Gibson-Graham, 1996) implies … … building flat theories—intellectual constructs not dominated by a vertical ontology … that presumes a hierarchy of scales from global to local" (Gibson-Graham, 1996, p. xxvi)—hence the importance of building generative theories such as grounded theory (GT), which would result in a mental (and emotional) liberation, with more energy devoted to details previously neglected as irrelevant or just unseen. Action-research and interventions would take the form of experimentation. Their results might induce us to review our own steps rather than create a clash between absolute models. Our energy would be most suitably expended building the new rather than destroying the old, seen as absolute evil. This also follows the movement from uni-disciplinary theoretical dominance to transdisciplinarity (Nicolescu, 2010).

An Enactive Approach in Social Sciences

In a previous essay (Giorgino, 2016) I dealt with this issue, making a specific reference to Kirchhoff and Hutto (2011) about their critical assessment of Varela's neurophenomenology, in which first-person inquiry and third-person inquiry are assumed to be methods at the same level. I also recalled Eugene Gendlin's contribution to an experience-based, non-representational model of knowledge.

What I propose is grounded on an embodied, interactional and enactive definition of experience. Embodied means that "cognition depends upon the kinds of experience that come from having a body with various sensorimotor capacities and second, that these individual sensorimotor capacities are themselves embedded in a more encompassing biological, psychological and cultural context" (Varela, Thompson, & Rosch, 1991, p. 173). The enactive approach "consists of two points: (1) perception consists in perceptually guided action and cognitive structures emerge from the recurrent sensorimotor patterns that enable action to be perceptually guided" (ib., p. 173). Varela et al. follow Minsky's approach about our cognitive functions: "brains use processes that change themselves and this means that we cannot separate such processes from the products they produce. In particular, brains make memories, which change the ways we'll subsequently think. The principal activities of brains are making changes in themselves". The world is not seen any more as an independent structure out there; it is interactional and intrinsic to these processes of self-modification: "instead of *representing* an independent world, [these systems] *enact* a world as a domain of distinctions that is inseparable from the structure embodied by the cognitive system" (Varela et al., 1991, pp. 139–140).

As Johnson writes: "Meaning includes patterns of embodied experience and preconceptual structures of our sensibility…, These embodied patterns do not remain private or peculiar to the person who experiences them. Our community helps to determine the nature of our meaningful, coherent understanding of our 'world'" (in Varela et al., 1991, p. 150). In fact, the social space can include also sensorial processes: social processes are constituted by bodily based interactions, not yet patterns, as Eugene Gendlin suggests (1992). *Felt sensations* are often the precipitate of previous interpretations of the world, but the process occurs *beyond* patterns. In other words, the creation of meaning does not have a symbolic base, firstly because experiencing exceeds concepts, and secondly because it is not the external conditions that make experience possible (Gendlin, 1997).

The strength of this vantage point resides in its apparent weakness. Sociology—and social sciences in general—does not lay its foundations for itself. From a more careful and closer observation, it follows that the usual approach toward the *one-dimensional reflective actor* ought to be substituted by an approach considering the multidimensional and apparent incoherence of the actor with different degrees of awareness, which are not the consequence of a spontaneous personal endowment, but more simply the consequence of self-work (working on the self).

As in personal experience, a wisdom-based approach is a method for *un*learning certain social habits and simplifying life. This approach suggests new forms of social action and expresses an innovative model of awareness that changes at any societal level. Five learning outcomes are of main interest here (Baer et al., 2006), concerning the recognition and development of what can be defined as "life skills":

- Attention skills
- Emotional awareness
- Sensorial awareness
- Self-observational labeling skills
- Non-judgmental attitude and acceptance skills

Scientists and humans in general deal with the same building blocks as members of the same species. More than ever, soft skills and life skills are important to contribute to our collective knowledge of processes that sustain life. Whether they are applied to science or to everyday life, their function is indispensable just like the "core economy" is indispensable for formal work in the market or state economy.

So far, this is also an emotional journey and a way to uncover "ourselves" while knowing the place for the first time, as the poet declaims. The first step is right in front of us: the world "outside" us and the world "within us" are part of the same world and they interact unceasingly, shaping our process of understanding. The foundations of a contemplative approach in the social sciences is a matter of boundaries: you can approach both realms, from one side toward the other, integrating existential suffering and social and economic suffering via methodologies and methods to deal with them. Working with the boundaries of both means many things. In the case of contemplative knowledge, it means being open to an inquiry into the social foundation of their practices, the evaluation of their effects, and the redefinition of them from a lay perspective. From a social science perspective, it means to put under scrutiny both the neo-positivist and the constructivist approaches. The enactive perspective seems the approach best equipped to take this responsibility and carry out this task.

The ambition of this text is to open up a dialogue with radical knowledge in the social field and proceed together in the co-design of a networking society that faces transition. If there is a point where the work to be done takes on an applied value, it will concern the role that soft skills and life skills play in human interactions. In particular, co-designing urban or community platforms makes this point unable to be deferred.

Conclusive Remarks

In 1994, Jon Kabat-Zinn reflected on our society, mentioning its high technological advancements and the need for turning attention to the inner technologies of contemplative practices. It was a sort of contemplative manifesto, and yet 23 years have passed. Obviously, many things have changed. Some social processes have been quite unexpected, and they are here shaping our current lives, forcing us to elaborate conceptual and practical tools to accommodate them.

We see these latest developments as opportunities of a *Second Renaissance* (Kabat-Zinn), much more visible and stronger than in 1994. If personal engagement and experimentation are the highways for the development of new forms of social learning and action, it is also clear that this will be possible beyond any particular religion. We can go forward with a fully secular orientation that translates the traditions of wisdom we have inherited so far. And, again recalling Kabat-Zinn's remarks, this must be pursued beyond any individual or personality, as usually happens in history. This opens up the opportunity to reflect about contemplative practices as a commons.

"The question for us now is how to further the emergence of such a profound and complex cultural transformation, which in some ways is already unfolding" (Kabat-Zinn, 1994). The political and organizational capital accumulated on the basis of industrial society is obsolete. We need new methods of research and action appropriate to the *Anthropocene*. Improving life's condition requires personal work that supports the desired transformation. The opening toward a systematic integration of social sciences with contemplative knowledge on a secular basis is what could make the difference in the near future. A contemplative lay culture seems to fit well in a setting of collaborative commons between caring individuals.[6]

Notes

1. "In the bitcoin protocol, hash functions are part of the block hashing algorithm which is used to write new transactions into the blockchain through the mining process. In bitcoin mining, the inputs for the function are all of the most recent, not-yet-confirmed transactions. To successfully 'solve' a block, miners try to combine all of the inputs with their own arbitrary piece of input data in such a way that the resulting hash starts with a certain number of zeroes. proof of work" http://www.coindesk.com/bitcoin-hash-functions-explained/
2. In 2009, it began with 25 BTCs, halving every four years: now it is 12.5 BTCs. In fact, miners are currently paid through a combination of BTC's block reward and transaction fees. The former still provide the majority of earnings.

   Once the majority of BTCs have been mined, the block reward will become an insignificant percentage of miners' overall earnings. https://www.bitcoinmining.com/bitcoin-mining-fees/

   BTCs are designed as limited in quantity to a capped amount of 21 million units in 2040. New currency (in blocks) is being issued at a regular and known pace, with about 16.4 million units (https://blockchain.info/charts/total-bitcoins) currently outstanding https://www.bitcoinmining.com/bitcoin-mining-fees/

3. See the documentary about a BTC mining company in China: https://bitcoinworldwide.com/mining/china/ A founding partner explains that they get 120 BTCs (about €256,000) per day for hashing activity (about 20–25 BTCs per day per site). There are about 3000 miners in six different factories; electricity costs amount to $80,000 per month (about €70,000).
4. The word "fork" in this context originates from open source software. "... The development of software like this would allow to draw trees: each time the code was copied separately there would be a new branch. This would be called 'forking', since the same code would then develop in two parallel directions.... What happens when the blockchain forks? You get two chains with a shared genesis and are identical up until the forking point, after which they exist exclusively in parallel (unless one is completely abandoned), creating two separate networks. Coins in my possession (all transactions leading up to that) before the fork remain mine on both chains after the fork, and both chains agree on those transactions since they were all before the fork. After the fork, each transaction takes place exclusively on each separate chain... The economies around each of these chains inherit the economies from the shared economy before the fork, so even though there are now twice as many coins, there is not twice as much value" (Danova, 2015).
5. A "software-based organizations [that] ... can re-implement certain aspects of traditional corporate governance using software, enabling parties to obtain the benefits of formal corporate structures, while at the same time maintaining the flexibility and scale of informal online groups. These organizations also can be operated autonomously, without any human involvement. They can own, exchange, or trade resources and interact with other humans or machines, raising novel questions around traditional notions of legal personality, individual agency, and responsibility" (Dupont, 2017).
6. As clearly expressed by Richard Bartlett, co-founder of Loomio, we should support a "net of networks of small groups rather than a mass movement of many individuals" (Bartlett, 2017). In my view, it also responds to a dynamic interplay of economic forms based on interoperability and primarily oriented to collaborative commons, "an emptiness [in which]. the practice ... is a fluid process of continual resignification" (Gibson-Graham, 1996, p. xv).

References

Alcock, R. (2015). The politics and economics of attention. Bristol seminar on the *politics of attention*, Bristol University. https://psychologicalgovernance.wordpress.com/resources/the-politics-and-economics-of-attention/

Andreessen, M. (2014, January 21). Why bitcoin matters. *The New York Times*. Retrieved from https://dealbook.nytimes.com/2014/01/21/why-bitcoin-matters/?_php=true&_type=blogs&_r=0

Baer, R., et al. (2006, March). Using self-report assessment methods to explore facets of mindfulness. *Assessment, 13*(1), 27–45.

Bartlett, R. D. (2017). 5 reasons to build a network of small groups, rather than a mass movement of individuals. *Enspiral Tales blog*. Retrieved from https://medium.com/enspiral-tales/5-reasons-to-build-a-network-of-small-groups-rather-than-a-mass-movement-of-individuals-46f2ea72b6b2

BAT. (2017). Basic Attention Token (BAT) blockchain based digital advertising. Brave software. *White Paper*, May 29. Retrieved from https://www.basicattentiontoken.org/

Bauwens, M. (2005). The political economy of peer production. *CTheory.net*. Retrieved from https://www.ctheory.net/articles

Bauwens, M., & Kostakis, V. (2014). *Network society and future scenarios for a collaborative economy*. London: Palgrave Macmillan.

Bearman, J., & Hanuka, T. (2015, May–June). The rise and fall of Silk Road, Part 1 and Part 2. *Wired*. Retrieved from https://www.wired.com/2015/04/silk-road-1/; https://www.wired.com/2015/05/silk-road-2/

Beck, U., & Beck-Gernsheim, E. (2002). *Individualization. Institutionalized individualism and its social and political consequences*. London: Sage.

Bollier, D., & Helfrich, S. (2015). *Patterns of commoning*. Amhert, MA: Levellers Press.

Castells, M. (1996/2010). *The information age. Economy, society, and culture. Volume I: The rise of the network society* (2nd ed.). Chichester: Wiley-Blackwell.

Callon, M. (1998). *The laws of the market*. Oxford: Blackwell Publishers.

Cicero, S. (2015). On the role of platform based peer production and the commons in the dynamics of innovation. Retrievd from www.meedabyte.com

Clippinger, J. H. (2014). Why self-sovereignity matters. In Clippinger & Bollier, 2014.

Clippinger, J. H., & Bollier, D. (Eds.). (2014). *From bitcoin to burning man and beyond*. Amherst, MA: Off the Commons Books.

Cognizant. (2017). Demystifying blockchain. *White Paper*, Cognizant, USA. Retreived from https://www.cognizant.com/whitepapers/demystifying-blockchain-codex2199.pdf

Conhill, J., et al. (2015). *Otra vida es posible. Prácticas económicas alternativas durante la crisis*. Barcelona: Editorial UOC.

Cooperativa Integral Catalana. (2014). Building a new economy. Retrieved from https://fair.coop/building-a-new-economy/

Crogan, P., & Kinsley, S. (2012). Paying attention: Toward a critique of the attention economy. *Culture Machine, 13*, 1–29.

Danova, H. (2015, September 2). What is bitcoin fork? *Bitcoin Dictionary*. Retrieved from https://blog.cex.io/bitcoin-dictionary/what-is-bitcoin-fork-14622

Dodd, N. (2014). *The social life of money*. Princeton: Princeton University Press.

Dodd, N. (2015, March). Bitcoin, utopianism and the future of money. *KR Magazine*.

Dodd, N. (2017). Utopian moneis: Complementary currencies, bitcoin, and the social life of money. In N. Bandelj, F. F. Wherry, & V. A. Zelizer (Eds.), *Money talks. Explaining how money really works*. Princeton: Princeton University Press.

Doran, P. (2013). A call for a new political economy of attention: Mindfulness as a new commons. In Dupont 2017. Retrieved from https://mindfulcommons.org/

DuPont, Q. (2018). Experiments in algorithmic governance: A history and ethnography of "The DAO," a failed decentralized autonomous organization. In Campbell-Verduyn, M. (Ed.). (2018). *Bitcoin and Beyond: The Challenges and Opportunities of Blockchains for Global Governance*, London, Routledge (in press; preprint).

ECSA. (2017). What, why and how ECSA. Retrieved from https://medium.com/new-economic-spaces/economic-spaceward-ho-231ba740f642; http://economicspace.agency/

Gendlin, E. T. (1992). The primacy of the body, not the primacy of perception. *Man and World, 25*(3–4), 341–353.

Gendlin, E. (1997). *The process mode*. Nyack, NY: The Focusing Institute.

Gibson-Graham, J. K. (1996). *The end of capitalism as we knew it. A feminist critique of political economy*. Cambridge, MA: Blackwell.

Gibson-Graham, J. K. (2006). *A postcapitalist politics*. Minneapolis: University of Minnesota Press.

Gibson-Graham, J. K. (2007). Cultivating subjects for a community economy. In Tickell A. et al. (Eds.), *Politics and practice in economic geography*. London: Sage.

Gibson-Graham, J. K. (2014). Rethinking the economy with thick description and weak theory. *Currrent Anthropology, 55*(9), 147–153.

Gibson-Graham, J. K., & Roelvink, G. (2011). The nitty gritty of creating alternative economies. *Social Alternatives, 30*(1), 29–33.

Giddens, A. (1999). *Runaway world: How globalization is reshaping our lives*. London: Profile Books.

Giorgino, V. M. B. (2013). A contemplative approach to clinical sociology. *Studies of Changing Societies: Comparative and Interdisciplinary Focus, 3*(7), 107–120.

Giorgino, V. M. B. (2014a). Happiness is an art of living: Towards a contemplative perspective on economy as relational work. In V. M. B. Giorgino (Ed.), *The pursuit of happiness and the traditions of wisdom*. Dordrecht, The Netherlands: Springer.

Giorgino V. M. B. (2014b, December 10). Oltre il capitalismo: un nuovo mondo è già tra noi. Riflessioni sull'economia da un punto di vista contemplativo buddista. Presentation at the Dialogue Conference between Buddhists and Christians *Costruire sentieri per il nostro tempo. Le ricadute antropologiche della crisi*, Pontificia Università Urbaniana – Citta del Vaticano.

Giorgino, V. M. B. (2016). Contemplative knowledge and social sciences: Close encounters of the enactive kind. In V. Bentz & V. M. B. Giorgino (Eds.), *Contemplative social research caring for self, being, and lifeworld*. Santa Barbara: Fielding University Press.

Graeber, D. (2011). *Debt. The first 5000 years*. New York: Melville House.

Hampshire, M. (2017a). Unpacking micropayments part 1: Lightning, scalability and going off-chain. Retrieved from www.networkcultures.org/moneylab/2017/03/14/unpacking-micropayments-part-1-lightning-scalability-and-going-off-chain/

Hampshire, M. (2017b). Unpacking micropayments part 2: User base dichotomies, and a cyberpunk sensibility. Retrieved from www.networkcultures.org/moneylab/2017/03/30/unpacking-micropayments-part-2-user-base-dichotomies-and-a-cyberpunk-sensibility/

Hawken, P. (2008). *Blessed unrest. How the largest social movement in history is restoring grace, justice, and beauty to the world*. London: Penguin Books.

Kabat-Zinn, J. (1994). Catalyzing movement towards a more contemplative/sacred-appreciating/non-dualistic society. Meeting of the Working Group—The Contemplative Mind in Society, Pocantico, September 29–October 2.

Kirchhoff, M. D., & Hutto, D. D. (2011). Never mind the gap: Neurophenomenology, radical enactivism, and the hard problem of consciousness. *Constructivist Foundations, 11*(2), 302–309.

König, T., & Duran, E. (2016). FairCoin 2.0. *White Paper*. Retrieved from https://fair-coin.org/faircoin2-white-paper
Kostakis, V., Bauwens, M., & Niaros, V. (2015). Urban reconfiguration after the emergence of peer-to-peer infrastructures: Four future scenarios with an impact on smart cities. In D. Araya (Ed.), *Smart cities as democratic ecologies*. New York: Palgrave Macmillan.
Lewis, A. (2015a). A gentle introduction to the blockchain technology. Retrieved from https://bravenewcoin.com/assets/Reference-Papers/A-Gentle-Introduction/A-Gentle-Introduction-To-Blockchain-Technology-WEB.pdf
Lewis, A. (2015b). A gentle introduction to Ethereum. Retrieved from https://bitsonblocks.net/2016/10/02/a-gentle-introduction-to-ethereum/
Lewis, A. (2016). A gentle introduction to smart contracts. Retrievd from https://bitsonblocks.net/2016/02/01/a-gentle-introduction-to-smart-contracts/
Maurer, B. (2017). Blockchains are a diamonds best friend: Zelizer for the bitcoin moment. In N. Bandelj, F. F. Wherry, & V. A. Zelizer (Eds.), *Money talks. Explaining how money really works*. Princeton: Princeton University Press.
Mcmillan, R. (2014, March 3). Story of Mt. Gox, Bitcoin's $460 million disaster. *Wired*. Retrieved from https://www.wired.com/2014/03/bitcoin-exchange/
Mougayar, W. (2015, January 16). Understanding the blockchain. Retrieved from https://www.oreilly.com/ideas/understanding-the-blockchain
Nakamoto, S. (2008). Bitcoin: A peer-to-peer electronic cash system. Retrieved from https://bitcoin.org/bitcoin.pdf
Nelson, J. A. (2006). *Economics for humans*. Chicago: University of Chicago Press.
Nicolescu, B. (2010, December). Methodology of transdisciplinarity—Levels of reality, logic of the included middle and complexity. *Transdisciplinary Journal of Engineering & Science, 1*(1), 19–38.
Robles, D. (2014, November 27). Future of money part 2. *The Ingenesist Project*. Retrieved from http://www.ingenesist.com/future-of-money-part-2/
Ruppert, A. (2017, June 1). Mapping the decentralized world of tomorrow. *Medium.com*. Retrieved from https://medium.com/
Swan, M. (2015). *Blockchain: Blueprint for a new economy*. Farnham: O'Reilly Media.
Szabo, N. (1997). The god protocols. Retrieved from http://nakamotoinstitute.org/the-god-protocols/
Varela, F. J., Thompson, E., & Rosch, E. (1991). *The embodied mind: Cognitive science and human experience*. Cambridge, MA: The MIT Press.
Vigna, P. (2016, August 1). The great digital debate: "New" Ethereum vs Ethereum "Classic". *The Wall Street Journal*.

Wright, A., & De Filippi, P. (2015, March 10). Decentralized blockchain technology and the rise of lex cryptographia. Available at SSRN: https://ssrn.com/abstract=2580664

Zelizer, V. (2012). How I became a relational economic sociologist and what does that mean? *Politics & Society, 40*, 145–174.

Vincenzo Mario Bruno Giorgino (PhD in sociology) is an aggregate professor at the Department of Economic and Social Sciences, Mathematics and Statistics, University of Torino, Torino, Italy. Since 1998, he has been primarily devoted to the integration of contemplative knowledge and sociology in action-research and higher education, with a focus on transformative methodologies. In 2016, he co-edited with Valerie Malhotra Betz the book *Contemplative Social Research: Caring for Self, Being, and Lifeworld* (Fielding University Press).

3

Navigating the Great Transition Via Post-capitalism and Contemplative Social Sciences

Zack Walsh

Economies in Transition

Since Paul Crutzen popularized the term in 2000, there has been growing recognition that we live in the Anthropocene, a geological epoch characterized by ever-greater human involvement in Earth systems. Alongside this awareness, there has been an ever-increasing need to reorganize and redesign social systems to support planetary flourishing in an era of anthropogenic climate change. Given the inextricable link between capitalism and climate change, it is worth rethinking the Anthropocene as the Capitalocene, or the "Age of Capital." Whereas the Anthropocene mischaracterizes the problem of climate change as a human problem, the Capitalocene more clearly recognizes the historicity of the climate crisis, accounting for the particular social, economic, and political conditions that gave rise to it in the first place (Moore, 2016). With this clarity, the

Z. Walsh (✉)
Institute for the Postmodern Development of China, Claremont, CA, USA

Toward Ecological Civilization (EcoCiv), Claremont, CA, USA

Institute for Advanced Sustainability Studies, Potsdam, Germany

V.M.B. Giorgino, Z. Walsh (eds.), *Co-Designing Economies in Transition*,
https://doi.org/10.1007/978-3-319-66592-4_3

central task facing humanity today becomes the search for a sustainable alternative to our global political economy: systems change, not climate change (Klein, 2014). Inspired by the vision of a Great Transition to planetary civilization (Raskin et al., 2012), this book describes how humanity might construct socially desirable and ecologically sustainable ways of life. Its mission is to co-design economies in transition, recognizing that the term "economies in transition" denotes the emergent landscape of alternative political and economic arrangements enabled by recent social and technological advancements.

It is clear that the current political and economic landscape is undergoing structural transformations marked by extraordinary promise and peril. In 2015, the former U.S. Treasury Secretary and Economic Advisor Lawrence Summers said we had entered "a new macroeconomic epoch where the risk of deflation is higher than that of inflation, and we cannot rely on the self-restoring features of market economics." As Robert Gordon (2016) illustrates in *The Rise and Fall of American Growth*, the growth of the global economy has steadily declined since 1970, and there are no prospects for rising levels of growth in the foreseeable future. Rapid economic growth was in fact a one-time-only event, spurred by technological revolutions between the mid-nineteenth and twentieth centuries. Over the same 40-year period that global growth rates declined, neoliberal policies enabled a massive redistribution of wealth, so that the political and economic elite gained most of the new wealth created, while driving down the wages and purchasing power of everyone else (Saez & Zucman, 2014). Between 1979 and 2009, there was an 80% increase in productivity, while the average hourly compensation increased by only 8% (Reich, 2011). According to the latest Oxfam data (Just 8 men, 2017), the eight richest men now own half the world's wealth.

Inequality doesn't just appear without gross imbalances in political power, which is why there has concurrently been a steady erosion and growing distrust of political institutions. "In 1964, Americans agreed by 64% to 29% that government was run for the benefit of all the people. By 2012, the response had reversed, with voters saying by 79% to 19% that government was 'run by a few big interests looking after themselves'" (Reich, 2015). The recent global rise of populism clearly constitutes a growing revolt against the political and economic elite. Neoliberalism has suffered a sustained legitimacy crisis since the 2007–2008 financial crisis, and even conservative economic institutions like the IMF now question its legitimacy (Ostry, Loungani, & Furceri, 2016). The terminal decline of the capitalist world system marks the break-up of conventional worlds and introduces two alternative futures—Barbarization or Great Transition.

There are already signs indicating both possibilities. The dangers of barbarization, for example, are apparent in the current rise of authoritarianism, nationalism, right-wing populism, and white supremacy. Given the diminishing prospects for long-term growth and widening levels of inequality, there is a greater sense of uncertainty and anxiety about the future, especially since millennials are the first generation to be worse off financially than their parents (Barr & Malik, 2016). For those unable to imagine a Great Transition, there is a strong desire to maintain any remaining sense of privilege or entitlement. However, if we remain attached to crumbling identities and worldviews, we will likely experience a Hobbesian struggle in which violence becomes the primary means for maintaining order amidst the ruins of conventional world systems. The most statistically significant variable predicting whether a voter elected Donald Trump was authoritarianism (Macwilliams, 2016), and this is not surprising considering that many people turn to crisis cults during times of collapse. "Make America Great Again!" was Trump's campaign slogan precisely because it spoke to the collective desire of his primary voting bloc, feeding illusions of recovered grandeur and empowerment.

In line with the trend toward barbarization, Slavoj Žižek (2011) has suggested that capitalism will restructure itself in more authoritarian forms. The increasing popularity of the China model as a viable political response to the catastrophes of the twenty-first century supports this view (Kurlantzick, 2013). Since Trump's election, the Chinese government has indicated that it hopes to overtake the USA as the world leader of global trade and international security (Huang, 2017). Increasingly, American imperialism and the Pax Americana seem poised to be replaced by Chinese imperialism and a new Pax Sinica, as China's increasingly aggressive military-backed foreign policy challenges the USA, while protecting its foreign-based investments across Asia, Africa, and Latin America (Hung, 2015; Krauss & Bradsher, 2015; Mingfu, 2015). China is now the world leader in renewable energy (Blackwell, 2016), green finance (Lehr, 2016), smart cities (Sellebraten, 2016), automation (Chu & Davis, 2015), and peer-to-peer platforms (Netessine & Solodkiy, 2016), clearly signaling its desire to control the future, though its development of the latter to form a nation-wide social credit system raises alarming concerns about human rights in an era of authoritarian capitalism (Hatton, 2015; Osborne, 2015; Yang, 2017). Climate fiction author, Margaret Atwood (2015), declares "there are two threats to our society that are even greater than the 2008 financial meltdown … environmental damage due to climate change, and the possible failure of China." Evidently, China will substantially determine the world's political and economic strategy (Summers, 2015), and given Trump's canceling of U.S. commitments to the Paris agreement, China will lead the world's climate negotiations and green investment strategy (Hilton, 2016).

To curtail the influence of authoritarian capitalism and decrease the likelihood of barbarization, we must envision feasible political and economic alternatives. Most people, however, depend on business-as-usual and fail to conceive its alternatives. As Mark Fisher (2009) wrote, it's easier to imagine the end of the world than the end of capitalism. The slogan "There is no alternative" (TINA), popularized by British Prime Minister Margaret Thatcher, has implicitly shaped mainstream ideology, upholding neoliberalism as the only possible reality, and demotivating people from imagining a transformation in the political economy. Though the 2007–2008 financial crisis questioned neoliberalism's legitimacy, capitalist realism has persisted, as if, Slavoj Žižek (1994) says, "liberal capitalism is the 'real' that will somehow survive even under conditions of a global ecological catastrophe" (p. 1). The immense popularity of dystopian climate fiction like Mad Max, Snowpiercer, and The Day After Tomorrow is testament to the failure of popular narratives to imagine a Great Transition.

The remarkable disconnect between the public's concern about the effects of climate change and their willingness to make sacrifices remains one aspect of the problem. Although an overwhelming majority (88%) of Americans support protecting the Earth's environment, only 52% support enacting policies that entail specific economic costs, and only 18% said enacting legislation to address climate change should be their highest priority, below chiefly economic concerns like improving the job situation

(58%), reducing the budget deficit (45%), and reducing healthcare costs (45%) (Piacenza, 2015). In another study from the Australian public, 54% of people said they believe our way of life will most likely end within the next 100 years and 24% said humans will most likely be wiped out. There is very little discussion of how an alternative political economy could feasibly provide for their needs and support the flourishing of the Earth's systems at the same time. Nevertheless, in the same survey, 75% responded actively, agreeing that "we need to transform our worldview and way of life if we are to create a better future for the world," whereas 44% responded with nihilism and 33% with religious fundamentalism, viewing the end of the world as a battle between good and evil (Randle & Eckersley, 2015). So, despite a large minority of people reverting to established views and behaviors in times of crisis, there does in fact exist an alternative will to work toward the Great Transition.

Yet another sign of hope is that people are increasingly recognizing that neoliberal capitalism is not universally accepted, and that globalization, in the singular, no longer covers our fractured and multi-temporal present. The global rise of nationalism is but one symptom of a larger phenomenon. For decades, people have become disillusioned with the myth of progress, and increasingly, they recognize the future as a cultural construct, more aptly characterized by a plurality of possible futures, as expressed in the World Social Forum's slogan: "Another World is Possible" (Williams, 2016). Taking a nonessentialist view of the political economy and recognizing that it is socially and culturally constructed, contingent on many economic and noneconomic factors, is the first step toward transformation. Like all aspects of life, economics is the result of decisions, prevailing prejudices, and leaps of faith, and as Ha-Joon Chang (2010) demonstrates, neoliberalism is replete with its own myths and questionable dogmatic assumptions. Once people begin to look at the system on which they depend as somehow strange and alien, they create space for a much more objective, demystified view of the political economy, its contingencies, and the possibility of its alternatives.

Fortunately, there are already emergent alternatives to capitalism, as the Next System project makes abundantly clear (Speth, 2016). André Gorz (2010) argues, "The exit from capitalism will happen... one way or another, either in a civilized or barbarous fashion." The likelihood of realizing a Great Transition therefore depends primarily on our capacity to discern the trends and practices that herald its possibility—to describe the political and economic conditions under which a sustainable future is possible. Discerning the active forces in the present that lead to a more liberative future has always been the work of historical materialists. As Walter Benjamin (2008) said, to see "the work of the past as still uncompleted … Every epoch… not only dreams the one to follow but, in dreaming, precipitates its awakening" (p. 109). Once the existing mode of production has been thoroughly demystified and denaturalized, one can begin to understand the dialectical processes currently at work and map the potentials for their successors—post-capitalism.

Post-capitalism

Post-capitalism names a reality which already exists, but which is little recognized by current thinking beholden to conventional worlds. As with the end of feudalism 500 years ago, the emergence of a new world system is occurring in the cracks of the old, in the spaces where capitalism cannot contain new noncapitalist forms of ownership, funding, decision-making, communication, and subjectivity. Post-capitalism has become the subject of much recent debate in political economy, spurred by notable publications by Jeremy Rifkin (2015), Paul Mason (2016), J.K. Gibson-Graham (2006), and Left accelerationists like Nick Srnicek and Alex Williams (2015). Though there is not uniform agreement among its proponents, post-capitalism generally describes building alternatives to capitalism within the existing system using technologies, business models, and forms of social organization focused on prefiguring the Great Transition. Whereas anti-capitalist politics generally follows an oppositional logic of resistance, post-capitalist politics redeploys existing infrastructure for activist causes. As Srnicek and Williams (2013) argue, "the material platform of neoliberalism does not need to be destroyed. It needs to be repurposed towards common ends." In particular, Left accelerationists reject the exclusive focus on what is often described as organic, grassroots, local, horizontal, or decentralized politics at the expense of systemic concerns, bureaucratic planning, technology, and transnational coordination (Fisher, 2011).

A detailed exploration of post-capitalism, the important differences between its major proponents, and its various critiques is beyond the scope of this book (see Pettifor, 2015; Postcapitalist ecology, 2015; The ground beneath, 2015; (Why we can't), 2015). In fact, none of our authors in this edited volume specifically reference post-capitalism; rather, post-capitalism indexes an abiding concern with transitional pathways toward an alternative political economy. There currently exist vast new technologies capable of disrupting or alternatively restructuring capitalism, including artificial intelligence and machine learning, robotics, nanotechnology, the Internet of Things, 3D printing, blockchain, biotechnology, and smart systems. There also exist novel ways to reorganize society, including emergent anti-proprietary and gift culture movements, the collaborative commons, guaranteed basic income, worker cooperatives, community land trusts, decentralized renewable energy, DIY and hacker culture, happiness economics, the circular economy, bioregionalism, ecovillages, and permaculture. The fact that these new technologies and forms of social organization exist, however, does not ensure a successful Great Transition. Instead, they only create its conditions of possibility. Realizing a Great Transition will depend on the capacity for new technologies and social relations to alter the balance of political and economic power. The most likely outcome will probably lie somewhere between today's imagined utopias and dystopias.

For example, there is evidence that many of the latest advances just mentioned have already been co-opted and contributed to the restructuring of capitalism. In the case of the sharing or gig economy, the digital revolution has only reinforced capitalist social relations, creating platform capitalism and a new class of precarious workers in its wake (Srnicek, 2016). However, the same digital technologies that constitute the sharing economy could be alternatively used to support noncapitalist relations in the form of platform cooperativism. Whether they do depends on whether new modes of production shift the balance of political and economic power. Emerging political movements indicate there is already a struggle underway. In the past few years, the world has witnessed a surge of anti-austerity, left-wing populism, and anti-capitalist movements responding to the crisis of neoliberalism. Examples include the Occupy movement, the indignados, the grassroots solidarity projects in Greece, transition towns and community currencies, Rojava's experimentation with stateless democracy, the Democracy in Europe Movement 2025 (DiEM25), the Nuit Debout movement in France and the electoral manifestations of these movements with Syriza and Popular Unity in Greece, Podemos in Spain, the Pirate party in Sweden and Iceland, the Left and Workers' Front in Argentina, Jeremy Corbyn in Britain, and Bernie Sanders in the USA. Each of these movements exploits the new technical infrastructure to launch programs of resistance and attempts to prefigure new models of social reproduction, which are independent of capitalism to varying degrees.

To focus on just one example in the USA, the Bernie Sanders campaign demonstrated that the American public was willing to debate systems change in mainstream media for the first time in recent memory (Nichols, 2015; Sanders' strength?, 2015). Sanders garnered massive grassroots support following a democratic socialist platform that sought to repoliticize the economy, extend democracy to the workplace, create new forms of participatory democracy, and limit the influence of a professional political class. He also represented the strongest position on climate legislation in the Senate (Adler, 2015), and defended many of post-capitalism's basic proposals, including guaranteed basic income and worker-owned cooperatives (Santens, 2016; Worker-owned businesses, 2014). Though his presidential campaign ultimately failed, it generated new political organizations that continue to amass popular support for his agenda.[1] Though Bernie's campaign cannot be equated with the aforementioned political movements, they share common aspects that are mutually reinforcing and indicative of a broader movement toward post-capitalism. In most cases, each was supported by a different model of social organizing that combined both social media and off-line organizing. Bernie Sanders, for instance, could not have gained prominence without the technical capacity to crowdsource his campaign, both through public funding via online contributions and grassroots political organizing. Globally, social movements have likewise evolved by incorporating social media and open-source technology, allowing for direct actions to be spontaneously organized and modified in real-time, so that they strategically adapt to changing conditions and constraints (Franco, Loewe, & Unzueta, 2015). While this new technical infrastructure has enhanced public participation in new political movements that contest capitalism, it has also created the conditions for a political economy based on new social relations to model alternative futures as the primary form of resistance (Buckland, 2016).

Overall, the best characterization of the next system is arguably defined by a reemergence of the commons. The enclosure of the commons was one of the primary historical conditions shaping the transition from feudalism to capitalism (Shiva, 2005). Since "the means of production are increasingly coextensive with our relationships in civil society," Kevin Carson (2016) exclaims, we only "need to tear down [the state's and capitalism's] enclosures of the social economy we've already built—and that can be done, to a large extent, by circumvention rather than conquest" (p. 26). The political economy of the commons, as supported by the transformational politics just mentioned, constitutes "what has been called plan C… an alternative to the failed plan A (austerity) and untested, but flawed, plan B (Keynesian growth based on further indebtedness)" (Kothari, Demaria, & Acosta, 2015). How exactly a common-based political economy could be achieved is, of course, a matter of debate among post-capitalists. Jean Lievens (2015) charts three possible pathways whereby a peer-to-peer society could develop either (1) after an economic collapse, (2) through neo-Keynesianism, or, preferably, (3) through a reformed state armed with a commons transitional plan that exploits new technology and modes of production to realize socialism. The democratic socialist platforms of Jeremy Corbyn and Bernie Sanders arguably represent examples of this third option.

Given both the increasing urgency of the Great Transition and the diversity of geopolitical reactions to neoliberalism, it is further necessary to conceive of alternative post-capitalisms. The concept itself holds no uniform meaning, and its multivalence indicates that post-capitalism merely characterizes a possibility space, affording opportunities for both openings and closures. Though pregnant with potential, the same material and social technologies born of post-capitalism harbor opportunities for capitalism's restructuring as much as they signify the potential for a next system. Utopian and dystopian possibilities compete side by side (Berger, 2015). Though the authors in this book each hold different assumptions and cover different aspects of the Great Transition, they all analyze the possibility space generated by post-capitalism with a keen understanding of its promises and perils.

Radical Approaches in Dialogue with Contemplative Social Sciences

Together, the authors in this book consider how radical knowledge-practices and contemplative social sciences might productively inform the technological and social advances of the Great Transition. The conversation between different radical knowledge-practices—such as feminist theory, post-growth environmentalism, the open-source approach to digital technologies, and social justice theories—and the emerging transdisciplinary field of contemplative social sciences is intended to transgress disciplinary boundaries and invent methods and concepts for better apprehending the immense challenges we face. The Anthropocene (or Capitalocene) will invariably alter humanity's self-understanding and unsettle the entrenched binaries, which shaped modernity and which generated its social and ecological crises. Modern divisions between nature and culture, subject and object, mind and matter can no longer be maintained, and we now require new forms of knowledge that are creative, offering syntheses of complex information that grasp the intricacies of life. The accelerated pace of technological development, the complexification of social organization, and the entanglement of the human and nonhuman, living and nonliving across vast spatial and temporal scales all create the conditions for progressive thought to flourish.

Contemplative social sciences respond to the need for progressive thought to encourage more conscious and sustainable patterns of life. Within academia, contemplative studies has become a uniquely transreligious and transdisciplinary field for cross-cutting inquiries. Traditional scientific understandings that take modern binaries for granted are losing ground to new methods and concepts for understanding complex and dynamic brain–body–world systems. Embodied, embedded, extended, and enactive (4E) approaches to cognition have introduced new ways to understand how nature and culture, subject and object, mind and matter are in fact co-produced. The old scientific models of inputs/outputs and stimuli/responses have become outdated. Research subjects are now attributed inner mental states, and increasingly, a degree of mentality seems to exist in every realm of matter. In the journal *Nature*, Richard

Conn Henry (2005) says, "The substratum of everything is of mental character"—a position expanded in Whitehead's process philosophy under the name of panexperientialism, which has also gained traction in the philosophy and science of mind through David Chalmer's (2013) theories of panpsychism and panprotopsychism.

Whether or not one fully subscribes to panexperientialism, it has nevertheless become clear that animals are active reality-testers, engaged in processes of speculative extrapolation and experimentation to modify their perception and behavior in dialogue with the environment. Science, like art, is now rightly understood as a social practice embodying and instantiating certain cultural values. Minds and bodies are now understood to be co-produced in their interaction with environments, and there is no longer any rational basis for maintaining an inside/outside split. As such, contemplative social sciences should extend and apply such innovative methods and concepts to our understanding and design of social organizations. In overcoming the traditional binaries of modernity, this will also help us better understand and negotiate our relations to the human and nonhuman world and help address important ethical questions.

Contemplative traditions have always challenged the modern distinctions between minds and bodies, the individual and the social, self and nonself, science, art, and philosophy by grasping their productive interconnections. And unlike positivistic science, a social science informed by contemplative wisdom would not view interdependence as a web of external relations somehow correlated, but, rather as an internal connection immediately present to one's inner awareness. As Alfred N. Whitehead (1926) wrote, "every entity is in its essence social," constituted by its relations to others, and immediately "present in other actual entities" (p. 108). Whitehead's process philosophy provides a naturalistic basis for understanding that individuals are both whole and part of a greater whole—a society of even greater societies. A contemplative social science thus informed would be in a unique position to discern the connections between individuals, societies, and ecologies using the methods of contemplative science.

Heretofore, contemplative studies has focused excessively on secular mindfulness techniques, though there exist a rich variety of contemplative practices and traditions available to future research. If these practices were studied using recent developments in 4E cognition, they could deepen and clarify our understanding of cognition in social and ecological systems. Whereas current secular mindfulness techniques tend to limit their interest to the instrumental benefits of practice, a contemplative social science might study the contemplation of everyday objects and social interactions. Everyday objects constitute the greater part of our ecology, they inform who we are, and they provide extraordinary insight into our social constitution. By contemplating my relation to everyday objects, for example, I can perceive how I am related to a complex web of human–nonhuman, living and nonliving, organic and mechanic interactions constituting myself and the whole geosocial landscape.

As the Anthropocene makes painfully clear, nature is just such a co-production of various assemblages. So, why not use contemplation to develop better ways to understand how our self-natures are always co-constituting social and ecological systems? In this way, contemplative practice could conceivably include everything and train us to perceive the intimacy of all things. Furthermore, since we are fundamentally sympoietic, world-making beings, we share a responsibility for making a better world for Earth's fellow creatures and future generations. Contemplative social sciences could thus also investigate the contingencies of responsibility and how to become more responsible in an era of anthropogenic climate change. These multiple commitments might form the foundations of contemplative social sciences through an ethico-onto-epistemology—an appreciation of the intertwining of ethics, knowing, and being, inspired by recent post-structural and process philosophies (Barad, 2007).

The consequences of taking this approach are not merely philosophical, but pragmatic. In *Inquiry into the Modes of Existence*, Bruno Latour (2013) explains that our attachments define us more than any essence or identity. The material goods, ideas, and passions that we are attached to constitute our being. Materiality and value, pragmatics and morality are always intertwined. Contemplative social sciences could use contemplation to understand how we are implicated in social and ecological systems, and how those systems could be more consciously and sustainably designed. Contemplative practices are natural allies for achieving these goals, because they have a unique capacity to train people to perceive complex interconnections and disentangle people from destructive attachments. In *A New Buddhist Path*, David Loy (2015) similarly argues that meditation can put us in greater touch with the immanent world, and engage a process of deconstructing and reconstructing the self in relation to that world. With this intention, contemplative social sciences might help us understand, for example, how the food we eat, our last trip to the shopping mall, or our daily use of information technology implicate us in the degradation of social and environmental systems and offer opportunities for living more sustainably not just personally, but structurally.

In her book *The Mushroom at the End of the World: On the Possibility of Life in Capitalist Ruins*, Anna Tsing (2015) argues that we should pay greater attention to the arts of noticing. Though Jedediah Purdy (2015) claims contemplative training is a privilege ill-fit to address political and economic concerns, I would argue that it has the greater capacity to enhance responsibility and solidarity when expressed as an ethico-onto-epistemology. Much of the modern philosophic foundations for today's political economy were inspired by the philosophy of mechanism, as interpreted by Thomas Hobbes and empowered by the idea of atomistic individualism, national sovereignty, and technocratic bureaucracy (Merchant, 1980, pp. 208–209). Similarly, modern production processes that dominate capitalist economics were born out of mechanistic philosophy and its resistance toward the organic (Giedion, 1969). This places contemplative social sciences as informed by post-structural and process philosophies on a radically different track, one which offers a strikingly different vision of political economy. It links the capacity to intimately understand one's situatedness with the traditional concerns of the social sciences, historically tied together in the interdisciplinary study of political economy.

Notes

1. See, Our Revolution, https://ourrevolution.com/; Brand New Congress, https://brandnewcongress.org/; Justice Democrats, https://justicedemocrats.com/

Bibliography

Adler, B. (2015, May 7). Here's how Bernie Sanders, the greenest presidential candidate, could get even greener. *Grist*. Retrieved from http://grist.org/politics/heres-how-the-greenest-presidential-candidate-bernie-sanders-could-get-even-greener/

Atwood, M. E. (2015, July 27). It's not climate change—It's everything change. *Medium*. Retrieved from https://medium.com/matter/it-s-not-climate-change-it-s-everything-change-8fd9aa671804

Barad, K. (2007). *Meeting the universe halfway: Quantum physics and the entanglement of matter and meaning*. Durham, NC: Duke University Press.

Barr, C., & Malik, S. (2016, March 7). Revealed: The 30-year economic betrayal dragging down generation Y's income. *The Guardian*. Retrieved from https://www.theguardian.com/world/2016/mar/07/revealed-30-year-economic-betrayal-dragging-down-generation-y-income

Benjamin, W. (2008). *The work of art in the age of technological reproducibility and other writings on media*. Cambridge, MA: Harvard University Press.

Berger, E. (2015, August 13). Into the mystic: Capitalism and the structuralization of spirituality. [blog]. Retrieved from https://deterritorialinvestigations.wordpress.com/2015/08/13/into-the-mystic-capitalism-and-the-structuralization-of-spirituality/

Blackwell, R. (2016, January 18). China now the largest installer of clean energy, report says. *The Globe and Mail*. Retrieved from http://www.theglobeandmail.com/report-on-business/industry-news/energy-and-resources/china-now-the-largest-installer-of-clean-energy/article28237771/

Buckland, K. (2016, March 22). Cultural shifts in the climate justice movement. *Roar*. Retrieved from https://roarmag.org/essays/paris-attack-climate-justice-movements/

Carson, K. A. (2016, Spring). Techno-utopianism, counterfeit and real. *Center for a Stateless Society Paper No. 20*.

Chalmers, D. J. (2013). Panpsychism and panprotopsychism. *The Amherst Lecture in Philosophy, 8*, 1–35. Retrieved from http://www.amherstlecture.org/chalmers2013/

Chang, H. J. (2010). *23 things they don't tell you about capitalism*. New York, NY: Bloomsbury Press.

Chu, K., & Davis, B. (2015, November 23). As china's workforce dwindles, the world scrambles for alternatives. *The Wall Street Journal*. Retrieved from https://www.wsj.com/articles/as-chinas-workforce-dwindles-the-world-scrambles-for-alternatives-1448293942?tesla=y

Fisher, M. (2009). *Capitalist realism: Is there no alternative?* Winchester, UK: O Books.

Fisher, M. (2011, November 16). The political aesthetics of postcapitalism. [Video file]. Retrieved from https://www.youtube.com/watch?v=GAQ6lhpVIss

Franco, M., Loewe, B., & Unzueta, T. (2015, June 22). How we make change is changing, part I open source campaigns for the 21st century. *Medium.* Retrieved from https://medium.com/@marisa_franco/how-we-make-change-is-changing-part-i-5326186575e6

Gibson-Graham, J. K. (2006). *A postcapitalist politics.* Minneapolis, MN: University of Minnesota Press.

Giedion, S. (1969). *Mechanization takes command: A contribution to anonymous history.* New York, NY: W.W. Norton & Company.

Gordon, R. (2016). *The rise and fall of American growth: The U.S. standard of living since the civil war.* Princeton, NJ: Princeton University Press.

Gorz, A. (2010, March). The exit from capitalism has already begun. *Cultural Politics, 6*(1), 5–14.

Hatton, C. (2015, October 26). China 'social credit': Beijing sets up huge system. *BBC News.* Retrieved from http://www.bbc.com/news/world-asia-china-34592186

Henry, R. C. (2005, July 7). The mental universe. *Nature,* 436. Retrieved from http://henry.pha.jhu.edu/The.mental.Universe.pdf

Hilton, I. (2016, November 21). With Trump, China emerges as global leader on climate. *Yale Environment 360.* Retrieved from http://e360.yale.edu/features/with_trump_china_stands_along_as_global_climate_leader

Huang, Z. (2017, February 22). Chinese president Xi Jinping has vowed to lead the 'new world order'. *Quartz.* Retrieved from https://qz.com/916382/chinese-president-xi-jinping-has-vowed-to-lead-the-new-world-order/

Hung, H. F. (2015, December 10). China fantasies. *Jacobin.* Retrieved from https://www.jacobinmag.com/2015/12/china-new-global-order-imperialism-communist-party-globalization/

Klein, N. (2014). *This changes everything: Capitalism vs. the climate.* New York, NY: Simon & Schuster.

Kothari, A., Demaria, F., & Acosta, A. (2015, July 21). Sustainable development is failing but there are alternatives to capitalism. *The Guardian.* Retrieved from https://www.theguardian.com/sustainable-business/2015/jul/21/capitalism-alternatives-sustainable-development-failing

Krauss, C., & Bradsher, K. (2015, June 24). China's global ambitions, cash and strings attached. *The New York Times.* Retrieved from https://mobile.nytimes.

com/2015/07/26/business/international/chinas-global-ambitions-with-loans-and-strings-attached.html
Kurlantzick, J. (2013). *Democracy in retreat: The revolt of the middle class and the worldwide decline of representative government*. New Haven, CT: Yale University Press.
Latour, B. (2013). *Inquiry into the modes of existence: An anthropology of the moderns*. Cambridge, MA: Harvard University Press.
Lehr, D. (2016, October 16). Why successful global green finance is all about the colour of private money. *South China Morning Post*. Retrieved from http://www.scmp.com/comment/insight-opinion/article/2028129/why-successful-global-green-finance-all-about-colour-private
Lievens, J. (2015). Can capitalism reform itself and move towards a p2p society? *Revista P2P e INOVAÇÃO, 2*(1), 6–24. Retrieved from http://www.brapci.ufpr.br/brapci/v/a/17333
Loy, D. R. (2015). *A new Buddhist path: Enlightenment, evolution, and ethics in the modern world*. Boston, MA: Wisdom Publications.
Macwilliams, M. (2016, January 17). The one weird trait that predicts whether you're a Trump supporter. *Politico Magazine*. Retrieved from http://www.politico.com/magazine/story/2016/01/donald-trump-2016-authoritarian-213533
Mason, P. (2016). *Postcapitalism: A guide to our future*. New York, NY: Farrar, Straus and Giroux.
Merchant, C. (1980). *The death of nature: Women, ecology, and the scientific revolution*. New York, NY: Harper & Row.
Mingfu, L. (2015). *The China dream: Great power thinking and strategic posture in the post-American era*. New York, NY: CN Times Books.
Moore, J. (Ed.). (2016). *Anthropocene or capitalocene?: Nature, history, and the crisis of capitalism*. Oakland, CA: PM Press.
Netessine, S., & Solodkiy, V. (2016, May 6). Five major fintech trends where China is leading the world. *South China Morning Post*. Retrieved from http://www.scmp.com/business/article/1941692/five-major-fintech-trends-where-china-leading-world
Nichols, J. (2015, October 14). The real debate last night was between democratic socialism and casino capitalism. *The Nation*. Retrieved from http://www.thenation.com/article/the-real-debate-last-night-was-between-democratic-socialism-and-casino-capitalism/
Osborne, S. (2015, December 22). China has made obedience to the state a game. *The Independent*. Retrieved from http://www.independent.co.uk/news/world/asia/china-has-made-obedience-to-the-state-a-game-a6783841.html

Ostry, J. D., Loungani, P., & Furceri, D. (2016, June). Neoliberalism: Oversold? *Finance & Development*. Retrieved from http://www.imf.org/external/pubs/ft/fandd/2016/06/pdf/ostry.pdf

Oxfam International. (2017, January 16). Just 8 men own same wealth as half the world. Retrieved from https://www.oxfam.org/en/pressroom/pressreleases/2017-01-16/just-8-men-own-same-wealth-half-world

Pettifor, A. (2015, November 6). Is capitalism 'mutating' into an infotech utopia? *Open Democracy*. Retrieved from https://www.opendemocracy.net/ann-pettifor/is-capitalism-mutating-into-infotech-utopia

Piacenza, J. (2015, April 22). On Earth day, Americans support principle of environmental protection, but divided over policy. *PRRI*. Retrieved from http://www.prri.org/spotlight/on-earth-day-americans-support-environmental-protection-divided-policy/#.VTenWFJHbCQ

Postcapitalist ecology: A comment on inventing the future. (2015, November 4). [blog]. Retrieved from http://thedisorderofthings.com/2015/11/04/postcapitalist-ecology-a-comment-on-inventing-the-future/

Purdy, J. (2015, October 8). The mushroom that explains the world. *New Republic*. Retrieved from https://newrepublic.com/article/123059/foraging-meaning

Randle, M., & Eckersley, R. (2015). Public perceptions of future threats to humanity and different societal responses: A cross-national study. *Futures*. Retrieved from https://doi.org/10.1016/j.futures.2015.06.004

Raskin, P., Anuri, T. B., Gallopin, G., Gutman, P., Hammond, A., Kates, R., et al. (2012). *Great transition the promise and lure of the times ahead*. Boston, MA: Stockholm Environment Institute. Retrieved from http://www.greattransition.org/documents/Great_Transition.pdf

Reich, R. (2011, September 3). The limping middle class. *The New York Times*. Retrieved from http://www.nytimes.com/2011/09/04/opinion/sunday/jobs-will-follow-a-strengthening-of-the-middle-class.html?src=rechp

Reich, R. (2015, August 2). The revolt against the ruling class. [blog]. Retrieved from http://robertreich.org/post/125702366950

Rifkin, J. (2015). *The zero marginal cost society: The internet of things, the collaborative commons, and the eclipse of capitalism*. New York, NY: St. Martin's Griffin.

Saez, E., & Zucman, G. (2014). Wealth inequality in the United States since 1913: Evidence from capitalized income tax data. *NBER Working Paper 20625*. Cambridge, MA: National Bureau of Economic Research. Retrieved from http://gabriel-zucman.eu/files/SaezZucman2014.pdf

Sanders' strength? Millennials back socialism. (2015, October 28). *MSNBC*. Retrieved from http://www.msnbc.com/watch/sanders-strength-millennials-back-socialism-553967171746

Santens, S. (2016, January 29). On the record: Bernie Sanders on basic income. *Medium*. Retrieved from https://medium.com/basic-income/on-the-record-bernie-sanders-on-basic-income-de9162fb3b5c#.vigc8geh1

Sellebraten, M. (2016, May 16). Sensity aims for China's smart city market. *Enterprise IoT Insights*. Retrieved from http://industrialiot5g.com/20160516/smart-cities/sensity-chinas-smart-city-market-tag29

Shiva, V. (2005). *Earth democracy: Justice, sustainability, and peace*. Berkeley, CA: North Atlantic Books.

Speth, G. (Ed.). (2016, April 1). New systems: Possibilities and proposals. Retrieved from http://thenextsystem.org/new-systems-possibilities-and-proposals/

Srnicek, N. (2016). *Platform capitalism*. Cambridge, UK: Polity.

Srnicek, N., & Williams, A. (2013, May 14). #Accelerate manifesto for an accelerationist politics. *Critical Legal Thinking*. Retrieved from http://criticallegalthinking.com/2013/05/14/accelerate-manifesto-for-an-accelerationist-politics/

Srnicek, N., & Williams, A. (2015). *Inventing the future: Postcapitalism and a world without work*. New York, NY: Verso.

Summers, L. (2015, October 7). The global economy is in serious danger. *The Washington Post*. Retrieved from https://www.washingtonpost.com/opinions/the-global-economy-is-in-serious-danger/2015/10/07/85e81666-6c5d-11e5-b31c-d80d62b53e28_story.html

The ground beneath the screens. (2015, October 28). *boundary2*. Retrieved from http://boundary2.org/2015/10/28/the-ground-beneath-the-screens/

Tsing, A. L. (2015). *The mushroom at the end of the world: On the possibility of life in capitalist ruins*. Princeton, NJ: Princeton University Press.

Whitehead, A. N. (1926). *Religion in the making*. New York: Fordham University Press.

(Why we can't) let the machines do it: A response to inventing the future. (2015, November 5). [blog]. Retrieved from http://thedisorderofthings.com/2015/11/05/why-we-cant-let-the-machines-do-it-a-response-to-inventing-the-future/

Williams, R. J. (2016, Spring). World futures. *Critical Inquiry, 42*(3), 473–546. https://doi.org/10.1086/685603

Worker-owned businesses. (2014, June 2). Retrieved from https://www.sanders.senate.gov/newsroom/recent-business/worker-owned-businesses-2014

Yang, Y. (2017, February 15). China penalises 6.7m debtors with travel ban. *The Financial Times*. Retrieved from https://www.ft.com/content/ceb2a7f0-f350-11e6-8758-6876151821a6

Žižek, S. (Ed.). (1994). *Mapping ideology*. London, UK: Verso.

Žižek, S. (2011). *Living in the end times*. London, UK: Verso.

Zack Walsh (Claremont School of Theology, USA) is a research specialist at Toward Ecological Civilization, the Institute for the Postmodern Development of China, and the Institute for Advanced Sustainability Studies in Potsdam, Germany. His research is transdisciplinary, exploring process-relational, contemplative, and engaged Buddhist approaches to political economy, sustainability, and China.

4

Having, Being, and the Commons

Ugo Mattei

Einstein used to say that the distinction between past, present, and future is only a stubbornly persistent illusion. The founder of relativity is one among a handful of intellectual giants (among them Plank, Heidegger, Eisenberg, and Husserl) that, thus far with modest practical success, have delegitimized the common sense of modernity, the mechanistic vision of reality, and the positivistic distinction between the domain of facts and that of values (Capra & Mattei, 2015).

Sometimes, such discredited epistemological distinctions emerge as an opposition between positive and normative propositions, such as "economics is the queen of social sciences" and "economics should be the queen of social sciences." I have not chosen my example randomly. Rather, the epistemological status of economics as "a social science" is due to the capacity of its experts to disagree *politically* on whether the diet in a nursery school should favor meat or fish, but to agree *scientifically* on factual propositions such as "if the price of meat goes up, then the quantity of fish consumed increases."

U. Mattei (✉)
University of Turin, Turin, Italy

V.M.B. Giorgino, Z. Walsh (eds.), *Co-Designing Economies in Transition*,
https://doi.org/10.1007/978-3-319-66592-4_4

Ironically, the scholarly stature of inquiry devoted to the commons has increased tremendously since Elinor Ostrom received the Nobel Prize (granted *only* to economics as the queen of social sciences). Nevertheless, the most promising work on the commons shows that the distinction between *facts* and *values*, like that between the domain of *having* and the domain of *being*, are "stubborn illusions" of a positivistic paradigm that Ostrom shares.

The crisis of perception within modernity that so many scholars have denounced for quite a long time only became worse, rather than being cured, in the last thirty years as its dramatic impact on our ecology became more and more apparent. Scholars have discussed the phenomenon of "cognitive capture" (Lakoff), which has limited critical thinking's capacity to influence mainstream thought. This capture, which has mostly affected the political left, is generated by a very radical transformation in the economy precipitated by "cognitive capitalism," which describes post-Fordist modes of production based on a dematerialized marketplace (Marrazzi).

What Althusser used to call the "ideological apparatuses of the State" are now powerful ideological apparatuses of globalized economic power. Their main achievement has been the construction of a business environment where consumerism, rather than being questioned, is promoted and advertised as the only and best way of life. They have kept discourse within borders that constrain the rational, possible, and politically viable to this reality, as if it were the only desirable reality.

"Stubborn illusions" preclude appropriate understandings of becoming, making it possible to conceive infinite growth on a finite planet, and making it possible to maintain a notion of development where the global south must follow the path already walked in the past by the "more advanced" economies. Much of mainstream academia currently works as a vehicle to implement such stubborn refusals to cope with reality. In such a climate, the notion of the commons is at high risk. Indeed, even a cursory look into the idea of becoming demonstrates the power that segregated, disciplinary perspectives typical of modern scientific positivism have, in keeping a *status quo*, been simply incapable of caring about the future. Thus, one generation is separated from another, becoming a discrete "object of observation" that as such can be studied and possibly measured. This perception is static and quite arbitrary.

Continuity, communication, incremental substitution, and becoming are what characterize the life of a living creature such as Gaia, our living planet. Each second, scores of individual human beings are born and substitute those that are dead, as it happens with the cells of every living creature or with the passage from one season into the other, or with every landscape and ecological system from the micro to the macro level. Whose well-being should we consider? What comprises a generation? How can it be located in the past, present, or future? Who belongs to a given generation? The old man in his deathbed? The baby just born? Those that happen to be thirty-five years old in that given moment? Generations and individuals within a generation are like the water in a river. The flux of change is so intimately part of it that every distinction, carrying some ontological status, can only be arbitrary. We should focus on the well-being of the whole ecosystem of the river. This is the challenge of dealing with the notion of becoming.

Thus, our discourse on the well-being of "future generations," to be interesting or even relevant, must be deeply contextualized in order to elucidate its purpose. What do we mean when we talk of "rights protected in the interest of future generations," as, for example, was done in the definition of "the commons" as attempted in Italy by the Civil Code reform proposed by the so-called Rodotà Commission? What apparatus of ideas do we need in order to introduce a modicum of long-term perspective into institutions that are currently designed around property rights that ideologically shift from having to being and back again, in order to facilitate short-term extraction and exploitation?

I would like to clarify here the genuine epistemological revolution that we need in order to deploy the notion of the commons as a cure to the aforementioned cognitive capture. There is a preliminary urgency to avoid the commons suffering the same sad fate of some other very promising notions, such as that of "sustainability," which has been fully naturalized within mainstream academia.

Words do have power. Certain words have been capable of suddenly subverting meaning that appears as stable, immutable, and institutionalized. By so doing, such powerful words can transform history and social events. On the contrary, other words, endowed with the very same potential, are condemned to remain missed opportunities. In secularized Western modernity, potentially subversive concepts are connected with the domain of the economic system, and connect it to law, politics, and philosophy, thus producing common sense across institutions. Let's take the experience of two such institutionally loaded words in recent history: "privatization" and "sustainability." The first has been capable of subverting and transforming history. The second, pacified incrementally over time, has lost its power to subvert and transform the *status quo*. Which one will be the fate of "the commons"?

Privatization dominates the current commonsense. It has disrupted civilizational history, which once posited faith in the notion of the Welfare State. The institutional outlook of capitalism throughout the Cold War era was based on a strong sovereign state, endowed with sufficient authority and power to mediate the conflict between capital and labor. At the end of the 1970s, a long and stubborn resistance against Keynesianism, the economic policy produced by such compromise, began to emerge. Its seeds were planted, beginning in the aftermath of World War II, by an academic group, the Montpellerin Society, whose membership included some of those who later became the masterminds of neoliberalism: Von Hayek, Von Mises, and Friedman. The main idea was "privatization." In the hands of talented politicians such as Reagan and Thatcher, privatization served as a weapon against the Welfare State, which proved much more lethal than expected. The Welfare State was less resilient than one might have thought. Once naturalized after the fall of the Berlin Wall as a bipartisan political platform, the concept of privatization has destroyed Keynesianism and changed the world in its wake. Privatization dominates today's common sense. It has successfully torn us away from a period in civilizational history that placed hope for inclusivity in government programs and the Welfare State.

On the opposite front, in the late 1960s, when the Keynesian model was not yet in terminal crisis, deep ecological thought emerged. Rachel Carson was the first notable figure to begin the movement. Fritz Schumacher translated it into economic strategies endowed with the tremendous prestige bestowed upon them as a beloved protégé of Lord Keynes himself. The notion of "sustainability" is thus born, beautiful in its simplicity. An economic system was considered sustainable so long as it did not consume more resources than it could regenerate. In other words, we must not confer the planet to *future generations* in a worse condition than we have received it from *past generations*. Despite the "stubborn illusion" denounced by Einstein, the target of this message is clear even within the narrow limits of institutional policy-making. It targets the *current generation* of powerful political and economic decision makers that can affect the becoming of the Anthropocene (Purdy, 2015).

The idea of sustainability is the foundation of an intellectual approach aimed at severing economic analysis from the mechanistic paradigm of scientific positivism. It searches for sufficiency, not growth. Sustainability is articulated within the context of "economic conversion": from "more" to "enough." Alex Langer emphasized that nature is not only material, but thoroughly spiritual and intimately personal (Viale, 2011). The break with economic orthodoxy and with the very common sense of modernity could not be more radical. Schumacher remained a highly heterodoxic economist, deeply critical of the dominant idea of development, which grounds the imperialist policies of market globalization promoted worldwide after the process of formal decolonization. His book, *Small is Beautiful*, is a cult hit in the current movement of "transition economics." However, following an early subversive phase, the idea of sustainability has been progressively normalized by the ideological apparatuses of global capitalism. "Sustainable growth" (or development), a clear oxymoron, is today a dominant notion in the comprehensive development plans (once Structural Adjustment Plans) of the World Bank and the IMF.

A fundamentally fraudulent idea of a green economy works as a fig's leaf for the new technological frontier of capitalism's exploitation of nature (and human beings). Fertile lands are covered with solar panels whose energy is used to exploit rare minerals from the land and transfer them from the south to the north, causing huge amounts of pollution from transportation. Soybean and corn monocultures eradicate other varieties of plants, increase the price of tortillas in the global south, and go to fill up the tanks of our biodiesel SUVs. The barrier between the food and fuel markets is thus diminished, as are those between them and financial speculation. The outcome of these irresponsible policies, destructive of any form of resiliency, can only be dependency and famine. The U.S. President Barack

Obama is the champion of such masterful hypocrisy. Paradoxically, President Trump, a climate change denier, may be more environmentally friendly than Obama, with all his green rhetoric, by increasing local production in the United States and thus limiting transportation.

Today, the commons must be appreciated as a field of contestation between two opposing views of the world. On the one hand, there is a revolution aiming at the construction of a new common sense and generative of a new paradigm (Bollier & Helfrich, 2012). On the other hand, precisely because it constitutes such a genuinely novel political emergence, this worldview is the object of attempts to subvert its meaning—a sort of spectacular reactionary "detournement" to use Gui Debord's idea. As in every attempt to produce false consciousness, this clash is a highly complex social phenomenon whose understanding requires sophisticated tools of critical analysis.

In the academic domain where ideological production is strongest, the idea of the commons was launched most famously by Garret Hardin, the biologist–economist–demographer and author of a very famous essay, *The Tragedy of theCommons*. His work has been interpreted as a sort of evolutionary theory legitimizing private property, wherein the institution of private property is reinforced within a narrow application of the "homo oeconomicus" paradigm. Beginning in the late 1980s, Elinor Ostrom, a political scientist and economist intellectually close to the so-called neo-institutionalism, organized a series of important inquiries to demonstrate that the commons were not a place without law, as argued by Hardin. Rather, they have proved capable of sustaining, sometimes for centuries, sharing arrangements capable of providing stable, virtuous, social equilibrium outside of any tragedy whatsoever. In 2009, Ostrom received a Nobel Prize for economics—the highest form of academic recognition. Mainstream economicshave attempted to revitalize the concept, after being burned by the financial crisis produced to a considerable extent by the implementation of the ideas of so many neoliberal Nobel Prize winners (Friedman, Baker, and Coase are just the best known to the larger public). Scholars such as North, Stiglitz, Kahneman, Krugman, and Williamson are among those whose theories have attempted to reintroduce realism into economic analysis.

Global resistance, as seen in Chapas, Cochabamba, and Seattle, for instance, shows that although Ostrom's critique of Hardin is decisive as a critique of the behavior of flesh and blood individuals (more often *homo civicus* than *homo oeconomicus*), it misses the mark politically. In fact, on the one hand, Ostrom spares the corporation (which is the true all mighty *homo oeoconomicus*), and on the other hand, she reinforces the dominant positivistic economic model by contributing to a fine-tuning of its less robust aspects (such as the assumption of rationality).

Hence, the Nobel Prize, as the standard of maximal mainstream recognition, has been granted to a vision whose political impact does not contribute to assigning responsibility for the current global tragedy of the commons. What really threatens the chances of "future generations" to *become* is indeed the predatory corporation behaving in a global environment that is significantly helpless in any effort to counteract its influence (in practice, a world of no law as suggested by Hardin).

Ostrom's contribution does not distinguish physical persons from moral persons, such that global corporations' predatory, extractive behavior is perfectly predicted by Hardin, both in the causes (short-term profit maximization) and in the consequences (overexploitation and tragedy). By failing to discuss (or even to recognize) such a distinction, Ostrom constructs an underlying ambiguity regarding the commons' political, cultural, and semantic significance, thereby exposing it to the risk of being subsumed by the positivistic paradigm of mainstream economic "science," and thus sharing the same fate as the potentially subversive idea of "sustainability."

Despite this risk, the scholarly work conducted worldwide on the paradigm of the commons has produced much more than a general awareness of its being alternative to the modern notions of "the private" (market) and "the public" (state). After the fall of the Berlin Wall, the privatization of the public sector (especially from the point of view of its motivations) became itself a factor explaining the global tragedy of the commons. The privatization of the public sector has been carried out in concert with cognitive capture, which is responsible for the current global "economic realism" (There Is No Alternative) supported by scores of philosophers in the New Realist Philosophical Manifesto (De Caro & Ferraris, 2012).

Only a deeply revolutionary program carried out at a variety of levels can resist the predominant common sense. Such a program must refuse the positivistic paradigm based on the distinction between facts and values and between science and politics. A revolutionary interpretation of the commons, which is the only one capable of avoiding the tragedy of the commons and restoring hope for future generations, cannot remain at the theoretical level, but requires concrete struggle (Capra & Mattei, 2015). Such struggle cannot consist of randomly disconnected episodes of resistance, but must be transformed into a renewal of commoning across institutions and must be connected to a network capable of transforming extractive institutions into generative ones from the bottom-up (Quarta & Spanò, 2016).

Practiced in this way, the commons is capable of providing alternatives to neoliberal policies through a radical, diffused, and relentless opposition toward any new enclosures, both physical and cognitive. Only a complete awareness of the commons in its physical form can overcome the process of cognitive capture, which forces even people in good faith to keep insisting on a pattern of behavior incompatible with long-term survival.

A collective reinterpretation of common space provides the theoretical power to envision a political economy of the commons. The motto that "Another world is possible" effectively motivates the political struggle of "global civil society," and demonstrates in the praxis of political commoning, even more than in the phenomenological critique of scientism, the theoretical weakness of the opposition between facts and values, which grounds both dominant economics and the new philosophical realism. Like a mole, the "commons" erode the roots of both private property and the state. In addition, we see in action a third dimension beyond the opposition between the "is" and the "ought to be" that erodes both the realism of the former and the dogmatism of the latter. It is the dimension of the "could be" that stimulates collective dreaming. The fantasy and the hope of commoning change the world by bringing the future generations already with us into the present.

Bibliography

Bollier, D., & Helfrich, S. (Eds.). (2012). *The wealth of the commons. A world beyond market and state*. Amherst, MA: Levellers Press.

Cacciari, P., Carestiato, N., & Passeri, D. (Eds.). (2012). *Viaggio nell' Italia dei beni comuni*. Napoli: Marotta & Cafiero.

Capra, F., & Mattei, U. (2015). *The ecology of law*. Oakland: Berrett Koheler.

Chignola, S. (Ed.). (2012). *Il diritto del comune. Crisi della sovranità, proprietà e nuovi poteri costituenti*. Verona: Ombrecorte.

De Caro, M., & Ferraris, M. (Eds.). (2012). *Bentornata realtà, Il nuovo realismo in discussione*. Torino: Einaudi.

Mattei, U. (2011). *Beni comuni. Un manifesto*. Bari: Laterza.

Merchant, C. (2009). *Ecology*. Amherst, MA: Humanity Books.

Negri, A., & Hardt, M. (2010). *Commonwealth*. Cambridge, MA: Harvard UP.

Ostrom, E. (2015). *Governing the commons*. Cambridge, UK: Cambridge University Press.

Pilger, J. (2002). *The new rulers of the world*. London: Verso.

Purdy, J. (2015). *After nature. A politics for the anthropocene*. Cambridge, MA: Harvard UP.

Quarta, A., & Spanò, M. (2016). *Beni Comuni 2.0*. Roma: Derive Approdi.

Rebelpainting. (2012). *Beni comuni e spazi sociali: una creazione collettiva*. Pisa: Rebeldia Edizioni.

Reich, R. B. (2008). *Supercapitalism*. New York: Vintage Books.

Settis, S. (2012). *Azione popolare. Cittadini per il bene comune*. Torino: Einaudi.

Teatro Valle Occupato. (2012). *La rivolta culturale dei beni comuni*. Roma: Derive Approdi.

Viale, G. (2011). *La conversione ecologica*. Rimini: Nda Press.

Ugo Mattei is the Alfred and Hanna Fromm Professor of International and Comparative Law at the University of California, Hastings College of the Law in San Francisco, and a full Professor of Civil Law at the University of Turin, Italy. He is the Academic Coordinator of the International University College of Turin (IUC), Italy—a radically new school where issues of law and finance in global capitalism are critically approached. He has recently oriented the focus of his research on the study of commons. He is leading a project on commons with Saki Bailey (IUC) and Filippo Valguarnera (Örebro University) in the context of the Common Core of European Private Law.

5

Par Cum *Pari*: Notes on the Horizontality of Peer-to-Peer Relationships in the Context of the Verticality of a Hierarchy of Values

Michel Bauwens

Definition and Description of the Peer-to-Peer Social Dynamic

We define peer-to-peer as the relational dynamic in distributed networks. Distributed networks are networks where individuals do not need permission to undertake actions and engage in relationships, because they are in control of their own productive resources, and therefore can undertake the production of common value through the self-aggregation of resources.

In our contemporary context, this means access to our own creative capacities, computing power and access to the communication networks, so that production of common 'immaterial' value can occur.

The following essay is a reworking of an earlier presentation: Pursuing the Common Good: How Solidarity and Subsidiarity Can Work Together Pontifical Academy of Social Sciences, Acta 14, Vatican City 2008 www.pass.va/content/dam/scienzesociali/pdf/acta14/acta14-bauwens.pdf

M. Bauwens (✉)
P2P Foundation, Chiang Mai, Thailand

V.M.B. Giorgino, Z. Walsh (eds.), *Co-Designing Economies in Transition*,
https://doi.org/10.1007/978-3-319-66592-4_5

As distributed networks, mostly in hybrid formats but nevertheless allowing for an unprecedented level of self-aggregation, are becoming the mainstay of our technical and social organization, our societal organization is in for an unprecedented overhaul. It is important to note that this model is now moving to more deeply influence all forms of material production as well, through the development of much cheaper distributed and networked machines that are connected to open design communities. Makerspaces and fablabs are prototyping these new industrial forms. Early production networks based on shared designs, such as Arduino or Atelier Paysan, have formed, and a vision of cosmo-local production, where 'everything that is light is global, and everything that is heavy is local' has been formulated elsewhere by this and other authors.

Some important characteristics are the following:

> As long as the self-aggregation occurs on the level of immaterial resources (i.e. resources that are copy-able and capable of being distributed on a massive scale at marginal cost), the creation of social value can occur outside the institutional field of both corporations and the state, even if for scaling purposes, the resources controlled by the two latter fields may be necessary for further transformations to occur.

Amongst the more important new social dynamics associated with these developments are:

- Peer production, as the generalized ability to create social value through self-aggregation
- Peer governance, as the generalized ability to manage this self-aggregation outside of market pricing, hierarchical mobilization of resources, or democratic negotiation (all three needed as potential mechanisms allocating scarce resources, but not in a sphere of self-aggregating abundant resources)
- Peer property, as the ability to protect the common value creation from private appropriation. This takes the form of new non-exclusionary, shared property formats, such as the Creative Commons and General Public License, which differ both from public/state/collective and from private exclusionary property.

Peer production has created an emerging model of production which has created three interdependent dynamics. This 'commons-centric economy' consists of:

1. productive communities engaged in the self-managed production of common artefacts;
2. aided by for-benefit institutions who manage the infrastructure of cooperation without a for-profit motivation; and
3. surrounded by an ecology of businesses creating 'scarce' and marketable added value around that commons.

A key question here is whether the relation between the commons and the market forms is 'extractive', that is, are the entrepreneurial entities unduly capturing the value of this human cooperation without an adequate return; or 'generative', that is, are these entities creating just and ecologically sustainable livelihoods. A recent report by the P2P Foundation, "Value in the Commons Economy" (2017), outlines some of the techniques used by 'value sovereign' productive communities, to avoid such types of capture. Value sovereignty refers to the capacity of these communities to independently evaluate and reward all contributions, independently of the market value assigned to it.

The Ethical Evaluation of P2P Dynamics: P2P is a Social Process Based on Equipotentiality

What are the ethical and inter-subjective implications of this emergence?

In this section, we would like to attempt an explanation on why peer production is such a strong candidate for a new social model.

What transpires from Pierre Levy's examination of both social control and power over nature is the increasing ability to start from the building blocks of matter, life and mind themselves. The broad movement is from a limited ability to influence nature and sociality as it is given 'externally', in a very broad 'holistic' way (premodernity), to the ability to influence collective 'molar' building blocks of such systems, that is, a mass or group orientation (modernity), and finally to the level of individuality (postmodernity).

This is true for the mastery of organic life processes through knowledge of genetics dealing directly at the DNA level, for the control of inorganic matter through material sciences involving an ability to work at the molecular and atomic level with nanotechnology and for the intellect and cultural/social sphere, which is moving from institutional/organizational intervention to the self-organized peer-to-peer level. A negative example is the level of deep behavioural and neural control now exercised by platforms like Facebook, which can intervene in our choices at this micro-level. Cambridge Analytica, a consulting company that was instrumental in the Brexit and Trump Insurgency wins, is an example of political capture. But again, the same techniques can be used for emancipatory purposes and human autonomy, depending on context and so forth.

In a positive and emancipatory context, the evolution of peer-to-peer dynamics can be seen to be in line with a broad evolution towards direct intervention through self-organized systems. Practices at this level of complexity, which tend to be more efficient and productive than previous models, create more surplus value and innovation in the societies practising them. The surplus of peer production tends to occur at this stage at the level of immaterial, cultural, intellectual, relational and spiritual wealth, in a way that can complement but also replace current logics of material accumulation.

It is here that I would like to introduce equipotentiality as the metaphysical basis of peer-to-peer relationships (i.e. the underlying view of the place of the human in the universe), as it is even more fine-grained than the individuality and individualism that was developed through modernity.

We could say that just as modernity developed all the implications of individuality, peer-to-peer processes develop all the implications and potentialities of relationality. Indeed, equipotentiality means the capacity of social systems to directly access the various skills of individuals, which can be aggregated selectively by the individuals themselves. Through equipotentiality, individuals allocate partial skills and effort to common value creation, finding identity and recognition through their engagement in such common projects. It's an object-oriented sociality, organized around transcendent objects and goals, that structure the peer-to-peer social system and the individuals within it.

This means that everyone can potentially cooperate in a project, that no authority can prejudge the ability to cooperate, but that the quality of cooperation is then judged by the community of peers, that is, through communal validation. In other words, distributed production is matched with distributed control mechanisms, through collective choice systems that avoid the emergence of 'representative' collective individuals, which would crystallize to take control of the social process. In equipotential projects, participants self-select themselves to the module to which they feel able to contribute.

In his landmark book on *The Wealth of Networks*, Yochai Benkler (2006) explains how open source communities coordinate themselves. Leadbeater (2007) paraphrases his argument:

> Open source communities resolve the difficulties of assessing creativity and quality by decentralising decision making down to individuals and small groups. They decide what to work on, depending on what needs to be done and what their skills are. There is little sense in working on a project that is already well staffed and where your contribution will add very little. It is very difficult to pull the wool over the eyes of your peers: they will soon spot if the contributions that you make do not really come up to scratch. That allows people to work on just their bit of the puzzle. Good central design rules allow the whole thing to add together. Work in open source communities gets done when creative people self-distribute themselves to different tasks, they submit their work to open peer review to maintain quality and the product has a modular design so that individual contributions can be clicked together easily. (Chap. 8, part 3)

Equipotentiality is an important concept in this context, and is a new view of humanity as a complementary contributor in the co-construction of common projects.

The ethical implications of equipotentiality are well drawn out by Jorge N. Ferrer, Ramon V. Albareda and Marina T. Romero (2011):

> An integrative and embodied spirituality would effectively undermine the current model of human relations based on comparison, which easily leads to competition, rivalry, envy, jealousy, conflict, and hatred. When individuals develop in harmony with their most genuine vital potentials, human relationships characterized by mutual exchange and enrichment would naturally emerge because people would not need to project their own needs and lacks onto others. More specifically, the turning off of the comparing mind would dismantle the prevalent hierarchical mode of social interaction—paradoxically so extended in spiritual circles—in which people automatically look upon others as being either superior or inferior, as a whole or in some privileged respect. This model—which ultimately leads to inauthentic and unfulfilling relationships, not to mention hubris and spiritual narcissism—would naturally pave the way for an I-Thou mode of encounter in which people would experience others as equals in the sense of their being both superior and inferior to themselves in varying skills and areas of endeavor (intellectually, emotionally, artistically, mechanically, interpersonally, and so forth), but with none of those skills being absolutely higher or better than others. It is important to experience human equality from this perspective to avoid trivializing our encounter with others as being merely equal. It also would bring a renewed sense of significance and excitement to our interactions because we would be genuinely open to the fact that not only can everybody learn something important from us, but we can learn from them as well. In sum, an integral development of the person would lead to a 'horizontalization of love'. We would see others not as rivals or competitors but as unique embodiments of the Mystery, in both its immanent and transcendent dimension, who could offer us something that no one else could offer and to whom we could give something that no one else could give. (p. 5)

An additional insight comes from John Heron (2006) who writes about the co-evolution of hierarchy and participation:

> There seem to be at least four degrees of cultural development, rooted in degrees of moral insight:
>
> 1. autocratic cultures which define rights in a limited and oppressive way and where there are no rights of political participation;

2. narrow democratic cultures which practice political participation through representation, but have no or very limited participation of people in decision-making in all other realms, such as research, religion, education, industry etc.;
3. wider democratic cultures which practice both political participation and varying degree of wider kinds of participation;
4. commons p2p cultures in a libertarian and abundance-oriented global network with equipotential rights of participation of everyone in every field of human endeavor.

Heron adds that

> These four degrees could be stated in terms of the relations between hierarchy, cooperation and autonomy.
>
> 1. Hierarchy defines, controls and constrains co-operation and autonomy;
> 2. Hierarchy empowers a measure of co-operation and autonomy in the political sphere only;
> 3. Hierarchy empowers a measure of co-operation and autonomy in the political sphere and in varying degrees in other spheres;
> 4. The sole role of hierarchy is in its spontaneous emergence in the initiation and continuous flowering of autonomy-in-co-operation in all spheres of human endeavor.

The crucial insight is this: until the advent of peer production, individual autonomy in cooperation was limited to small groups, which were unable to scale because the transactional cost of organizing commonality required hierarchical structures. However, peer production is the ability to globally coordinate a multitude of cooperating individuals and small groups, and in such a way that small group dynamics, that is, peer governance as the ability to manage such common projects, remain at the core of the process of value creation, and no longer at the periphery. There may be new forms of hierarchy (of merit, engagement and entanglement within the networks), but they cannot be equated with command and control mechanisms. This means that productive processes can now be autonomous and cooperative, which is a potentially important social advance. Until today, democracy and participation were limited to choosing representatives in the political field, while production itself remained a hierarchical and non-participatory process.

We should further note that peer production is not limited to the business or economic field, but can be applied to every form of value creation. Autonomy-in-cooperation becomes scalable throughout the social field.

There is, of course, much to say about peer governance itself, where power becomes interdependent, since it is based on voluntary contributions and not on wage-dependency, and such power can only be consensual. However, power can and does hide in the invisible architectures of the design of such social systems, requiring a literacy of cooperation from the cooperating communities, who need to become adept at value-sensitive design, so that diversity and autonomy are stimulated.

As John Heron (2006) says in concluding his examination, "the sole role of hierarchy is in the spontaneous emergence in the initiation and continuous flowering of autonomy-in-cooperation, in all spheres of human endeavour".

Passionate Production as a Superior Modality of Value Creation

In this section, we offer a series of arguments of why peer production is potentially a more efficient form of value creation.

Let's start with motivation. Precapitalist models of the division of labour, such as slavery and feudalism, were based on coercive cooperation, whereby the real producers of wealth had to respectively give away the totality (slaves) or a part (serfs) of their production. While the motivation of serfs would be obviously superior to that of slaves, neither group would be motivated to produce beyond subsistence without coercive pressure, and while slavery-based societies are said to be characterized for their lack of technical innovation regarding human work, medieval feudal societies fare better, but are still characterized by very slow productivity growth compared to capitalism, with the majority of the population not moving substantially beyond subsistence levels. Both systems are of course determined by 'extrinsic negative' motivation, that is, ultimately fear, possibly the lowest possible form of human motivation in terms of efficiency.

One could argue that the great social advance of the capitalist mode is to change the extrinsic negative motivation into a positive one, that is, mutual self-interest. Ideally, all parties exchange equivalent value with each other. The result has been an unprecedented rise in productivity and efficiency, but with a high social and natural cost. Indeed, while coercive modes can be characterized (in game theory format) as win–lose dynamics, capitalism's win–win is still very limited (and, of course, in reality, that ideal is rarely attained): parties in a market exchange cannot and do not take into account any externalities, whether it be social or natural.

This is why a for-profit enterprise can only innovative relatively, that is, strive for relative quality, while a for-benefit community cum institution can and does strive for absolute quality. What is remarkable for example is to note the absence of any 'planned obsolescence'-based design in open design projects.

Peer production is therefore characterized by the filtering out of both negative and positive extrinsic motivation, leaving only intrinsic positive motivation as the sole motivator. In other words, this system of voluntary contributions thrives on human passion and the search for creative expression, social recognition and the need for meaning in the process of common value creation.

Peer production is therefore highly efficient, based on a quest for absolute quality, and wherever this mode becomes economically feasible because of the drop-in coordination and transaction costs, it will generally tend to drown out competing modes.

However, in the transition period where peer production is in a seed form, it will give rise to many different hybrid formats, involving cooperation with both state and private forms of production and governance.

The Non-Reciprocal Logic of Peer Production

Historically, we have seen a succession of a tribal economy, primarily based on symmetrical reciprocal gift-giving, tributary economies based on a-symmetrical hierarchical allocation of goods according to social rank, and finally the dominance of market pricing mechanisms according to a logic of equivalent exchange.

What kind of social logic is behind peer-to-peer? As we will see, it is definitely not a gift economy based on direct reciprocity!

We are using the definitions of anthropologist Alan Page Fiske (1993), who uses a fourfold typology of possible inter-subjective relationships based on his research in his book, *The Structures of Social Life*, which he says are a valid 'relational grammar', for all cultures and temporalities.

According to Fiske (n.d.), this would give the following:

Dominant in the tribal gift economy:

In Equality Matching (EM) relationships, people keep track of the balance or difference among participants and know what would be required to restore balance. Common manifestations are turn-taking, one-person one-vote elections, equal share distributions.

Dominant in the tributary economies:

In Authority Ranking (AR), people have asymmetric positions in a linear hierarchy in which subordinates defer, respect and (perhaps) obey, while superiors take precedence and take pastoral responsibility for subordinates. Examples are military hierarchies (AR in decisions, control and many other matters), ancestor worship (AR in offerings of filial piety and expectations of protection and enforcement of norms), monotheistic religious moralities (AR for the definition of right and wrong by commandments or will of God).

Dominant in capitalist economies:

Market Pricing relationships are oriented to socially meaningful ratios or rates such as prices, wages, interest, rents, tithes or cost–benefit analyses. Money need not be the medium, and Market Pricing relation-ships need not be selfish, competitive, maximizing or materialistic—any of the four models may exhibit any of these features. Market Pricing relationships are not necessarily individualistic.

However, it is clear that the peer-to peer-dynamic is not covered by any of the first three definitions. As a reminder, peer-to-peer is based on voluntary contributions on the input side, but not to another individual, but rather to the whole collective project, and by universal availability on the output side. One can take without giving, and one can give without receiving anything back, though one has access, as have the non-givers, to the totality of the commons that has been created through this self-aggregation of effort.

Clearly, we are talking here about non-reciprocal, 'generalized' exchange, which do not fit the previous models. We therefore turn to Fiske's fourth model, which does give a correct definition of the inter-subjective logic of peer-to-peer.

He calls it 'Communal Sharing', and it is dominant in the emerging peer-to-peer modes:

> Communal Sharing (CS) is a relationship in which people treat some dyad or group as equivalent and undifferentiated with respect to the social domain in question. Examples are people using a commons (CS with respect to utilization of the particular resource), people intensely in love (CS with respect to their social selves), people who 'ask not for whom the bell tolls, for it tolls for thee' (CS with respect to shared suffering and common well-being), or people who kill any member of an enemy group indiscriminately in retaliation for an attack (CS with respect to collective responsibility).

We would therefore like to present an alternative account of social evolution, formulated by the Dutch author Wim Nusselder (2003), which beautifully summarizes the point we are trying to make:

> The primary economy is based on reciprocity, which derives from common ancestry or lineage. It is based on families, clans, tribes and exchange mostly operates through gifts which create further obligation. The division of labor is minimal and most often related to gender and age. The key question is 'to belong or not to belong'. Social groups are based and bounded by real or symbolic lineage. Wants are defined by the community. Leadership is in the hands of the lineage leadership.

The secondary economy arises together with power monopolies, which engender coercion as a means to force cooperation. We enter the domain of class societies, and production is organized by the elite in power, which holds together through the symbolic power, which transforms power into allegiance. Respect for power, in the form of tribute, taxes and so forth is normative. Distribution depends on your place in this chain of symbolic power. Wants are defined by the symbolic power, with symbolic markers monopolized. The key question is: 'to deserve power or to deserve subjection'. Social groups are bound by allegiance to power. Leadership is political and religious. Relationships, that is, allegiance, is highly personal.

The tertiary economy arises with the entrepreneur and capitalism. It is based on 'equivalent', that is, 'fair' exchange, which is normative. Power arises from relative productivity, relative monopoly over a needed good and the wage relationship, which creates dependence. Social groups are loose, and wants are determined by advertising and mimetic desire. Cooperation is no longer correlated to belonging. Relationships are impersonal.

The quaternary economy, based on peer-to-peer processes, is based on 'ideological leaders', which can frame common goals and common belonging and is based on membership and contribution. Contributing to the best of one's ability to common goals is normative, and the key question becomes: to follow an existing group or to create one's own, that is, to convince or be convinced. Contributions to many groups can overlap. Power is dependent on the power to convince.

From all of these that have been mentioned, we are tempted to formulate a temporary conclusion: that peer production based on the intersubjective logic of 'communal shareholding', that is, characterized by non-reciprocal generalized exchange between the individual and the collective, now a seed form present in a transitional economic regime, may well be the emerging logic of social and economic organization of a new political economy and civilization yet to arise.

What we arrived at as a preliminary conclusion is that peer-to-peer modes are highly efficient, and are based on advanced modes of motivation and cooperation, and on an ethic of non-reciprocal giving and sharing.

Peer-to-Peer in the Light of the Social Doctrine of the Catholic Church

An interesting point of comparison is to compare our findings regarding peer production, with the social doctrine of the Catholic Church, as it similarly puts civil society at the centre and sees the state and market forms as servants of civil society.

Let us briefly review the four pillars of the social doctrine, and make a preliminary examination of how the emergence of peer-to-peer modes may affect it. The four pillars are the recognition of personhood, the centrality of the common good as ideal standard for human behaviour, subsidiarity, as the necessity to exercise power at the lowest most appropriate level, and solidarity, stressing the interdependency of human action.

- Regarding personhood, there is no doubt that peer-to-peer modes respect personhood, and represent a 'relational augmentation' of individuality. Equipotentiality as the ethical and metaphysical principle underlying peer-to-peer does not endanger any concept of personhood. We would argue that it represents a deepening of personhood and the possibilities of self-realization and autonomy-in-cooperation.
- Regarding the common good, the peer production of common value is more respectful of the common good than market relations, which are genetically unable to take into account the necessary social externalities. Constitutively, peer-to-peer includes the convergence of individual and collective interest, so that individual effort strengthens the commons, which is universally available to all who need it. Some would suggest that forms of giving and sharing that do not require reciprocity would be ethically inferior to reciprocal giving, but I would suggest that the kind of giving and receiving that occurs in peer-to-peer is related to the common and represents an extension of the circle of care. But rather than rely on altruism, it relies on designing social systems so that individual and collective interests are aligned. Peer-to-peer dynamics do create strong personalized relationships amongst the core producers, but also allow for impersonal collaboration, while crucially enabling cooperation amongst strangers.
- Peer-to-peer modes strengthen subsidiarity, in the sense that civil society organizations, in the new more 'informal' form that it takes in the P2P context, increase their ability to create common value and decrease the necessity for both the market and the state to intervene. Both market and state remain complementary, and can play a substantial role in enabling and empowering the direct production of social value, through open business models that include benefit-sharing practices, and partner state policies which strengthen the infrastructure of social

cooperation. However, we would argue that peer production truly 'realizes' subsidiarity, as it enables all types of value creation which were hitherto monopolized by private entities and subject to commodification and market relations.

- The challenge of peer-to-peer lies in the fourth pillar of the social doctrine: solidarity. It's an issue which peer production cannot solve on its own.

Peer-to-peer modes, because they rely on voluntary contributions, are sustainable collectively, but not on the individual level. Projects can sustain themselves if they maintain the level of volunteering, but no individual can permanently maintain him or herself outside of the monetary system. P2P projects are essentially 'agnostic' as to the individual situation of the volunteers, as they rely on the surplus and abundance that they are able to mobilize through self-aggregation. It has no answer to the individual who cannot mobilize such resources (though it does create vast wealth in a commons mode, which is universally available), and it has no mechanisms to monetarily sustain the volunteers, beyond the creation of satellite economies around the commons.

This poses not just a problem for the individual, but for society, as it creates a 'crisis of value' for present market society. Indeed, as increasing numbers of individuals choose passionate production and the infrastructure for peer production continues to improve, the ability to directly create use value increases exponentially, but the ability of the market to monetize such social utility only rises linearly, creating a huge gap between the desire and potential for peer production, and the ability of individuals to sustain such choices. This is, in our opinion, one of the constitutive causes of precarity and precariousness amongst the new generations.

Society therefore needs a new mechanism of solidarity, but which cannot be a monetization based on profit-sharing, as this would simply 'crowd out' the willingness for non-reciprocal contributions. The solution then would seem to be very similar to the one familiar to the Catholic Church in the Middle Ages, when nearly one-quarter of the male population was supported in their spiritual production, through gifts to the Church. In contemporary terms, this could mean an unconditional form of support in the form of a basic income.

Such a basic income should not be seen as welfare, but as recognition by society and the market that social innovation has become the primary vehicle for value creation, and it would, in a transitory period, allow citizens to move more easily in and out of the market sphere, and manage their careers over the longer term, so that periods of peer production could be more easily inserted. Europe is already moving in that direction, through transitional labour market policies being developed in various countries, but it is still based on the premise that transitional periods are less productive than formal labour, while the new emerging realities point to the opposite, namely, that value creation is highest through peer production, and not in the market sphere, which is becoming increasingly derivate *vis-à-vis* social innovation in the P2P sphere.

Before such basic income becomes a reality, open business models based on benefit sharing and partner state policies should be supported.

In the longer term, we have to ask the question about moving from a political economy where peer-to-peer is a subset of market relations in a context of infinite-growth capitalism, to a political economy where the market for scarce goods is a subset of a peer to peer economy and a civilization centred around the notions of the commons and direct value creation through civil society.

If infinite growth is indeed a logical and physical impossibility in the context of finite natural resources; and when the artificial scarcities currently impeding social cooperation and innovation will be increasingly seen as counterproductive, then such a shift might be seen as a conditional inevitability.

If we find a solution for the solidarity issue, and the right interface and combination between non-reciprocal peer production in the immaterial field and cost-recovery mechanisms for the production of scarce rival goods, then the resulting society would be seen to be a more adequate expression of the value system expressed by the social doctrine.[1]

Notes

1. Nota Bene: For extensive documentation on the emergence of peer to peer formats throughout the social field, see https://wiki.p2pfoundation.net

Bibliography

Bauwens, M., & Niaros, V. (2017). Value in the commons economy: Developments in open and contributory value accounting. Berlin: Heinrich Boll Foundation.

Benkler, Y. (2006). *The wealth of networks*. New Haven, CT: Yale University Press.

Ferrer, J., Albereda, R., & Romero, M. (2011). Embodied participation in the mystery: Implications for the individual, interpersonal relationships, and society. *Revision, 27*(1). Retrieved July 4, 2017 from http://www.estel.es/EmbodiedParticipationInTheMystery,%201espace.doc

Fiske, A. (1993). *Structures of social life*. New York, NY: Free Press.

Fiske, A. (n.d.). Relational models theory. Retrieved July 4, 2017 from http://www.rmt.ucla.edu/

Heron, J. 2006. Personal communication to the author. Retrieved July 4, 2017 from https://wiki.p2pfoundation.net/4.3._Evolutionary_Conceptions_of_Power_and_Hierarchy

Leadbeater, C. (2007). We think: The power of mass creativity. London, UK: Profile. Retrieved July 4, 2017 from http://wethink.wikia.com/wiki/Chapter_8_part_3

Nusselder, W. (2003). What is the present economy. Retrieved July 4, 2017 from http://wim.nusselder.antenna.nl/schrijfsels/what_is_the_present_economy.htm

Michel Bauwens is the founder of the P2P Foundation, based in Chiang Mai, Thailand, and works in collaboration with global researchers in the exploration of peer production. Michel is also research director of CommonsTransition.org, a platform for policy development aimed towards a society of the commons and a founding member of the Commons Strategies Group, which has organized major global conferences. He is the (co-) author of three recent books, including'*Network Society and Future Scenarios for a Collaborative Economy*. In 2017, Michel Bauwens crafted a Commons Transition Plan for the city of Ghent in Belgium.

6

Economics Beyond the Self

Laszlo Zsolnai

Henrik Ibsen's famous figure Peer Gynt can be considered as an ideal type of today's profit-seeking, globally oriented, greedy entrepreneur who wants to realize himself via money. In Ibsen's play, Peer Gynt, a successful businessman at an age about 60, reflects on his life and then discovers that his life-journey was without meaning. Finally, he begins to pose questions like: "What does it mean to be oneself?" and "Who have I been in all my life?" (Ims & Zsolnai, 2010).

The self of Peer Gynt was an all desiring and never insatiated ego. The Gyntish self is about a universal pursuit of money, material possessions and power. Aiming at realizing his self, Peer Gynt became a global entrepreneur engaged in dirty businesses of many kinds. Close to the end of his life, Peer Gynt learns from the Button-molder that he has never been himself. Peer Gynt asks the Button-molder what is it "being oneself." He got the answer: "To be oneself, Peer Gynt, the self must die."

Almost all wisdom traditions of humankind require some form of self-transcendence of the person to achieve a meaningful and ethical life. This

L. Zsolnai (✉)
Business Ethics Center, Corvinus University of Budapest, Budapest, Hungary

V.M.B. Giorgino, Z. Walsh (eds.), *Co-Designing Economies in Transition*,
https://doi.org/10.1007/978-3-319-66592-4_6

paper uses the example of Buddhism to show how "going beyond the self" can be realized in economic and social contexts. Mindfulness and compassion are at the heart of Buddhist way of life whose noble goal is to end suffering of all sentient being (human and non-human alike).

Buddhism in the Context of Global Capitalism

In his article "From Western Marxism to Western Buddhism," philosopher Slavoj Žižek (2001) argues that "although Western Buddhism presents itself as the remedy against the stressful tension of capitalist dynamics, allowing us to uncouple and retain inner peace and Gelassenheit, it actually functions as its perfect ideological supplement." He adds that the Buddhist meditative stance is an efficient way for many Western people to fully participate in the capitalist economy while retaining the appearance of mental sanity.

There is a lot of truth in Žižek's view. Elements of Buddhist thought and practice are used in many business organizations. Global technology companies including Google are connecting to the power of mindfulness and meditation to drive happiness in their business functioning. They employ the advice of the famous Zen master Thich Nhat Hanh and other Buddhist thinkers on how practicing mindful meditation at the workplace help companies to improve their bottom line. (Confino, 2014).

The question remains whether "doing things right" without "doing the right things" can contribute to realize ethics and meaning in a true sense. The noble goal of reducing suffering of human and non-human sentient beings cannot be achieved without adopting the ethics of true compassion.

In his insightful essay "Buddhists Must Awaken to the Ecological Crisis," philosopher and Zen teacher David Loy (2016) argues that for many modern Buddhists "the path is sometimes understood as a program of psychological development to help us let go of afflictive emotions and resolve personal problems." But he adds "there is a difficulty if one believes that all problems are due to the way the mind works; the solution, then, is simply to change the mind rather than change the system."

In agreement with David Loy, we can say that the goal of traditional Buddhism is to transcend (in one way or another) the unsatisfactory world. But modern Western Buddhism is helping people to adapt to the unsatisfactory world better.

Loy (2016) emphasizes that Buddhism provides a wonderful archetype that can bring individual and social transformation together: the bodhisattva. "Bodhisattvas have a double practice—as they deconstruct and reconstruct themselves, they also work for social and ecological change. We need to develop less self-centered and more compassionate ways of living in the world. (…) By devoting ourselves to the well-being of others, including the health of the earth's ecosystems. Such concerns are not distractions from our personal practice but deeper manifestations of it."

Innovative Buddhist entrepreneurs in Bhutan, Europe, USA and elsewhere are working in the bodhisattva style to achieve or at least to get closer to a sustainable and peaceful world.

Principles of Buddhist Economics

Modern Western economics promotes doing economic activities in self-interested, profit-maximizing ways. It cultivates desires. People are encouraged to develop new desires for things to acquire and for activities to do. The profit motive of companies requires creating more and more demand. Modern Western economics aims to introduce markets wherever social problems need solving. In modern Western economics, the value of an entity (be it a human being, another sentient being or an object) is determined by its marginal contribution to the production output. An economic project is considered worthy of undertaking if and only if its discounted cash flow is positive. There is only a limited place for ethics in modern Western economic thinking. The profit-seeking economic players can consider the interest of others only if it serves their own interest, at least in the long term.

Buddhist economics challenges the basic principles of modern Western economics and proposes alternative principles such as (I) minimizing suffering, (II) simplifying desires, (III) non-violence, (IV) genuine care and (V) generosity. The main principle promoted by Buddhist economics is to *minimize suffering* of all sentient beings concerned, including non-human sentient beings. From a Buddhist viewpoint, a project is worthy to be undertaken if it reduces the suffering of those who are affected. The suffering-minimizing principle can be formulated to reveal that the goal of economic activities is not to produce gains but to decrease losses. Since humans (and other sentient beings) display loss sensitivity, it is worthy trying to reduce losses for oneself and for others rather than trying to increase gains. Losses should not be interpreted only in monetary terms or applied only to humans. The capability of experiencing losses, that is, suffering, is *universal* in the realm of both human and non-human kingdoms.

Buddhist economics suggests not to multiply but to *simplify human desires*. Above the minimum material comfort, which includes enough food, clothing, shelter and medicine, it is wise to reduce one's desires. Wanting less could bring substantial benefits for the person, for the community and for nature as a whole. Buddhism recommends moderate consumption and directly aims at changing one's preferences through meditation, reflection, analyses, autosuggestion and the like.

Non-violence (ahimsa) is the main guiding value of Buddhist economics for solving social problems. It is required that an act does not cause harm to the doer or the receivers. Non-violence prevents doing actions that directly cause suffering for oneself or others and urges participative and communicative solutions. Community-based economy models are good examples of potential solutions. Communities of producers and consumers are formed to meet their needs at the lowest cost and to reduce risk through long-term arrangements. Community-based economies use *local resources* to meet the needs of *local people* rather than the wants of markets far away. They are based on partial or complete self-reliance. (Douthwaite, 1996).

Buddhist economics favors practicing *genuine care*. Robert Frank (2004) developed five distinct types of cases when socially responsible organizations are rewarded for the higher cost of caring.

1. Opportunistic behavior can be avoided between owners and managers.
2. Getting moral satisfaction, employees are ready to work more for lower salaries.
3. High-quality new employees can be recruited.

4. Customers' loyalty can be gained.
5. The trust of subcontractors can be established.

Caring organizations are rewarded for the higher costs of their socially responsible behavior by their ability to form commitments among owners, managers and employees and by their ability to establish trust with customers and subcontractors.

Buddhist economics suggests that *generosity* might work in business and social life because people behave like *Homo reciprocans*. They tend to reciprocate what they get, and often they give back more than they received. Samuel Bowles, Robert Boyd, Ernst Fehr and Herbert Gintis (1997) summarize the model of Homo reciprocans as follows: Homo reciprocans comes to new social situations with a propensity to cooperate and share, responds to cooperative behavior by maintaining or increasing his or her level of cooperation and responds to selfish, free-riding behavior by retaliating against the offenders, even at a cost to himself/herself, and even when he or she could not reasonably expect future personal gains from such retaliation.

The contrast between mainstream Western economics and Buddhist economics can be illustrated as two frameworks in opposition (Zsolnai, 2007). Mainstream Western economics represents a *maximizing framework*. It wants to maximize profit, desires, markets, instrumental use and self-interest, and tends to build a world where "bigger is better" and "more is more." Buddhist economics represents a *minimizing framework* where suffering, desires, violence, instrumental use, and self-interest must be minimized. This is why "small is beautiful" and "less is more" nicely express the essence of the Buddhist approach to economic questions (Table 6.1).

Table 6.1 Mainstream Western economics versus Buddhist economics

Mainstream Western economics	Buddhist economics
Maximize profit	Minimize suffering
Maximize desires	Minimize desires
Maximize markets	Minimize violence
Maximize instrumental use	Minimize instrumental use
Maximize self-interest	Minimize self-interest
"Bigger is better"	"Small is beautiful"
"More is more"	"Less is more"

Realizing Buddhist Principles in Business

In her book on Buddhist Economics, UC Berkeley scholar Claire Brown (2017) suggests that Buddhist principles should be realized at the level of individual and the level of government. However, the main players in modern economic life are business organizations. So, the real challenge is to realize Buddhist principles in business. The paper presents working examples from the USA, Africa and Thailand to illustrate the possibility of doing Buddhist business in today's real-world context.

Greyston Bakery Inc. is a for-profit social enterprise founded in 1982 by a Zen Buddhist meditation group led by Bernard Glassman. The company is famous for producing high-quality baked goods and ice cream products. It practices an "open hiring" policy, which means that anyone can apply to work with them, regardless of his or her background, including people with a criminal record. Besides the bakery, Greyston also has a foundation, which comprises an integrated network of not-for-profit and for-profit entities in Yonkers, New York, that provides jobs, work force development, affordable housing, community gardens, youth services, child care and health care to the local community. (Zsolnai, 2015).

Greyston Bakery incorporates a positive societal agenda into its core business by hiring individuals who have been chronically unemployed due to their lack of skills or education, homelessness, drug addiction or imprisonment. Greyston is a force for self-transformation and community economic renewal through its activities. Besides operating a profitable business, the company serves the community in many forms in an area where the level of poverty and the unemployment rate is high.

In 2014, the Greyston Bakery generated more than ten million dollars in revenues. Greyston became the first Benefit Corporation (B-Corp) in New York State, operating with a "triple bottom line": prioritizing profits, social contributions and environmental impact.

The company's mission is to make a positive impact on society while engaging in transparent business operations with a commitment to maintaining customer satisfaction. From the beginning, Greyston has had a focused mission to reinvigorate the impoverished community of Southwest Yonkers in New York State and set an example for other socially conscious businesses to follow. It is constantly striving to make a long-term, sustainable impact on the local community and the situation of individuals. Greyston is a successful enterprise with a compassion-based philosophy that fuels community development and commitment to human growth. The company is managed in the belief that everything is interconnected, and that one cannot afford to ignore sections of society. Based on Zen traditions, Greyston places great emphasis on personal empowerment and transformation. Employees are encouraged to develop a sense of responsibility for themselves, their families and their co-workers. Gainful employment is seen as the first step on an individual's path toward success. Social justice, economic development and personal empowerment are the important building blocks that support the operations of the company.

The company is famous for baking brownies for Ben & Jerry's ice cream and producing a line of brownies and cookies that can be found at Whole Foods shops. Over time, the business has evolved into a gourmet wholesale–retail bakery that operates a state-of-art facility, producing high-quality baked goods. Greyston Bakery also financially supports Greyston Foundation, which promotes holistic solutions for helping break the cycle of poverty.

Apopo is a Belgian social enterprise with headquarters in Tanzania and operations in Mozambique, Angola, Thailand and Cambodia that researches, develops and implements landmine detection technology for saving human lives and preventing human suffering. It was founded by Bart Weetjens in 1995 when he developed a unique solution for the global landmine problem. Weetjens realized that rats as intelligent and widespread animals can be used to detect mines and even tuberculosis in underdeveloped countries. In two decades, Apopo helped to destroy more than 100,000 landmines by which 900,000 people were freed from the threat of explosives and more than 2160 hectare land was released for local communities. In addition, more than 11,000 tuberculosis cases were detected and more than 80,000 positional tuberculosis infections were halted.

The *Santi Asoke* is a Buddhist reform movement in Thailand which aims to realize Buddhist community-based economic model. Asoke communities are organized around the principle self-transcendence, specified in the slogan "Consume Little, Work Hard and Give the Rest to Society" (Essen, 2011). Residents in the Asoke communities limit their consumption by adhering to the Buddhist precepts, sharing communal resources and following the rules of frugality, namely, recycle, reuse, repair, reject. Deeply concerned with the problems of greed, Asoke members prefer being content with little. They also emphasize sufficiency, which follows the Buddhist Middle Way doctrine (neither asceticism, nor luxury).

Work serves as a primary method of meditation in Asoke committees. Members practice open-eye meditation continuously as they work and interact with others within their community. They believe that "giving the rest to society" is a way to selflessness. They contribute to the material and spiritual development of Thai society through a variety of means. For instance, they run vegetarian restaurants and non-profit markets that simultaneously provide the Thai public with healthy food and useful goods at low cost while promoting the concepts of selflessness and generosity.

Conclusion

Buddhist economics represents a strategy, which can be applied in a variety of contexts. Buddhist economics may help Buddhist and non-Buddhist people alike to create livelihoods which aim to reduce the suffering of human and non-human beings by practicing non-violence, caring and generosity.

Buddhist economic and business models are only a subset of a much broader set of spiritually inspired models which are based on the intrinsic motivation of economic actors for serving the common good, and suggest measuring success in a holistic, multidimensional way. In these models, profit and growth are not final ends but only elements of a broader set of objectives. Similarly, cost–benefit calculations are not the only means of economic decisions but integrated into a more comprehensive scheme of wisdom-based economizing. (Bouckaert & Zsolnai, 2012).

References

Bouckaert, L., & Zsolnai, L. (Eds.). (2012). *The Palgrave handbook of spirituality and business*. London: Palgrave Macmillan.

Bowles, S., Boyd, R., Fehr, E., & Gintis, H. (1997, June 7). *Homo reciprocans: A research initiative on the origins, dimensions, and policy implications of reciprocal fairness*. Research Initiative on Reciprocal Fairness, University of Massachusetts, Boston.

Brown, C. (2017). *Buddhist economics. An enlightened approach to the dismal science*. Bloomsbury Press.

Confino, J. (2014, March 28). Thich Nhat Hanh: Is mindfulness being corrupted by business and finance? *The Guardian*. Retrieved December 30, 2016 from https://www.theguardian.com/sustainable-business/thich-nhat-hanh-mindfulness-google-tech

Douthwaite, R. (1996). *Short circuit. Strengthening local economics for security in an unstable world*. Dublin: The Lilliput Press.

Essen, J. (2011). Economic sufficiency and Santi Asoke. In L. Zsolnai (Ed.), *Ethical principles and economic transformation—A Buddhist approach* (pp. 61–77). Berlin: Springer.

Frank, R. (2004). *What price the moral high ground? Ethical dilemmas in competitive environments*. Princeton and Oxford: Princeton University Press.

Ims, K., & Zsolnai, L. (2010). Self-realization in business: Ibsen's peer Gynt. In R. Ghesquière & K. Ims (Eds.), *Heroes and anti-heroes. European literature and the ethics of leadership* (pp. 137–150). Garant. Antwerp/Apeldoom.

Loy, D. (2016, August 23). Buddhists must awaken to the ecological crisis. *Lion's Roar*. Retrieved December 30, 2016 from http://www.lionsroar.com/can-we-awaken-to-the-ecological-crisis/

Žižek, S. (2001, Spring). From Western Marxism to Western Buddhism. *Cabinet Magazine*, Issue 2. Retrieved December 30, 2016 from http://www.cabinet-magazine.org/issues/2/western.php

Zsolnai, L. (2007). Western economics versus Buddhist economics. *Society and Economy, 29*(2), 145–153.

Zsolnai, L. (2015). *Post-materialistic business: Spiritual value-orientation in renewing management*. New York, NY: Palgrave.

Laszlo Zsolnai is a professor and Director of the Business Ethics Center at the Corvinus University of Budapest, Hungary. He is Chairman of the Business Ethics Faculty Group of the CEMS (Community of European Management Schools–The Global Alliance in Management Education). He is President of the European SPES Institute in Leuven, Belgium. His recent publications include "Post-Materialistic Business: Spiritual Value-Orientation in Renewing Management" (Palgrave, 2015), "The Spiritual Dimension of Business Ethics and Sustainability Management" (Springer, 2015), "Ethical Leadership. Indian and European Spiritual Approaches" (Palgrave, 2016) and "Economics as a Moral Science" (Springer, 2017).

7

The Koan of the Market

Julie A. Nelson

Introduction

In Zen Buddhism, koans are stories or questions that serve as invitations to investigate—to investigate the universe, to investigate our lives as they are, and to investigate the present moment. Practitioners using one famous Korean koan continually ask of everything, "What is this?" A bird—"What is this?" A breeze—"What is this?" Such constant questioning encourages us to not fall back on what we think we already know. It opens us to taking a fresh look. It opens us to the possibility of being surprised! I suggest we treat "the market" and "capitalism" as concepts to be investigated by means of the koan, "What is this?" Many writers on mindfulness and economics claim to already know the "nature" or "essence" of markets and capitalism. But do they?

My approach is rather different from that of many Buddhist scholars who write on social issues. I've been a student of Zen for a number of years, and am a senior dharma teacher in the Boundless Way Zen school. And I

J.A. Nelson (✉)
Department of Economics, University of Massachusetts, Boston, MA, USA

V.M.B. Giorgino, Z. Walsh (eds.), *Co-Designing Economies in Transition*,
https://doi.org/10.1007/978-3-319-66592-4_7

am also an economist, by training and by profession. I'm a rather unusual one, having specialized in the areas of feminist and ecological economics, which are distinctly marginalized within the profession. What my exploration of economics has told me is that much of the writing done on Buddhism and economics is *insufficiently radical*. And it is so for precisely the same reasons that seem to mark it as "radical" for many. Let me explain, starting by summarizing a common story line.

The Usual Mindfulness-and-the-Economy Story

First, a Buddhist speaker or writer calls attention to the immense suffering going on in the world that is related to the economy. We point out—correctly—that, for example, rampant consumerism doesn't lead to happiness, and instead leads to over-exploitation of the natural world. We cite statistics about widening inequalities in income and wealth, and about the persistence of poverty. We relate stories of abuses committed by corporations in the name of profits and free markets. These facts are undeniable. We clearly need to point these out and work to relieve them. The question is how. What is the cause? What is the cure?

Then, many writers—including, for example, Helene Norberg-Hodge (2002), Ken Jones (2003), David Loy (2008), and Joel Magnuson (2008)—go on to make further assertions. They claim that the cause of the suffering we see is a capitalist, market system that is inherently based on greed and exploitation. The claim is made that, simply *of its nature*, "the market" is solely and inexorably characterized by competition, self-interest, global expansion, and domination. Our current economic system "institutionalizes greed," writes David Loy, for example. It is dominated by corporations that "tend to take on a life of their own as new types of collective ego," he claims, and whose CEOs find it impossible to pursue any goal other than profit (2008, pp. 88–89).

Lastly, a solution is proposed. Clearly, if that is the nature of the system that we are in now, then in order to stop the suffering, we need to make an enormous leap into some completely different system. This different system is usually defined in terms of characteristics that are diametrically opposed to those said to characterize our present system. The new, mindful economy, it is said, must be based on values of cooperation and on small, local, egalitarian, non-profit, and non-monetized types of organizations (Magnuson, 2008; Norberg-Hodge, 2002). Because the envisioned change is large, this is often considered a radical proposition. But "radical" comes from the Latin word for "root," and this solution, based on conventional understandings of economic life, does not come close to going to the root of the problem. For that, we have to dig deeper, and understand the root of those conventional beliefs.

Critique #1: There Is No "Essential" Market

The first part of the usual mindfulness-and-economics story aligns well with the canonical teachings of Buddhism. The bodhisattva Avalokiteshvara (also called Guanyin or Kanzeon) is the symbolic embodiment of the Buddhist practitioner who "hears the cries of the world." Buddhist teachings call on us to release our focus on our idea of ourselves as separate entities, to pay attention to the suffering of others, to not make divisions of "us" and "them," and to act with compassion.

But the next step—the further assertions about "the nature" of markets and capitalism—is bad economics. It is bad economics not because it's "too radical," but because it fails to look beyond the common myth that there is a particular unchanging, essential, simple "nature" to our current economic system. Both critics of market systems and proponents of market systems now tend to buy into the idea that capitalist market economies are all about calculation and self-interest. This is what has been promulgated by economists and disseminated by the business media. The idea that firms are "driven" to "profit maximize," however, while now bandied about as a truism, was actually *invented* by economists as *a theory*. Economists wanted our field to imitate physics, a "hard" science, in order to prevent it being classified with the "soft" fields of sociology and the humanities. The theory of profit maximization elegantly boils down the whole messy process of running a business into a simple matter of applying calculus to find the top point on a mathematical profit function.

Afflicted with physics-envy, economists confused math with scientific rigor—quite oddly, since the result is dogma rather than open-minded investigation. The eagerness to represent the world in simple, precise-looking models also motivated the invention of the image of rational, autonomous, self-interested "economic man," as well as ideas about "drives" (note the mechanical analogy) for accumulation and growth.

The idea that capitalist economies are based on self-interest, competition, and so forth, then, did *not* come from studies of actual businesses or actual markets. In reality, businesses and markets are far more than simple math problems. Actual businesses are places of complex social interactions, of complex social relations. Actual markets are also like that. They have elements of both competition *and* cooperation. They have both pecuniary (or monetary) interests going on *and* all sorts of other interests, good and bad.

For example, the real problem that has led to many outrageous chief executive officer (CEO) salaries and a pattern of widening inequality is *not* "too much competition." It is too much *cooperation*. What is actually happening is that CEOs are sitting on each other's boards. They are very chummy. There is lots of solidarity and cooperation going on, but it is going on within a very small group in positions of power, where they are able to arrange things to give themselves even more economic power. They use the excuse that there is a "competition" for CEO "talent" and claim that the market "dictates" ridiculously large compensation packages. That is a bunch of nonsense being used to rationalize greed and hide the real power dynamics.

It is often claimed that CEOs *cannot* choose to prioritize environmental concerns, creativity, or service to the community over profits (Loy, 2008, p. 88). This is also false. It turns out that if one actually studies the law, and one actually studies markets, one will discover that the idea that there is a "law" or "mandate" that firms have to maximize profits is not true (see Bratton, 2011; Nelson 2006, 2011, 2016b). As mentioned earlier, it was made up out of whole cloth by economists. In practice, the laws, the courts, and markets generally allow corporate leaders substantial leeway to make choices, whether for good (such as reducing negative environmental impacts) or for ill (including enriching themselves at the expense of workers and shareholders).

Capitalism has no unchanging "nature" or "essence." Economic systems are as impermanent as anything else. They are changeable. They are variable. I keep coming up against the idea that there are preexisting "essences" again and again in my work in social science. There is very interesting work in psychology that demonstrates how beliefs in essences arise as creations of the mind. Buddhism, of course, teaches us a great deal about the fallacy of mental creations, and how these mental creations stand in the way of skillful action.

Critique #2: There Is No Airplane to Florida

What about the solution? The usual story often ends with a dualistic contrast between a presumably evil, competitive, oppressive, global capitalism and a wonderful world of cooperative, egalitarian, and small-scale solidarity.

We have a saying in the sangha that I sit with, that "there is no airplane to Florida." Here in New England it is very snowy and cold in the winter, and people dream of a Florida vacation. One is supposed to be warm and happy when one gets there! What "there is no airplane to Florida" means is that there is never going to be a time when we can say that we've found the right sangha, the right teacher—the right economy!—and can just relax and say, "Ah, now I've found it! This is it!" The good news and the bad news of meditation practice is that one is right here. One is where one is. And even attachment to a teacher, even attachment to a sangha—even attachment to a particular vision of a better world—are not places we can rest.

If we think that small, non-profit institutions will somehow automatically give us good results, we might want to think again. Families, for instance, are very small, non-profit, very local, and presumably based on values of love. They are also too often sites of neglect, domestic violence, and even murder. Scandals about power, money, and sexual abuse in Zen centers also illustrate that small and non-profit does not mean ideal.

Total egalitarianism and democracy are also not necessarily the sort of solutions that they are sometimes envisioned to be. Total egalitarianism ignores differences in abilities. In my work as a feminist economist, I've done a lot of thinking about issues of caring labor, which has also caused me to think more about hierarchies of power. When I think about caring relationships between parents and children, and between nurses and patients, for example, it seems that some element of difference in power is unavoidable. Meanwhile, though total democracy may sound good, it can be bad news for people in a voting minority. Is it possible to have some levels of hierarchy or leadership—not extreme cases, but some levels of differentiation—in which respect and even care is still possible? I think it is, not only in intimate relations but also in relations of work and community (Nelson, 2016a).

In terms of social action, I think the conventional mindfulness-and-economics story also leads to a real temptation to get into adversarial, and even contemptuous, us-versus-them thinking. We have "us," the contemplative people, the people who want a new economy, who want a caring economy. And there are "them," the CEO of ExxonMobil, the heads of those organizations that have horrible actions going on. But to me, a very basic teaching of Zen is that "them" is "us." If I do not understand my own greed, anger, and ignorance, I am just going to continue to inflict them on the world. Importantly, I need to understand that the CEO of ExxonMobil is dealing with the same factors of greed, anger, and ignorance that I am, and that in the realm of emptiness there is no separation between that person and me. Only in this way can I come up with ways of action that do not demonize and dehumanize people on an imagined "other side." In no way is the refusal to engage in us-versus-them thinking a prescription for complacency. Rather, it is the root of the sort of non-violent action so impressively described and demonstrated by leaders such as Martin Luther King and Mahatma Gandhi.

So the standard sort of dualistic view—that we have to give up on the current economy and jump someplace else—is insufficiently radical. It still works within the categories set out by mainstream economics, and encourages us to focus too strongly on someplace other than where we are. So what *can* we hope for?

Conclusion

I'm a Zen practitioner, and Zen—at least in the form in which it is now being taught and practiced in contemporary Western societies—is just unrelentingly empirical. The fundamental teaching about maintaining a "'don't know' mind" means that there is nothing to grasp onto in terms of metaphysical beliefs. While teachers and texts can give guidance, fundamentally one has to keep on finding out things for oneself. So in regard to economic life, as well, I encourage people to keep finding out things for themselves. When one hears about a theory, does it jive with what one sees in one's daily life? And when we look at how economies actually function, rather than relying on ideological teachings about how they function, we will find both that there is a lot of suffering here and now, and that there are also places for action, here and now. We do not need to jump to someplace else to be able to do good. We need to enact our compassionate response here and now, where we actually are.

Let me end with the closing paragraphs of an essay I wrote a few years back on "The Relational Economy":

> Sometimes I am accused of being Pollyannaish—which means naïve—about large corporations and about economies, because I do not firmly condemn "greedy global corporate capitalism" and advocate some kind of new cooperative, local, solidaristic economy. But I do not think this is the case. Rather, I am an equal-opportunity skeptic. I do not believe that any sort of institution—business, government, non-profit, local enterprise, community, family, or, alas, even a Buddhist sangha—has an essential "nature" that makes it *automatically* serve human (and ecological) ends, because people are who we are. Our poisons, our thirst, our suffering, cannot be made to magically disappear by some perfection of system, structure, or scale. Yet, in each moment, we have an opportunity to respond.
>
> A key contribution of Buddhism, I believe, is in reminding us about non-attachment, and warning us against latching onto us-versus-them thinking. Applied to economic suffering, this does not mean inactivity, and

does not mean that attempts at transformation, including local community action, must be abandoned. But the teachings of Zen Buddhism and other contemplative practices, I suggest, should also encourage us to be alert to the temptations of self-righteousness and to be more open to wide and deep engagement *with* businesses, governments, and the larger, painful world. (Nelson, 2011)

References

Bratton, W. W. (2011). At the conjunction of love and money: Comment on Julie A. Nelson, does profit-seeking rule out love? Evidence (or not) from economics and law. *Washington University Journal of Law and Policy, 35*, 109–115.

Jones, K. (2003). *The new social face of Buddhism: A call to action.* Boston: Wisdom Publications.

Loy, D. R. (2008). *Money, sex, war, karma: Notes for a Buddhist revolution.* Boston: Wisdom Publications.

Magnuson, J. (2008). *Mindful economics: How the U.S. economy works, whit it matters, and how it could be different.* New York: Seven Stories Press.

Nelson, J. A. (2006). *Economics for humans.* Chicago: University of Chicago Press.

Nelson, J. A. (2011). The relational economy. In L. Zsolnai (Ed.), *Ethical principles and economic transformation: A Buddhist approach* (pp. 21–33). Dordrecht: Springer.

Nelson, J. A. (2016a). Husbandry: A (feminist) reclamation of masculine responsibility for care. *Cambridge Journal of Economics, 40*, 1–15.

Nelson, J. A. (2016b). Poisoning the well, or how economic theory damages moral imagination. In G. DeMartino & D. McCloskey (Eds.), *The Oxford handbook of professional economic ethics* (pp. 184–199). Oxford: Oxford University Press.

Norberg-Hodge, H. (2002). Buddhism in the global economy. In A. H. Badiner (Ed.), *Mindfulness in the marketplace: Compassionate responses to consumerism* (pp. 15–27). Berkeley: Parallax Press.

Julie A. Nelson is Professor of Economics at the University of Massachusetts, Boston, USA; a Senior Research Fellow at the Global Development and Environment Institute; and a senior dharma teacher in the Boundless Way Zen school. She is the author of *Economics for Humans* (2006) and many other books and articles examining the relationship of economics to feminism, ecology, and ethics. Among these are "A Buddhist and Feminist Analysis of Ethics and Business," *Development* 47(3), 2004, and "The Relational Economy" in *Ethical Principles and Economic Transformation—A Buddhist Approach*, ed. Laszlo Zsolnai, Dordrecht: Springer, 2011.

8

Epistemology of Feminist Economics

Zofia Łapniewska

Introduction

Economics is often portrayed as an objective and rigorous science, giving the impression of being one of the physical rather than social sciences (Longino, 1990; Nelson, 1996a). The principle of rational choice, as well as the implementation of game theory and mathematical formulas, allows economists to calculate the effects of certain phenomena, or to predict, not necessarily precisely, the outcomes of some economic decisions. Despite its imperfections, econometrics remains the mainstay method of analysis—perceived as not necessarily accurate, but the best reflection of our economic reality. But, as always, the question remains: can we quantify everything? Would it be possible to make economic forecasts based on animal spirits (human emotions motivating consumer and investor confidence (Keynes, 1936)) or cognitive biases such as the illusion of control, selective perception, illusion of validity, optimism bias, risk

Z. Łapniewska (✉)
Institute of Economics, Finance and Management,
Jagiellonian University, Kraków, Poland

V.M.B. Giorgino, Z. Walsh (eds.), *Co-Designing Economies in Transition*,
https://doi.org/10.1007/978-3-319-66592-4_8

compensation and so forth (Akerlof & Shiller, 2009)? Or, how about the way we value common goods and services that don't rely on notions from Hobbes' *Leviathan* to be governed and prosper (Hobbes, 2010 [1651]; Ostrom, 1990)? And finally, how can we use numbers to illustrate the emotions or affective and bodily sensations accompanying care (Deleuze & Guattari, 1987)? Feminist economics attempts to face these questions by referring to the ethics of care (Phillips, 2007; Tronto, 1987) and going beyond quantitative methods (Nelson, 1993; Poteete, Janssen, & Ostrom, 2010).

In this chapter, I put forward a thesis that feminist economics is an economics of becoming, focused on processes instead of only outcomes. To support it, I concentrate specifically on the epistemology of feminist economics. The first part of this text is dedicated to the premises of the ethics of care, its critique and prospects. In the second part, I introduce a selection of feminist epistemological concepts that are then used in determining research methods. The last part of this chapter recommends methods used by feminist economists and addresses new trends and discussions in this field.

Economics and Ethics of Care

Feminist economics is a critical field of study within economics, attempting to overcome androcentric biases in the discipline (cf. chapter by Margunn Bjørnholt in this volume). It is guided by the ethics of care, a framework for moral and political judgement, as well as by feminist epistemology as the basis for its methodology (Strassmann, 1999). Julie A. Nelson argues that feminist economics "challenges economic analyses that treat women as invisible, or that serve to reinforce situations oppressive to women, and develops innovative research designed to overcome these failings" (Nelson, 2008). Feminist economics shares research interests with other heterodox approaches, such as institutional economics and post-Keynesian or ecological economics; yet it also differs substantially from them due to its overriding feminist perspective. Some of its core areas of concern include care, social reproduction, the environment and well-being.

Moreover, as I propose in my thesis, feminist economics focuses on processes—including processes of "becoming"—and, given its various epistemologies, it differs from mainstream economics' interest in the figure of self-interested *homo economicus* at its core (Strober, 2003). The French philosopher Gilles Deleuze (2006) uses the term "becoming" to conceptualize "becoming different" from the identities present in our habitual thinking (Stagoll, 2005, pp. 25–27). For Deleuze, a human being is not a stable and rational individual that remains the same person despite various experiences and stimuli, but is a constantly changing being shaped by a moving order of forces. This dynamic approach to individuals is an important factor in care services. The "functionings" (Sen, 1993) of a caregiver and care-receiver evolve over time, and so does the relationship between them. Deleuze's becoming, which I interpret here as becoming different from the economic man, refers to bonds built with others, which Rosi Braidotti (2006) describes as:

> a faithfulness that is predicated upon mutual sets of inter-dependence and inter-connections, that is to say sets of relations and encounters. These compose a web of multiple relationships that encompass all levels of one's multi-layered subjectivity, binding the cognitive to the emotional, the intellectual to the affective and connecting them all to socially embedded forms of stratification. (p. 136)

Feminist economists share this point of view, seeing the world around us in terms of social constructions and perceiving people as connected and concerned with the well-being of others, and, hence, also emotional beings influenced by their environment in their decision-making (Folbre, 1994; Nelson, 1996b; Waring, 1988). Consequently, their research is guided by the ethics of care, which is not only important for feminist economics but also constitutes an integral component of other heterodox traditions.

The ethics of care is described by Joan C. Tronto (1987) as "a set of sensibilities that every morally mature person should develop, alongside the sensibilities of justice morality" (p. 662). These sensibilities are developed when individuals experience both caring for others and being cared for by others. Tronto (1987) concludes further that "[t]he dearth of caretaking experiences makes privileged males morally deprived" (p. 652). Care that mostly burdens women is often perceived as insignificant, hidden and belonging to the private sphere, even though it often leads to their time poverty and economic hardship. Feminist economists in their research aim to elevate the meaning of care by showing that the public/private split is artificial and harmful to both women and men. Clare Ungerson (1995) claims that to change our understanding of care and citizenship, it is essential to dispose of that split. Feminist economics shows that a more equal division of care responsibilities between women and men can improve the lives of women and men alike (Esplen, 2009). Numerous studies illustrate that care work contributes significantly to the economy, fosters reproduction and development of societies and provides equal chances for a good life for all (Budlender & Sharp, 1998; Elson, 1998).

It is also necessary to transform the dominant ethos away from individualistic perspectives to a more social and collective one based on reciprocity, solidarity and equal rights (Phillips, 2007). Seeing people as engaged in the relationships of care at every stage of their lives reformulates the definition of human nature in mainstream economics. It is no longer that of a rational self-made man maximizing his own interests. The ethics of care accepts the fact that relational responsibilities create a social order that may be incompatible with the full exercise of individual rights. Rosi Braidotti (2006) calls the forcible creation of such social identity "the death of the ego" (p. 155). She emphasizes that "ethical behaviour confirms, facilitates and enhances the subject's *potential*" (Braidotti, 2006, p. 134). This "becoming", or transformation, in people's lives can also be seen as a deep journey to our inner treasure—which Plato (1993) calls *agalma*—that makes us valuable persons. Such an evolved form of self-knowledge may lead to building "a society based on care [that] would perhaps be less violent, rageful, and unhappy than many current societies are" (Tronto, 1995, p. 148). The epistemology of feminist economics is guided by that logic.

Unfortunately, not all existing needs for care can be met, primarily due to the scarcity and commodification of care. In this respect, the analysis of care goes beyond gender issues and includes disadvantaged groups, such as ethnic minorities or the poor, that may have difficulties to access care (Duffy, 2011). This broader perspective is close to the approach of intersectionality. In this regard, Tronto's (1987) following questions are still relevant:

> [w]ho determines who can be a member of the caring society? What should be the role of the market in a caring society? (…) How much inequality is acceptable before individuals become indifferent to those who are too different in status? How well do current institutions and theories support the ethic of care? (p. 661)

Institutions, as well as people, function in a complex net of social relations, which is why the responsibilities they perceive as binding are also complex and sometimes competing. In addition, people tend to care more for those who are close to them—physically, emotionally or culturally. The question of context has always been important for feminist economists, as it enables them to situate the subjects and objects of their research in a particular time and culture/society. At the same time, feminist epistemology has rejected objectivity and pure rationality (Nelson, 1996b).

The market of care emerged for those without care relationships or with greater care needs than their social web could accommodate, resulting in the commodification of care and services provided by both public and private institutions. Efficiency seems to be the only factor impacting the market of care which encloses care within discourses focused on cost. Also for many individuals, buying care has become part of this reductive shortcut of bringing costs down, including capitalizing on resources offered by the black market of care services provided by migrant workers. These global care chains cause "care drain" in the migrants' countries of origin and can also take the form of modern-day slavery (Ehrenreich & Hochschild, 2004). Care, however, should not be perceived as simply another commodity dragged into the capitalist market logic of exploitation. The nature of care is more complex and is based on relational responsibilities between a caregiver and a care-receiver. Care as a process, in order to develop properly, requires that both parties work on their specific roles and on their "becoming" subjects, which means transforming themselves into more sensitive beings and feeling empathy with others. This corresponds with the position of Deleuze and other post-modern thinkers, for example Judith Butler (2004), that one's self does not remain the same stable, rational individual, but arises from confluences of expectations, societies, laws and other stimuli from their environment (Stagoll, 2005, p. 27). *Ipso facto* care, described earlier, should include attentiveness to the needs of others, taking responsibility for their own actions, gaining certain skills and finally responding adequately (Fisher & Tronto, 1990; Phillips, 2007). These qualities are not limited to care relations only, but they can be used as principles in all spheres of life. They can guide professional activities, contacts with family and friends, or our capacity for engaging in collective political actions or volunteer work. All these spheres and issues are also studied by feminist economists.

The intention of this part of the chapter was to present only the most important focal points of political and moral discussions that guide inquiries in feminist economics as an economics of becoming. By applying the ethics of care and relational responsibilities perspective to their research, feminist economists concentrate on equality, justice, relationships with others and context. In doing so, they distance themselves from an individualistic point of view, which makes them different from mainstream economists and their methods. Care, efforts to reinforce its status and its equitable distribution between women and men are undoubtedly key issues in feminist economics. Other key issues include trying to create better living conditions for women and the disadvantaged, while questioning the concepts of rationality, truth and objectivity. These aspects of feminist epistemology will be discussed in the next part of this chapter.

Feminist Epistemology

Feminist epistemology, defined as the feminist engagement with cognition, the production of knowledge and the perception of truth, coincides with the assumptions of feminist economics on at least four different planes: (1) a critique of rationality and dualism (Bordo, 1987; Lloyd, 1984), (2) gender biases in science (Code, 1996; Longino, 1990), (3) the re-envisioning and reconstruction of scientific practices through, for example, the inclusion of context, values and ethical opinions (Beneria, 2003; Nelson & Goodwin, 2005) and, finally, (4) the knowledge formed by, for example, ordinary experience and leading to the improvement of life (Harding, 1995a; Nussbaum, 2000). These planes are also mirrored in Deleuze's works, since he challenges Platonic theories privileging originality, essence and constancy (Deleuze & Guattari, 1987). Although feminist epistemology is complex and includes a diversity of theoretical positions, I introduce and discuss in more detail the four themes I consider to be the most well-represented in feminist economics.

The feminist critique of rationality and dualism has been initiated by Genevieve Lloyd (1979) and Susan R. Bordo (1987), among others. They argue that "the Man of Reason" is derived from the "Cartesian promise of absolute epistemic objectivity and ultimate foundations for knowledge" (Bordo, 1987, p. 2). Lloyd determines that our contemporary consciousness, which follows the ideal of rationality, also associates the "male" with the "rational" and the "female" with the "non-rational" (Lloyd, 1979, p. 18). Susan Hekman (1990) and Julie A. Nelson (1996b) quote further dualisms on which Enlightenment epistemology rests, such as the public/private, subject/object, culture/nature, formal/informal, individual/social and autonomous/dependent dualism, thereby showing the privileged character of the first element, mainly attributed to men, over the second element, most often recognized as distinctly feminine. They disagree with the Enlightenment's "claim that only rational, abstract, universalistic thought can lead to truth" (Hekman, 1990, p. 5), and argue that "social sciences are subjective, but that this subjectivity is their strength, not their weakness" (ibid.). Bordo (2002, p. 85) also refers to Aristotelian modes of knowing, namely *thought* (or reason), which is immaterial and universal, and *sensing*, which is the domain of the body that Bordo describes as material and precise. In contrast, Gilles Deleuze's and Félix Guattari's (1987) concept of affect maintains that sensing can also refer to the states of body and mind, which are difficult to grasp.

Feminist economic methodologies, which are described in more detail in the next section, move beyond these dualisms, aiming to destabilize and deconstruct them (Jennings, 1993; Ungerson, 1995). By perceiving the world as a social construct, feminist economists avoid using bold cognitive categories and reject dichotomous presuppositions to view social processes in their constant flux and forms of "becoming", which is consistent with my thesis that feminist economics is an economics of becoming. As a social scientist, I not only maintain a pluralistic understanding of truth and knowledge that is contextually dependent, but I also view sex and gender as changing (cf. Butler, 2004) according to the "patterns of culture" (Benedict, 1934). Bodily transformations which do not necessarily reflect the traditional duality of sexual identity are becoming more and more common, and the models and patterns of social behaviour are evolving. In addition, Lloyd (1984) indicates that "[d]econstructive strategies can assist our understanding of the symbolic content of the 'male' and 'female,' and our understanding of what is distinctive about the relations between women and the symbol structures which, as symbol users, they share with men" (p. IX).

This topic has been brought up by feminist economists for many years regarding political and social debates, such as in Nelson's article entitled "Would women leaders have prevented the global financial crisis? Teaching critical thinking by questioning a question" (2013). She argues that in order to develop critical thinking, students must notice "both difference *and* similarity" between genders and avoid simplistic binary thinking (Nelson, 2013, pp. 2–3). These observations apply not only to the employees of institutions in the global financial market, but also to the structures of academia. This reflection brings us closer to the next theme of feminist epistemology, which addresses gender biases in science.

The feminist critique of science studies, which involves revealing gendered biases embedded in scientific practices, has been articulated by feminist theorists such as Sandra Harding (1995a), Helen Longino (1990) and Julie A. Nelson (1996a). Harding (1995a) aptly notices that "assumptions have been those of the dominant groups, as in the racist, sexist and class-bound biological determinist ones" (p. 11). They limit the hypotheses and methods of scientific inquiry, which consequently do not result in plausible models and theories (Longino, 1993). Nelson (1996a) recognizes that "contemporary economic theorizing is based on a set of a priori postulates that focus on only selected aspects of human behavior", which covers "the 'tough' areas of public life (by which they mean markets and government)" and "the efficient use of economic resources, pushing aside the 'soft' areas of family finances and economic and social equity" (p. B3).

The selection of economics research methods used to follow a similar path, valuing quantitative methods (regarded as "objective", "formal" and "rational") over qualitative ones (seen as "informal" and "imprecise"). Many feminist economists, instead of adhering to previous models, call for treating all methods on equal terms and selecting them depending on research topic and needs (Goodwin, Nelson, Ackerman, & Weisskopf, 2005; Macdonald, 1995). Janet Seiz (1995) recommends positioning a researcher on the epistemological "middle ground" between the overconfident angle of trust in scientific knowledge and overdiffident angle of relativism, pointing out that moving closer to either of these extreme stances may diminish expected results such as the improvement of women's lives (p. 113). In order to advocate for social change and challenge the assumptions of mainstream economics, feminist economists must effectively communicate with a wider audience, including politicians, using language and arguments tailored to convince those who wield influence over social change. The difficulty lies in the fact that politicians have recently started making use of innovative psychographic micro-targeting (sending diversified and precisely adjusted announcements to their voters), based on big data (detailed data on millions of people—their "digital footprints"—that can be purchased on the Internet databases markets) and modelled by private research companies (Kosinski, Wang, Lakkaraju, & Leskove, 2016). Nonetheless, such companies or research centres need to build their models in correspondence with research questions or theses/hypotheses, and these are often based on qualitative evidence. It is important to mention that big data can be used not only for marketing purposes, but also for the common good (e.g. by combing data for patterns in health) or for promoting values on which fairer and more equal communities and local economies can be built. For that reason, it is still important to draw attention to the selection of models, methods and techniques used by economists in all areas of studies (with preference to interdisciplinary ones), as well as to focus on empirical and policy-oriented work rather than abstract theorizing.

Feminist economists argue that androcentric bias is not only present in the thematic areas and methods selected in research, but also in the selection of research subjects that ignore women as either subjects or objects of scientific inquiries (Nelson, 1996a, p. B3). Feminist economists advocate for more studies on gender in the formal and informal economy, more research grants for such analyses, and more space for economic courses to include gender aspects so as to enrich the discipline (Schneider & Shackelford, 2001). Finally, they ask for the power to shape the discipline, to push it towards more inclusivity as well as to develop new and more diverse curricula, depending, in part, on women's representation within the field. Sadly, economics still has the lowest share of women among full professors in the social sciences; therefore, the appeals of feminist economists in this regard should be taken seriously (Ceci, Ginther, Kahn, & Williams, 2014; Romero, 2013).

The demand for scientific pluralism is aligned with the third dimension of feminist epistemology: the re-envisioning and reconstruction of scientific practices through, for example, the inclusion of context, values and ethical opinions. In a similar vein, Donna Haraway (1988), another postmodern philosopher, argues that "[s]cience has been about a search for translation, convertibility, mobility of meanings, and universality—which I call reductionism only when one language (guess whose?) must be enforced as the standard for all the translations and conversions" (p. 580). To do away with the prevalent trend of looking for a universal pattern of scientific inquiries, Haraway proposes making use of the diversity approach and a wide network of connections in order to learn about different communities and their knowledge deriving from their particular contexts—qualities she dubs "situated knowledges". Additionally, Susan Bordo (1987) observes that "[p]hilosophy has been forced to recognize that its 'enduring' issues and 'timeless' concerns are the products of very particular cultural circumstances" (p. 3). The historical context in which certain lasting theories came into being is distinctive for economics. John Maynard Keynes (1936) and Michał Kalecki (1933) published at the same time. Their theories were used to justify the expansion of the welfare state as well as the introduction of, for example, the New Deal and the Marshall Plan after the Second World War (Hannsgen & Papadimitriou, 2009). Trends changed and in the 1970s the Chicago school of economics began to build the neoclassical empire (Klein, 2007, p. 7). Feminist economists have critiqued schools of mainstream economics and their influence on real economies and on the development of economics as a discipline (Ferber, 1995; Waring, 1988). They emphasize that not only do historical conditions change, but so do the cultures and places in which ideas are implemented. For example, capitalism had different faces in the United Kingdom, the United States, Haiti and Chile in the 1980s (Toussaint, 2012). In those societies, the position of women, their *habitus* and their economic power also differed; therefore, comparing their economies by relying only on numbers, which reflect wealth or growth for instance, blurs rather than accounts for their real status. In their book entitled *Microeconomics in Context*, Neva Goodwin et al. (2005) emphasize that ultimately people and societies have different goals and:

> there are costs as well as benefits to the continual expansion of human control over a finite material world, and to emphasizing wealth in our human relations. Looking at the complex fallout of our achievements—including environmental degradation, stress felt by families, and other social ills—it is clear that promotion of material wealth without concern for the ends to which wealth is used, or for the consequences of the manner in which wealth is pursued, may in fact work *against* the final goals we most desire. (p. 5)

Many feminist scholars have discussed ethical opinions about wealth accumulation, which are now strongly evident in the international economic debate (Atkinson, 2015; Piketty, 2014) and in the orientation towards goals other than just material affluence (Beneria, 2003). These alternative goals—namely, well-being, freedom, participation, meaning, ecological balance—could also have different meanings for women versus men, as well as for other groups within society. The feminist economic assessment of established ends and the ways to accomplish them include normative and descriptive components and are not value-free. Furthermore, feminist economists situate their theories and research in a particular context, address communities and relationships between people, and include care, thereby deconstructing androcentric and individualistic bias in scientific practices. Julie A. Nelson and Neva Goodwin

(2005) give special importance to this approach in their working paper on teaching ecological and feminist economics:

> …[t]he broader, final goal of "contextual economics" is well-being for all people, present and future, in all of their economic and social roles: not only as consumer and producer, but also as citizen, family member, teacher, and giver and recipient of nurturing care and other assistance. (p. 2)

The different social roles that we perform every day construct the context we live in; hence, they are part of our "situated knowledges" (Haraway, 1988) and relate to the fourth area of feminist epistemology discussed here: the knowledge derived from mundane experiences, aiming at the improvement of people's lives.

The function and utility of knowledge is often determined in communities or groups, which understand it better than individuals. All of us have different experiences and abilities. If we share our knowledge, we can have more confidence that it is comprehended appropriately and the process of discussing it can lead to the emergence of new qualities. Additionally, knowledge can emerge from deductive processes as well as from casual accounts and qualitative research (an inductive approach). Gaining grassroots knowledge through, for example, fieldwork often leads to the greatest success in creating better conditions for women's development and boosting their well-being. Sandra Harding (1995a) puts it this way:

> [i]n order to generate economic theory that is more comprehensive and accurate, research must value—be interested in—nature, childhood, bodily needs, human connectedness, women's work in the household, the gender-differing values and interests within every household and gendered power relations more generally. The neutrality ideal (ideal of "positivity") itself, they are arguing, has been shown to limit the empirical and theoretical adequacy of economic theories. (p. 10)

By focusing on the issues of domestic labour or unpaid work, feminist economists place economic provisioning at the centre of their studies (Power, 2004). Additionally, what is also distinctive for the feminist standpoint theory (Harding, 2004) is that feminist economists try to present their theories and research from the perspective of women's lives. Thus, they can be perceived as "outsiders within" (Collins, 1991), having an epistemic privilege as women that is contrary to their disadvantaged status within society. Harding (2004) emphasizes that this approach leads to the development of new research questions and goals, because the marginalized see problems differently. Furthermore, she calls for a "fundamental ethic of democracy: 'those who bear the consequences of decisions should have a proportionate share in making them'" (Harding, 1995b, p. 126).

The exclusion of local women's perspective from the process of implementation of the official employment programmes of the World Bank in sub-Saharan Africa is one of the more significant examples of that absence. Sarah Bibler and Elaine Zuckerman (2013) reviewed 36 projects conducted in Malawi, Mali, Niger and Rwanda, proving that 92 per cent of them were not effective because of the oversight of women's time poverty caused by the burden of care. Their report illustrates women's social marginalization and their invisibility in the decision-making process. Their lives were not adequately mapped nor needs identified; therefore, time poverty went unnoticed, and the programmes were introduced in vain. If only additional care services had been offered, the projects could have ended differently.

To achieve these different ends, however, local knowledge and norms have to be utilized first. Rules and social strategies which exist in dominant societies are not neutral, but are products of existing power relations. Gender is one of their many layers. That is why, before we start scientific inquiries, we have to re-envision our research premises to include the structures within the social matrix. The tools and methods which feminist economists use fit the epistemic assumptions discussed earlier. Now, in the next section, I will present some concrete examples.

Feminist Economic Methodology

The debate about methodology in feminist economics might be based on a false polarization between the application of qualitative and quantitative methods. Thus, as Irene van Staveren (2010) points out "[w]e need both quantitative and qualitative methods, in order to further our understanding of unpaid labour and care" (p. 26). As Shulamit Reinharz (1992) claimed over two decades ago, feminist economists have used a wide range of tools, including "all existing methods and have invented some new ones" (p. 4). I specifically mention the time frame because it is an important factor in the methodological field. Certain trends of using particular methods prevail at specific moments, including the recent trend of using big data (large datasets mentioned previously in this chapter) or certain research perspectives such as intersectionality. Later in the chapter, I outline the methodology of feminist economics and some old and new research approaches, accompanied by a number of examples illustrating their practical application. Due to the vastness of this thematic area, I do not show all academic discussions and arguments, but instead focus on the most common research practices.

Feminist methodology is defined as a feminist theory on the principles of conducting feminist research, indicating a course of application and thereby concentrating on the very process of doing feminist research (Harding, 1987; Jayaratne & Stewart, 1991). These principles are derived from the aforementioned approaches and viewpoints, such as the ethics of care and feminist epistemology. Feminist scholars propose to change economics as a discipline by accepting the vulnerability and interdependency of human beings as a core assumption, which contrasts with the existing figure of a rational economics man that underpins neoclassical economics (Blank, 1993). This figure of *homo economicus* is portrayed as a man that "springs up fully formed, with preferences fully developed, and is fully active and self-contained. He has no childhood or old age; no dependence on anyone; no responsibility for anyone but himself" (Nelson, 1996b, p. 31). To understand the economics of becoming, which constitutes the underpinnings of the feminist economics, as presented in the thesis of this chapter, is, however, to understand that "[h]umans are born of women, nurtured and cared for as dependent children, socialised into family and community groups, and are perpetually dependent on nourishment and shelter to sustain their lives" (ibid.).

According to Kenneth Boulding (1986), the presiding orientation of economics towards "how society was organized by exchange" rather than how "society was 'provisioned'" has contributed to the failure of modern economics. Feminist economists engage with caring and social provisioning as starting points in their methodologies and point out definitive goals such as "satisfaction of basic physical needs, realization of one's potential, fairness, freedom, participation, good social relations and ecological balance" (Goodwin et al., 2005, p. 9). These goals are very similar to the central human functional capabilities put forward by Martha C. Nussbaum (2000) in her book *Women and Human Development*. By naming ten particular capabilities, Nussbaum defends a set of universal values that could be read as "basic political principles" (p. 70) for the improvement of women's well-being. These basic principles follow "life of a normal length, bodily health, bodily integrity, being able to use the senses, to imagine, think and reason, emotions, practical reason, affiliation, other species, being able to laugh, to play, to enjoy, and control over one's environment: political and material" (pp. 78–80). The capabilities approach, introduced by Amartya Kumar Sen (1985) and developed by Nussbaum, inspired many economists in their practical, comparative and quantitative research on the quality of life. The work of the British economists Paul Anand, Graham Hunter, and Ron Smith (2005) exemplifies such applied research since they operationalize and test Nussbaum's approach by using data from the British Household Panel Survey. They "find evidence that a wide range of capabilities exhibit statistically significant relations to well-being [and] that the relations are complex and slightly different for men and women" (Anand et al., 2005, p. 9).

The Basic Capabilities Index developed by the Social Watch (Social Watch, 2015a) constitutes another example of applied research. Although statistical measurement is often reductive (losing specific context and culture dimensions), which is also the case if big data is used (e.g. a prevalence of "WEIRD" in samples—"WEIRD" standing for "Western", educated, industrialized, rich and democratic countries' citizens (Kosinski et al., 2016)), this index was created to demonstrate the critical deficiencies experienced by a large part of the world's population and to encourage countries in the Global North to keep their promises with respect to the Millennium Development Goals (reformulated as the Sustainable Development Goals in 2015). The indicator is based on three components: child mortality under 5, maternal reproductive health and education measured in registrations for primary schooling, literacy and the number of children finishing 5th grade (Social Watch, 2015a). A news release from 2007 states that "at the current rate of progress, universal access to a minimum set of social services will only be achieved in Sub-Saharan Africa in 2108" (Social Watch, 2015b). Undoubtedly, this message clearly expressed the gravity of the situation, and therefore meets the goals of the Social Watch. However, feminists often reject this kind of universalism. They view it as a reflection of the aims, values and experiences of dominant groups, in this case, as countries in the Global North imposing a certain vision of development on countries in the Global South. They also question the grounds on which its claims presumably meet a shared set of needs and interests between women or men or between any other homogenous groups, such as nations (Harding, 1999). Referring to Haraway's concept of "situated knowledges", Drucilla Barker (2003) posits that "collective subject positions are always socially constructed and partial" (p. 107). This brings us closer to the discussion on research methods used by feminist economists.

In order to reflect the complexity of economic phenomena, feminist economists are rather ambivalent about the exclusive use of formal mathematical methods and econometrics, even though they return very precise results if based on big data. Julie A. Nelson (1993) points out that the truth of economics can arise from a rigorous logical analysis, as well as from intuitive knowledge, reasoning beyond logic or imaginative rationality (pp. 29–30). Donald N. McCloskey (1993) proposes a new term for this combination called a *conjective* science that implies the use of both stories and metaphors for deeper argumentation, as well as facts, numbers and logic as traditional forms of evidence (p. 76). Toby E. Jayaratne and Abigail J. Stewart (1991) argue that using quantitative research methods has the following benefits: "power to change political opinion, advantage to change sexist belief systems or to support progressive legislation, ability to provide tests of theories, or identify the most effective strategies for implementing feminist goals" (p. 53). On the other hand, Amy R. Poteete et al. (2010) warn against the high levels of abstraction in mathematical models that may not be reflected in empirical studies (pp. 12–13). They recommend that "the external validity of general relationships can best be evaluated, however, through analysis of a large number of nonexperimental observations" (ibid.). In one study, for example, Jayaratne and Stewart (1991) argue that ignoring important qualitative data, such as the role of values and attitudes in girl's math performance, "which reasonably may have explained the sex difference in performance" (p. 52), illustrates the failures of using solely quantitative data (cf. Eccles & Jacobs, 1986). On the other hand, quantitative models based on big data, if appropriately applied, can be suitable for feminist economic ends. Of course, it is still essential to ensure that the models match the underlying assumptions about epistemology through sound theoretical argumentation. In addition, one must take a critical approach to the interpretation of results (both qualitative and quantitative), making sure that they lead to accurate findings and avoid misrepresentations and overgeneralizations. This problem is also taken up by scholars (Kosinski et al., 2016) who analyse big data mining. They pinpoint a problem of overfitting—an occurrence of a random error being defined as an underlying effect or beyond underlying effect in a model. They recommend either a cross-validation or reducing the number of variables in the data set.

More reflexive approaches to economics may be based on mixed/multi-methods (a combination of both qualitative and quantitative methods) and triangulation (the use of multiple data sources) (Reinharz, 1992, pp. 197–213; Starr, 2014). This combination of using multiple methods and data sources helps to compensate for the weaknesses of using only one (Jick, 1979). However, it is important to remember that collecting data through qualitative techniques, such as participant observations, interviews, focus groups, case studies, oral histories or archival research, only leads to meaningful and explanatory results when they are thoroughly planned. Certain issues must be reflected upon and understood by a scientist in advance in order to apply the given method properly. To conduct fieldwork, for instance, a researcher must often learn a local language and possess key observational skills, as well as extensive knowledge of the history and culture of the observed community or group. They must be able to grasp the local context, exhibit self-awareness and good ethical conduct in inter-personal relations, keep a thorough and transparent record and interpret the collected data accurately (Burawoy, 1998; Rochelau, 1995).

One example of a sensitive subject, one that requires the special preparation and sensitivity of researchers, is violence against women. Seema Vyas, Jessie Mbwambob, and Lori Heisec (2015) have conducted an exploratory study of the relationship between women's employment and the experience of violence from their intimate partners in 20 in-depth interviews among women aged 18–49 years in two different regions of Tanzania. Although a number of quantitative studies on that issue had already existed, they often showed contradictory findings. The research proved that:

> [a]mong these women, we found that their access to money did not necessarily strengthen their fallback position in terms of being able to negotiate for the violence to stop or even to leave the violent relationship. One of the main factors that facilitated women's ability to either permanently or temporarily leave the home was their strong social, especially natal, support (Vyas et al., 2015, p. 53).

This example illustrates the salience of qualitative methods in detailing the complexity of relationships by taking into consideration different processes, actors and influencing factors described by the women fully and in their own terms. With regard to such difficult subjects, feminist economists recommend carrying out interdisciplinary studies drawing especially from other social sciences, like cultural anthropology or psychology, preparing researchers for interviews appropriately and finding different ways to interpret the collected information (see Laurence, 1999).

In summary, feminist economists conclude that the dichotomy between qualitative and quantitative methods is erroneous. The methodology they use encourages empirical research, and it is open to different approaches and forms of interpretation. The ultimate aim of feminist economists remains to contribute to policy change for the improvement of women's lives, which is analogous to distancing themselves from the mainstream research on ontologies of the economic man, outlined at the beginning of this chapter. Although feminist economics is an established school of heterodox economics, mainstream economists tend to discount the results of its studies. They disregard the findings provided by methods they are unfamiliar with, often labelling them unscientific, and condemn the references to work in other fields or publications in journals from other disciplines including interdisciplinary ones. As a result, when methodological choices influence career incentives, many junior faculty may make a professional choice not to engage in broad collaborations and multi-method research (Poteete et al., 2010, pp. 20–21). Still, even if a single method is used by a single researcher, as Jayaratne and Stewart (1991) have accurately formulated it, "researchers need to consider practical issues such as the time, effort, money and other resources available to the research staff. It is our belief that any, even a limited, attempt at increasing the feminist value of research is worthwhile" (p. 53).

Conclusion

The absolute criterion for judging knowledge production in feminist economics is the ethics of care. The distinct concerns of feminist economists regarding care for others, relational responsibility and equal opportunity for a good life differ from mainstream economics and their privileging of rational, egoistic and individualistic behaviour. This crucial issue was discussed in the first section of my study. Thereafter, I discussed feminist epistemology and its four planes: the critique of rationality, the existing gender bias in science, the necessity for the inclusion of context and values and the improvement of people's lives. In the last section, I examined the unique methodology that these subjects require, linking qualitative and quantitative methods as well as deductive and inductive approaches. Together, the three thematic areas—ethics of care, feminist epistemology and diverse methods—present a coherent whole that supports the thesis that feminist economics is an economics of becoming—becoming different from the economic man. The answer to this essay's opening question is a resounding "no": we cannot quantify everything, and this admission shall be perceived as the strength, not the weakness, of social sciences.

Acknowledgements I would like to express sincere gratitude to Sara Cantillon for encouraging me to write this chapter, for drafting its initial structure and for discussing it at various stages. I am also grateful to Kirstin Mertlitsch for her continuous philosophical inspiration and feedback, and Stefan Łapniewski for his linguistic support.

References

Akerlof, G. A., & Shiller, R. J. (2009). *Animal spirits: How human psychology drives the economy, and why it matters for global capitalism*. Princeton: Princeton University Press.

Anand, P., Hunter, G., & Smith, R. (2005). Capabilities and well-being: Evidence based on the sen-nussbaum approach to welfare. *Social Indicators Research, 74*, 9–55. https://doi.org/10.1007/s11205-005-6518-z

Atkinson, A. B. (2015). *Inequality: What can be done?* London: Harvard University Press.

Barker, D. K. (2003). Emancipatory for whom? A comment on critical realism. *Feminist Economics, 9*(1), 103–108. https://doi.org/10.1080/13545700110059270

Benedict, R. (1934). *Patterns of culture*. New York: Mariner Books.

Benería, L. (2003). *Gender, development, and globalization: Economics as if people mattered*. London: Routledge.

Bibler, S., & Zuckerman, E. (2013). *The World Bank and women's unpaid care work in select sub-Saharan African countries*. Retrieved from http://www.genderaction.org/carereport.pdf

Blank, R. M. (1993). What should mainstream economists learn from feminist theory? In M. A. Ferber & J. A. Nelson (Eds.), *Beyond economic man: Feminist theory and economics* (pp. 133–143). Chicago: The University of Chicago Press.

Bordo, S. R. (1987). *The flight to objectivity: Essays on cartesianism & culture*. Albany: State University of New York Press.

Bordo, S. R. (2002). Selections from 'The flight to objectivity'. In G. Lloyd (Ed.), *Feminism and history of philosophy* (pp. 82–97). Oxford: Oxford University Press.

Boulding, K. (1986). What went wrong with economics? *The American Economist, 30*(1), 5–12.

Braidotti, R. (2006). The ethics of becoming imperceptible. In C. Boundas (Ed.), *Deleuze and philosophy* (pp. 133–159). Edinburgh: Edinburgh University Press.

Budlender, D., & Sharp, R. (1998). *How to do a gender-sensitive budget analysis: Contemporary research and practice*. Canaberra: Commonwealth Secretariat and Australian Agency for International Development.

Burawoy, M. (1998). The extended case method. *Sociological Theory, 16*(1), 4–33. https://doi.org/10.1111/0735-2751.00040

Butler, J. (2004). *Undoing gender*. New York: Routledge.
Ceci, S. J., Ginther, D. K., Kahn, S., & Williams, W. M. (2014). Women in academic science: A changing landscape. *Psychological Science in the Public Interest, 15*(3), 75–141. https://doi.org/10.1177/1529100614541236
Code, L. (1996). What is natural about epistemology naturalized? *American Philosophical Quarterly, 33*(1), 1–22.
Deleuze, G. (2006). *Two regimes of madness: Texts and interviews 1975–1995*. Los Angeles: Semiotext(e).
Deleuze, G., & Guattari, F. (1987). *A thousand plateaus: Capitalism and schizophrenia*. Minneapolis: University of Minnesota Press.
Duffy, M. (2011). *Making care count: A century of gender, race, and paid care work*. New Brunswick, NJ: Rutgers University Press.
Eccles, J. S., & Jacobs, J. E. (1986). Social forces shape math attitudes and performance. *Signs, 11*(2), 367–380. https://doi.org/10.1086/494229
Ehrenreich, B., & Hochschild, A. R. (Eds.). (2004). *Global woman: Nannies, maids, and sex workers in the new economy*. New York: Holt Paperbacks.
Elson, D. (1998). Integrating gender issues into national budgetary policies and procedures: Some policy options. *Journal of International Development, 10*, 929–941. https://doi.org/10.1002/(SICI)1099-1328(1998110)10:7<929::AID-JID563>3.0.CO;2-5
Esplen, E. (2009). *Gender and care cutting edge pack—Overview report*. BRIDGE. Brighton: Institute of Development Studies.
Ferber, M. A. (1995). The study of economics: A feminist critique. *The American Economic Review, 85*(2), 357–361.
Fisher, B., & Tronto, J. C. (1990). Toward a feminist theory of caring. In E. Abel & M. Nelson (Eds.), *Circles of care: Work and identity in women's lives* (pp. 35–62). Albany: State University of New York Press.
Folbre, N. (1994). *Who pays for the kids? Gender and the structures of constraint*. New York: Routledge.
Goodwin, N., Nelson, J. A., Ackerman, F., & Weisskopf, T. (2005). *Microeconomics in context*. Armonk: M.E. Sharpe Inc.
Hannsgen, G., & Papadimitriou, D. B. (2009). Lessons from the new deal: Did the new deal prolong or worsen the great depression? *Working Paper 581*. The Levy Economics Institute Working Paper Collection.
Haraway, D. (1988). Situated knowledges: The science question in feminism and the privilege of partial perspective. *Feminist Studies, 14*(3), 575–599. https://doi.org/10.2307/3178066
Harding, S. (Ed.). (1987). *Feminism and methodology: Social science issues*. Bloomington: Indiana University Press.

Harding, S. (1995a). Can feminist thought make economics more objective? *Feminist Economics, 1*(1), 7–32. https://doi.org/10.1080/714042212

Harding, S. (1995b). Bon voyage: Navigating through the contemporary epistemological landscape. *Feminist Economics, 1*(3), 125–127. https://doi.org/10.1080/714042254

Harding, S. (1999). The case for strategic realism: A response to lawson. *Feminist Economics, 5*(3), 127–133. https://doi.org/10.1080/135457099337842

Harding, S. (Ed.). (2004). *The feminist standpoint theory reader: Intellectual and political controversies*. New York: Routledge.

Hekman, S. (1990). *Gender and knowledge: Elements of a postmodern feminism*. Boston: Northeastern University Press.

Hill Collins, P. (1991). *Black feminist thought: Knowledge, consciousness and the politics of empowerment*. New York: Routledge.

Hobbes, T. (2010 [1651]). *Leviathan* (Revised ed., A. P. Martinich & B. Battiste, Eds.). Peterborough: Broadview Press.

Jayaratne, T. E., & Stewart, A. J. (1991). Quantitative and qualitative methods in the social sciences: Current feminist issues and practical strategies. In M. M. Fonow & J. A. Cook (Eds.), *Beyond methodology: Feminist scholarship as lived research* (pp. 44–57). Bloomington: Indiana University Press.

Jennings, A. L. (1993). Public or private? Institutional economics and feminism. In M. A. Ferber & J. A. Nelson (Eds.), *Beyond economic man: Feminist theory and economics* (pp. 111–130). Chicago: The University of Chicago Press.

Jick, T. D. (1979). Mixing qualitative and quantitative methods: Triangulation in action. *Administrative Science Quarterly, 24*(4), 602–611. https://doi.org/10.2307/2392366

Kalecki, M. (1933). *Próba teorii koniunktury*. Warszawa: Instytut Badania Koniunktur i Cen.

Keynes, J. M. (1936). *The general theory of employment, interest and money*. London: Palgrave Macmillan.

Klein, N. (2007). *The shock doctrine: The rise of disaster capitalism*. New York: Henry Holt and Company.

Kosinski, M., Wang, Y., Lakkaraju, H., & Leskove, J. (2016). Mining big data to extract patterns and predict real-life outcomes. *Psychological Methods, 21*(4), 493–506.

Laurence, L. (1999). Domestic abuse. In J. Peterson & M. Lewis (Eds.), *The elgar companion to feminist economics* (pp. 121–126). Cheltenham: Edward Elgar.

Lloyd, G. (1979). The man of reason. *Metaphilosophy, 10*(1), 18–37. https://doi.org/10.1111/j.1467-9973.1979.tb00062.x

Lloyd, G. (1984). *The man of reason: 'Male' and 'Female' in Western philosophy*. London: Routledge.

Longino, H. (1990). *Science as social knowledge*. Princeton: Princeton University Press.

Longino, H. (1993). Subjects, power and knowledge: Description and prescription in feminist philosophies of science. In L. Alcoff & E. Potter (Eds.), *Feminist epistemologies (thinking gender)* (pp. 101–120). New York: Routledge.

Macdonald, M. (1995). Feminist economics: From theory to research. *The Canadian Journal of Economics/Revue canadienne d'Economique, 28*(1), 159–176. https://doi.org/10.2307/136027

McCloskey, D. N. (1993). Some consequences of a conjective economics. In M. A. Ferber & J. A. Nelson (Eds.), *Beyond economic man: Feminist theory and economics* (pp. 69–93). Chicago: The University of Chicago Press.

Nelson, J. A. (1993). The study of choice or the study of provisioning? Gender and the definition of economics. In M. A. Ferber & J. A. Nelson (Eds.), *Beyond economic man: Feminist theory and economics* (pp. 23–36). Chicago: The University of Chicago Press.

Nelson, J. A. (1996a, June 28). The masculine mindset of economic analysis. *The Chronicle of Higher Education, 42*(42), B3.

Nelson, J. A. (1996b). *Feminism, objectivity and economics*. New York: Routledge.

Nelson, J. A. (2008). Feminist economics. In S. N. Durlauf & L. E. Blume (Eds.), *The new Palgrave dictionary of economics* (Vol. 3, pp. 282–285). London: Palgrave Macmillan.

Nelson, J. A. (2013). Would women leaders have prevented the global financial crisis? Teaching critical thinking by questioning a question. *Economics Faculty Publication Series*, 40. Retrieved from http://scholarworks.umb.edu/econ_faculty_pubs/40

Nelson, J. A., & Goodwin, N. (2005). Teaching ecological and feminist economics in the principles course. *GDAE Working Paper 05-05*. Teaching Ecological and Feminist Economics. Medford: Global Development and Environment Institute, Tufts University.

Nussbaum, M. C. (2000). *Women and human development: The capabilities approach*. Cambridge: Cambridge University Press.

Ostrom, E. (1990). *Governing the commons: The evolution of institutions for collective action*. Cambridge: Cambridge University Press.

Phillips, J. (2007). *Care*. Cambridge: Polity Press.

Piketty, T. (2014). *Capital in the twenty-first century* (A. Goldhammer, Trans.). Cambridge: Belknap Press.

Plato. (1993). The symposium. In W. S. Cobb (Ed.), *The symposium and the phaedrus: Plato's erotic dialogues* (pp. 11–60). Albany: State University of New York.

Poteete, A. R., Janssen, M. A., & Ostrom, E. (2010). *Working together: Collective action, the commons, and multiple methods in practice*. Princeton: Princeton University Press.

Power, M. (2004). Social provisioning as a starting point for feminist economics. *Feminist Economics, 10*(3), 3–19.

Reinharz, S. (1992). *Feminist methods in social research*. Oxford: Oxford University Press.

Rochelau, D. (1995). Maps, numbers, text, and context: Mixing methods in feminist political ecology. *The Professional Geographer, 47*(4), 458–466. https://doi.org/10.1111/j.0033-0124.1995.00458.x

Romero, J. (2013). Where are the women? *Econ Focus*. Second Quarter 2013, Federal Reserve Bank of Richmond.

Schneider, G., & Shackelford, J. (2001). Economics standards and lists: Proposed antidotes for feminist economists. *Feminist Economics, 7*(2), 77–89. https://doi.org/10.1080/13545700110059243

Seiz, J. (1995). Epistemology and the tasks of feminist economics. *Feminist Economics, 1*(3), 110–118. https://doi.org/10.1080/714042252

Sen, A. K. (1985). Well-being, agency and freedom: The Dewey lectures 1984. *The Journal of Philosophy, 82*(4), 169–221. https://doi.org/10.2307/2026184

Sen, A. K. (1993). Capability and well-being. In M. C. Nussbaum & A. K. Sen (Eds.), *The quality of life* (pp. 30–53). Oxford: Clarendon Press.

Social Watch. (2015a). *The basic capabilities index*. Retrieved from http://www.socialwatch.org/node/9376

Social Watch. (2015b). *Social watch: G8 countries have not met their promises*. Retrieved from http://www.socialwatch.org/sites/default/files/ICB_2007_eng/SocialWatch_NewsRelease.pdf

Stagoll, C. (2005). Becoming. In A. Parr (Ed.), *The Deleuze dictionary* (pp. 21–22). Edinburgh: Edinburgh University Press.

Starr, M. A. (2014). Qualitative and mixed-methods research in economics: Surprising growth, promising future. *Journal of Economic Surveys, 28*(2), 238–264. https://doi.org/10.1111/joes.12004

Strassmann, D. (1999). Feminist economics. In J. Peterson & M. Lewis (Eds.), *The Elgar companion to feminist economics* (pp. 360–373). Cheltenham: Edward Elgar.

Strober, M. H. (2003). The application of mainstream economics constructs to education: A feminist analysis. In M. A. Ferber & J. A. Nelson (Eds.), *Feminist economics today: Beyond economic man* (pp. 135–156). Chicago: University of Chicago Press.

Toussaint, E. (2012). *A glance in the rear view mirror: Neoliberal ideology from its origins to the present*. Chicago: Haymarket Books.

Tronto, J. C. (1987). Beyond gender difference to a theory of care. *Journal of Women in Culture and Society, 12*(4), 644–663.

Tronto, J. C. (1995). Care as a basis for radical political judgements. *Hypatia, 10*(2), 141–149. https://doi.org/10.1111/j.1527-2001.1995.tb01376.x

Ungerson, C. (1995). Gender, cash and informal care: European perspectives and dilemmas. *Journal of Social Policy, 24*(1), 31–52. https://doi.org/10.1017/S004727940002451X

Van Staveren, I. (2010). Feminist economics, setting out the parameters. In C. Bauhardt & G. Caglar (Eds.), *Feministische Kritik der politischen Ökonomie* (pp. 18–48). Wiesbaden: VS Verlag für Sozialwissenschaften.

Vyas, S., Mbwambo, J., & Heise, L. (2015). Women's paid work and intimate partner violence: Insights from Tanzania. *Feminist Economics, 21*(1), 35–58. https://doi.org/10.1080/13545701.2014.935796

Waring, M. (1988). *If women counted: A new feminist economics*. San Francisco: Harper & Row.

Zofia Łapniewska is an economist, an assistant professor in the Institute of Economics, Finance and Management at the Jagiellonian University in Kraków, Poland, and Women in Scotland's Economy Research Centre International Fellow at Glasgow Caledonian University. For two semesters in 2015, she was a Visiting Fellow at the Gender Institute at the London School of Economics and Political Science. She also spent more than two years in Germany between 2012 and 2014 as a post-doctoral fellow at the Humboldt-Universität zu Berlin, and later as a research fellow at the Technische Universität Berlin. Her areas of scientific interest are feminist economics, institutional economics and alternatives to capitalism.

9

How to Make What Really Matters Count in Economic Decision-Making: Care, Domestic Violence, Gender-Responsive Budgeting, Macroeconomic Policies and Human Rights

Margunn Bjørnholt

Introduction

How to make people matter and how to make economics and the economy promote well-being and the common good for all—women, men and children—is a common theme throughout feminist critique, theorizing and policy inputs. This directly relates to what should count as economic activity and economic decision-making, and helps to determine the place of women in the economy. More than a century has passed since Charlotte Perkins Gilman raised these issues in *Women and Economics* (1898). Since then, there have been many different approaches to give visibility to women's work and values, including critiques of the Gross Domestic Product (GDP) as a welfare measure, equal pay and income distribution, women and globalization and ecofeminism. The institutionalization of feminist cri-

M. Bjørnholt (✉)
Norwegian Centre for Violence and Traumatic Stress Studies, Oslo, Norway

V.M.B. Giorgino, Z. Walsh (eds.), *Co-Designing Economies in Transition*,
https://doi.org/10.1007/978-3-319-66592-4_9

tique in the economics discipline was precipitated by the Committee on the Status of Women in the Economics Profession in 1972, and in the 1970s and 1980s, there was a proliferation of gender-based critiques of traditional economics. From its inception, feminist economics has been interdisciplinary, overlapping with a growing body of feminist sociology examining household work and task-sharing in the household, as well as analyses of how gender divisions of breadwinning and care produce and sustain gendered hierarchies and gendered differences in earnings and power. With the founding of the International Association for Feminist Economics (IAFFE) in 1992 and with its creation of the journal *Feminist Economics* in 1995, feminist economics became an academic field in its own right.

Feminist economists critique core assumptions, concepts, methods and knowledge claims in mainstream economic theory. They also critique male dominance and androcentrism in the discipline and profession of economics (see Benería, Berik, and Floro (2016) for an updated overview of these critiques), and they argue for a reformulation of the economics discipline to include care, the value of unpaid household work and analyses of the economic consequences of gendered divisions of labour and the gendered consequences of economic decision-making at all levels. Feminist economists share with other heterodox economists the critique of neglecting the process of provisioning (Nelson, 1993) and the indifference of the discipline to shortfalls of provisioning in terms of poverty, lack of healthcare and deteriorating social conditions. Power (2004) identified the social provisioning approach as a common ground for feminist economists, including five main areas of agreement that characterize it: (1) The need to value caring work and to place it centrally in analyses, (2) the use of human well-being as the definition of economic success, (3) emphasizing human agency and processes as well as outcomes, (4) the validity and importance of ethical judgements and (5) acknowledging differences by gender, along with other stratifying factors such as race, ethnicity, class and sexual orientation (Power, 2004). Gendered hierarchies of values also become cultural metaphors with implications for how economic decision-making and policy understand core issues of the economy with regard to the core purpose of economics as social provisioning rather than maximization of wealth (Nelson, 1992).

Care figures centrally in feminist economic analyses. Today, feminist analyses of care include a continued concern for the value of unpaid work and its contribution to the economy, as well as theorizations of care as social investment (Himmelweit, 2013), as an input factor and as a necessary precondition for other production (O'Hara, 2014). The theorization of care in feminist economics sees care as the foundation and indeed the secret mechanism that makes the whole economy work, the invisible heart, argues Folbre (2001), alluding to and challenging Adam Smith's 'invisible hand.' Goodwin, Harris, Nelson, Roach, and Torras (2013) have recently developed a contextual approach to economics, in which household production, care and social provisioning feature centrally as the core sphere of the economy. The feminist economic approach emphasizes the use value of care and also presents a critique of the understanding of what constitutes the economy and economic production, in addition to central concepts in economic theory, such as the concept of 'goods.' According to Himmelweit, in contrast to goods in economic theory, which are seen as tradeable assets with a monetary value attached to them, goods in the real world are socially embedded and relational (Himmelweit, 2013). Care for children reminds us of the relational nature of care work motivated by love (Folbre & Nelson, 2000).

By addressing the crucial question of how to make what really matters count in economic decision-making, we immediately bring to our attention what matters most of all—our love for our parents and our hope for humanity, our children and their well-being, as well as how the conditions for children's well-being are shaped in the individual and societal trade-offs between love for what matters most and the demands and possibilities of economic life.

Over time, feminist economics has expanded to include a growing focus on institutions, states, macroeconomics, human rights and regulatory frameworks, including financial regulation (Balakrishnan & Elson, 2011). In the remainder of this chapter, I will briefly illustrate this further development by presenting some topics from the wide and diverse field of feminist economics and their link to social change, advocacy and policymaking at the national and international level.

The aim is to highlight some examples of attempts to make people count in economic thinking, methodology and decision-making. I will start with unpaid work, its exclusion from national accounting systems and the ongoing work to find ways of measuring and including it. Care for children is a large part of unpaid work in the household, and the relational nature of this work—the love for our children—calls for a careful, innovative and concerned approach to conceptualizing value assessments and considering their policy implications. Later, I will present gender-responsive budgeting (GRB) as a strategy for linking gender equality policy to public budgetary processes, which is a methodology, drawing on insights from feminist economics along with a more general concern with strategies of gender equality linking international commitments and implementation at state and sub-state levels.

My next area of concern will be violence against women. This is a key example of how an issue previously perceived as a private issue became a public responsibility as part of making the personal political during second-wave feminism. It also became an economic issue as a result of feminist economic insights, making women's lives 'count,' and changing the view of domestic violence from 'family trouble' to criminal acts, which have serious consequences for the health and well-being of large numbers of women worldwide. Subsequently, the introduction of cost analysis into this field (i.e. the analysis of the cost of domestic violence to individual women and to society) was a tool to give economic visibility to this undercommunicated problem.

Finally, I will draw attention to the most recent development of feminist economic analysis: macroeconomic policies and human rights. This will illustrate how feminist economics has expanded far beyond issues perceived as women's 'only' issues and towards a more general concern for ethical responsibility, justice and institutional accountability, as illustrated by the purpose statement of the journal *Feminist Economics*: *'to improve the conditions of living for all children, women, and men.'* Together, these cases will illustrate some of the dynamics between feminist economic critique, theorizing, advocacy and policy development, thus elucidating the interrelations between academic work and the ways in which theories, concepts and critiques may inspire, inform and underpin social change.

Counting Unpaid Work, But Does It Count?

Over the last century, critiquing national accounting systems for excluding the value of women's unpaid work has been a cornerstone of feminist critique. Charlotte Perkins Gilman raised these issues in *Women and Economics* (1898) and in *The Home: Its Work and Influence* (1903). This was echoed some decades later by Margaret Reid in *Economics of house hold production* (1934). In the early 1970s, Mariarosa Dalla Costa and Selma James (1973) and other Marxist feminists in the Wages for Housework campaign reshaped the discourse on women, reproduction and capitalism, viewing the exploitation of women's care and domestic work, and its role in producing labourers for the formal economy, as the key to women's oppression. In 1985, the value of subsistence production was an important topic at the UN women's conference in Nairobi, drawing heavily from these insights. In 1988, Marilyn Waring's seminal work *If Women Counted: A Feminist Economics* (Waring, 1988) brought together critiques of the exclusion of the value of unpaid work with the value of nature in economic thinking and national accounting. The book became very popular and stimulated academic work, activism and change across the world, including a change in the international standard of national accounts (UNSNA), which used these critiques as its main line of argumentation. In a text message to the author on March 9, 2015, Marilyn Waring recalls:

> at the meeting of the United Nations Statistical Commission in it must have been 1992, a number of the central and south American delegations were led by women. In particular, I was told this story by the deputy chief statisticians from Mexico and Chile. *Counting for Nothing* [Marilyn Waring's book, best known as *If Women counted*] had been published in Spanish. *'We carried your book like a bible'* they said to me. In the 1993 United Nations System of National Accounts (UNSNA) Revision there were a number of changes, one of the most important being the changes in the boundary of production, which was expanded to include a number of key subsistence activities: the carriage of water being a key addition. They were supported by many African statisticians. Of course, in terms of the outcome, most of the countries where the expanded production boundary would have been of the most use, the statistical and logistical capability, and the resources, were seldom there to collect this data. (Waring, 2015)

This case is illustrative of the ways in which scholarly work within feminist economics has been put to use to transform methods, policies and institutional practices. It was only a partial victory though. Unpaid household work that leads to the production of goods (food for one's own consumption, collection of firewood or water necessary for the household) is now considered part of the System of National Accounts. However, the unpaid time people devote to the care of family, friends and neighbours is still explicitly excluded, despite it being increasingly acknowledged that it is care work mostly undertaken by women that makes possible much of the paid work that drives the market economy (United Nations Development Programme (UNDP), 2015). A quarter century after Waring's groundbreaking book, Bjørnholt and McKay (2014) demonstrate the wide influence of Waring's work worldwide in a number of areas.

Valuation efforts have gradually been gaining ground in national income accounting, and estimates differ among countries that are attempting to measure the value of unpaid care work from 20 per cent to 60 per cent of GDP (Antopoulos, 2009). In India, unpaid care is estimated at 39 per cent of GDP and in South Africa 15 per cent (Budlender, 2010); among Latin American countries, in Guatemala it is estimated at between 26 and 34 per cent of official GDP and in El Salvador at 32 per cent (Durán & Milosavlejevic, 2012). In 2008, the Organization for Economic Cooperation and Development published estimates of household production in 27 countries and highlighted that the value of household production as a share of GDP varies considerably. It is above 35 per cent in several countries generally considered affluent—Australia, New Zealand and Japan, and below 20 per cent in Mexico and Korea (Ahmad & Seung-Hee Koh, 2011; Folbre, 2015.)

In Norway, unpaid work in the household was counted as production, and the first estimate of the value of housewives' unpaid production in the household was made as early as in 1882, and continued throughout the first decades of the twentieth century; but from the 1950s, it was no longer included when Norway adopted the new international standard of national accounts (UNSNA) (Aslaksen & Koren, 2014), which includes only monetary flows as opposed to the Scandinavian tradition of distinguishing between the real economy, the production of goods and services and the monetary economy. In Norway, unpaid work in the household is being counted once a decade using time use studies, and based on the data on time use, its monetary value is also being imputed every decade, since 1988, when a large group of women's organizations sent a common letter demanding that Statistics Norway should calculate the value of unpaid work. In 2010, unpaid household work was still the single largest sector of the economy, 26 per cent of GDP, although its share has declined since 1988 when it was estimated at 44 per cent of GDP (Koren, 2012). Drawing on the Finnish experience, Varjonen and Kirjavainen (2014) conclude that, in Finland, although unpaid work was counted, it was not very well understood in the public and it did not have the expected impact on policies. This is where gender-responsive public budgeting may serve to fill a substantial gap in knowledge on policy impacts.

On a more optimistic note, time use studies and efforts to valuate unpaid work have proliferated in recent years and may gain increasing importance (Folbre, 2015, 2016). However, Pearson and Elson (2015) recently argued that the lack of data on household production, due to lack of time use studies in Europe, severely impedes on the possibilities to study the impact of the economic crisis in Europe. Despite being measured, at least to some extent, unpaid work still remains outside of regular macroeconomic planning and decision-making processes, and it is ignored in the thinking and models that inform macroeconomic policy.

Ironically, unpaid household work continues to be ignored, even in alternatives to GDP, which have, to a large extent, been developed as a result of feminist critiques, and which are intended to recognize gender disparities such as the Gender-related Development Index (GDI) and the Gender Empowerment Measure (GEM) (Folbre, 2015). Women who are not fully employed in paid work are still routinely seen as not contributing fully to the economy, being treated as an available 'resource' and as a labour market reserve to be drawn upon at a low cost in times of need. This argumentation may come guised as 'empowerment of women' and economic growth, and has gained new momentum as part of the new sustainable development goals adopted by the UN Agenda 2030.

International Monetary Fund Director Christine Lagarde recently publicized estimates of GDP foregone by many developing countries as a result of restrictions on women's employment. Although policies that limit women's choices need to be criticized for a number of reasons, the underlying implication that women make no economic contributions outside the market illustrates how decades of feminist economic critique, theorization and the documentation of unpaid work's value as well as its contribution to the economy continue to be ignored (See Folbre (2015, p. 16) for an elaboration of this argument).

Unpaid household work was put back on the agenda by the Stiglitz, Sen and Fitoussi Commission, which assessed various measures of economic development (Stiglitz, Sen, & Fitoussi, 2009). It has always been recognized that GDP and per capita GDP cannot be interpreted as a measure of living standards. This was one of the reasons for the Commission's work. The committee pointed out the need for a broader measure of household income, which includes the value of unpaid household work. Furthermore, they argued that emphasis on market production may give a distorted picture of the standard of living, because part of what is measured as economic growth may just reflect a shift in production from household to market (35).

Charlotte Koren (2012) has demonstrated this shift in detail for Norway, arguing that the transformation from a housewife society to a dual-earner society meant that parts of the production that previously took place as unpaid work in the household were made visible as they were transferred to the market and became part of the monetary economy, leading to a steady rise in GDP, which was counted as economic growth. However, this growth did not reflect real growth in consumption goods, argue Aslaksen and Koren (2014), as the work already took place—it was just not counted. Growing understanding of the interconnections between paid and unpaid work and the understanding that unpaid household work is productive implies a theoretical critique of the way growth is being measured and a critique of what came to be seen as the normal growth rates for Organisation for Economic Co-operation and Development (OECD) economies over the last 50 years. This case illustrates how the discussion of the place of unpaid work in the economy is far from trivial, but addresses the core of economic thinking, practices and results with potentially wide-ranging implications for policymaking.

As pointed out by Marilyn Waring, this case runs parallel to the fact that nature with its irreplaceable qualities and values is not counted for in economic decision-making. Nature is only counted for in accounting when it is used as a resource for human production and consumption. The similar invisibility of women's work and nature is the core issue of ecofeminism (Mies & Shiva, 1993), feminist philosophies (Merchant, 1980; Warren, 1996) and an emerging topic in feminist economics (Aslaksen, Bragstad, & Ås, 2014; Mellor, 2005; Nelson, 1997).

As a strategy of gender equality, counting unpaid work also runs up against a deep division within the women's movement and the currently preferred strategies of gender equality in OECD countries, which increasingly rely on family policies aimed at reconciling paid work and care, as well as reallocating care from women to men, drawing on the vision of the 'universal carer model,' which, according to Nancy Fraser (1994), is the only family model that can deliver full gender equality, among the three models she presents as possible alternatives 'after the family wage.' The first alternative, making difference costless, compensating women's unpaid work within the male breadwinner/female home-maker model, has lost its appeal among feminists, and has increasingly come to be seen as incompatible with a modern gender equal life. Feminist economic arguments for valuing unpaid work and placing care centrally in economic analysis are no longer supported by a strong women's movement willing to lobby for and promote this strategy. This is in contrast to the 1970s and 1980s, when care ethics, gender difference and the value of women's experiences were still a stronger part of the feminist movement, providing a ground for making claims for the valuation of unpaid household work. Today, this branch of the women's movement has more or less dried up at least in developed countries. The dual-breadwinner model, which places both parents in employed work with little support for care, might become the chosen strategy in many countries, considering the strong focus on women's labour market participation as the preferred strategy of gender equality. This was the other of the two models that Fraser (1994) saw as unfit to deliver full gender equality, as it relied on women becoming like men, and it did not recognize unpaid work/care, but relied on full outsourcing of care. In addition, there has been a dramatic change in labour markets, job security and wages, making claims of valuation of unpaid work even more difficult.

This unilateral reliance on full-time paid work for parents as the main strategy of gender equality is particularly damaging in many countries with less developed family polices, but even in a developed country like Norway, which figures in international comparisons as a model of gender equality, the emphasis on paid work may become a new constraint. Norway provides a full package of policies for childcare, including a long and fully compensated parental leave with a quota for fathers, subsidized childcare for all children from the age of one and other entitlements for working parents. A recent study of parents of preschool children, however, found that the new model may not be unequivocally liberating and that it is also felt as a normative constraint among young Norwegian parents today (Bjørnholt & Stefansen, forthcoming). So, what about the well-being of children? How can public policy help make the well-being of children compatible with the well-being of parents, and alleviate the burden of trade-offs in parents' allocation of time between their work and care for children?

Gender-Responsive Budgeting

Gender-responsive budgeting (GRB) is a strategy that focuses on integrating a perspective on how to improve equality between women and men based on a gender analysis in every stage of planning, programming and execution of government budgets; in short, to assess how the governments' raising and spending of money contribute to the aim of achieving gender equality. While the main focus in gender budget work until recently has been on public expenditure, there is also an increasing focus on public revenue, how governments raise money through taxation and the consequences of taxation, including tax evasion. GRB is increasingly understood as a crucial driver of implementing policies of gender equality through financial frameworks and programmes. It was first launched in relation to the Beijing Platform for Action, arguing that '*limited resources at the state level*' should encourage implementation of gender equality policies and the mainstreaming of gender perspectives in all policy domains. It urged national governments to incorporate a gender perspective into the design, development, adoption and execution of all budgetary processes, as appropriate, in order to promote equitable, effective and appropriate resource allocation and establish adequate budgetary allocations to support gender equality and development programmes, which enhance women's empowerment and develop the necessary analytical and methodological tools and mechanisms for monitoring and evaluation (UN General Assembly, 2000).

Despite these commitments, progress was slow, and disproportionately relied on the advocacy and voluntary work of civil society. In this respect, the UK Women's budget group, founded in 1989, was a pioneer. It is a network of leading feminist economists, researchers, policy experts and campaigners committed to achieving a more gender equal future, with renowned feminist economists like Sue Himmelweit and Diane Elson in lead roles. The group is still at the forefront of scrutinizing government policy from a gender perspective, producing research and analysis, as well as running training workshops and developing resources to build the capacity of women and women's groups to participate in debates about economics and public budgeting.

In Scotland, Professor of Economics Ailsa McKay was similarly central in initiating and developing the Scottish women's budget group and later the research group, Women in the Scottish Economy (WISE). She became a respected partner and policy advisor to the first minister as well as to the ministers of finance (Campbell & Gillespie, 2016). In 2006, the European Gender Budget Network was founded, and in 2007, the network formulated a manifesto addressed to decision-makers in the European Union, urging the implementation of GRB: *'More than 10 years ago, governments committed themselves to Gender Budgeting at the World Women's Conference in Beijing. The call for gender budgeting is equally rooted in the EU commitment to gender mainstreaming and firmly based in the Treaty (…)'* (EGBN, 2007). It recalled a number of previous commitments and initiatives:

- The decision of the gender budgeting conference under the Belgium Presidency in 2001 to implement gender budgeting in all countries by the year 2015.
- The resolution of the European Parliament on gender budgeting and its recommendations.
- The opinion of the Advisory Committee on Equal Opportunities for Women and Men on gender budgeting and its proposals to take action.

- The opinion on Gender Budgeting by the Council of Europe.
- The recommendations of the European Women's Lobby on gender budgeting.
- The activities of WIDE, Women in Development Europe and IAFFE, the International Association for Feminist Economics, to promote the implementation of gender budgeting.

Another ten years on, after decades of initiatives, there has been continued advocacy and voluntary work at international, European and national levels. A recent survey of GRB initiatives initiated by the International Monetary Fund concludes that gender budgeting has led to significant changes in budget legislation and administrative practices in a number of European countries (Quinn, 2016). Nevertheless, an unpublished survey among members of the European Gender Budget (EGBR) network (Mader, 2014) ironically revealed that the main criterion of success of gender budget initiatives in Europe was the altruistic and often unpaid voluntary work of members in the network.

Although the role of civil society advocacy and capacity building in this field is recognized, the extent to which success relies on civil society engagement, including the engagement by dedicated academics in roles as experts and advocates, is not often fully described or understood. (See O'Hagan (2013) for a detailed comparative analysis of GRB-initiatives, providing a rich account of what it takes. Quinn, 2016, also includes civil society initiatives in her survey of GRB in Europe.) In the Nordic region, the Nordic Council of ministers all agreed to implement GRB (Schmitz, 2006). However, ten years on, only Sweden, Iceland and Finland are represented in the IMF survey of European GRB initiatives, while Denmark and Norway are missing (Quinn, 2016).

In Norway, which I know best, the commitment to gender-sensitive planning has *de facto* been scaled back. The reason is, in my view, that in contrast to Sweden, where the Swedish Women's lobby took a lead role in developing material, training and promoting GRB, in Norway, there has been no civil engagement with GRB. Thus, the resistance and lack of interest, will and know-how at political and administrative levels remain unchallenged and unchanged in Norway, in contrast to many other countries today, which increasingly see GRB as an important and necessary step towards improving democracy and providing justice for all. In 2016 and 2017, the International Monetary Fund has taken several initiatives to assess, disseminate and further develop GRB, drawing on and involving many of the key scholars and GRB advocates and practitioners (Quinn, 2016).

Violence Against Women—An Economic Issue?

Another area within which feminist economics has had an influence is the field of violence against women. Violence against women became a public concern in the 1970s, when experiences of violence, rape and sexual abuse were reframed from a private issue to a political issue under the slogan *'the private is political,'* and women's groups established shelters for victims of violence. In the beginning they were based on solidarity and voluntary work, and those shelters that were rooted in radical feminist ideology were keeping their distance from the state; but in many countries the shelter movement obtained public funding from an early stage, thus holding society responsible for providing services and providing justice for victims of violence and abuse. The first shelter in the UK was set up in 1971 (Pizzey, 2011), and was soon copied in other countries. Parallel to the development of shelters for victims of violence, the prevention of violence and protection of women and girls against violence was subsequently put on the political agenda of nation states as well as at the United Nations (UN) and at regional levels.

The UN 1993 Declaration on the elimination of violence against women was the first international instrument explicitly addressing violence against women, providing a framework for national and international action. Today, violence against women is on the agenda of several UN bodies. In 2011, the Council of Europe Convention on preventing and combating violence against women and girls became the second legally binding regional instrument on violence against women and girls. During the 2000s, national action plans and new legislation were introduced in many countries. The passing of international conventions and action plans as well as legislation at national, regional and international levels is the result of continuous feminist mobilization at all levels over decades.

As violence against women became a political priority at the international and national level, there was demand for action with budgetary consequences. Estimates of the cost of violence to society created an economic argument for violence prevention, as violence was found to be extremely costly to society, far exceeding public expenditure on violence prevention (Dolan, Loomes, Peasgood, & Tsuchiya, 2005; Kerr & McLean, 1996; Walby, 2004 [2009]; Yodanis, Godenzi, & Stanko, 2000). In this way, violence against women and child sexual abuse was linked to the economy as a whole. One impetus to calculate the costs came from work with victims. According to Jülich (2014), in her work with adult victims of child sexual abuse in New Zealand in the mid- to late 1990s, a frequent question was *'Don't they know what it [child sexual abuse] costs?'* (113). This led her to develop a costing method and spreadsheet calculators to be deployed by community agencies. Later, the cost of child sexual abuse was included in cost of crime analysis in New Zealand.

Today, estimates of the costs of violence have become part of the standard repertoire in framing the problem and of arguments for violence prevention at the international and national level. This includes the development of methods (see, for instance, the manual by the World Health Organization and Centers for Disease Control and Prevention (2008)). According to a multi-country study commissioned by the World Bank (Duvvury, Callan, Carney, & Raghavendra, 2013), the costs of domestic violence are estimated to amount to 1–2 per cent of GDP. Cost estimates vary, but may include the direct costs of violence in terms of public expenditure on treating and handling the consequences of violence in the health system, social system, educational system and legal system; as well as the potential costs such as the loss of future public revenue due to the loss of health (including death) and the loss of income-earning capacity among victims of violence, potentially with repercussions over generations. According to a recent fact sheet by the European Women's Lobby, EWL Observatory on violence against women (2016), "Violence against women costs 226 billion euros each year, which represent almost 2% of the annual EU budget."

Evaluating costs is, however, not without risks. First, there are methodological problems since there is insufficient data on violence and sexual abuse and since there is general agreement that crime statistics, health statistics and prevalence studies do not present the whole picture. In addition, the way violence is presented in statistics may underestimate domestic violence. For example, the method of capping does not count the actual number of incidents experienced by victims experiencing repeated violence. In the UK, the cap is set at five incidents, thus underestimating the total number of violent crimes and the degree of victimization experienced by the most exposed groups (Walby, Towers, & Francis, 2016). The problem of insufficient data is made worse by general problems in cost analysis, such as what to count and what price tag to use. In conclusion, any cost analysis and in particular any cost analysis based on limited and insufficient data, such as in the case of violence, will be speculative, and due to unaccounted costs, will probably present an underestimate.

Nevertheless, estimates of the costs of violence to society, although uncertain, highlight the extent and magnitude of the problem by translating it into what can be seen as policymakers' mother tongue: money. Estimates of economic costs can further provide activists and stakeholders with additional evidence to argue for public expenditure on prevention and services for victims of violence. Nevertheless, there is a danger in framing violence as an economic issue. Freedom from violence is recognized as a human right,[1] and human rights obligations are already legally binding for states. Further, the duty to raise the necessary resources for the realization of human rights is also mandated by human rights obligations. Consequently, no further argument should be needed for states to take action. If violence is framed simply as an economic issue, a cynical view could be that this is a cost societies can afford. Or, even worse, if hypothetically, the costs of violence were found to be lower than the costs of prevention, violence could be ignored, because prevention would not be economically worthwhile. Note that this is hypothetical, keeping in mind that, today, the estimated costs, which are most probably underestimates, are huge, as compared to the amount of money used on prevention. This argument runs parallel to the ecofeminist debate about whether harm to Mother Earth can and should be brought onto the policy agenda by monetary value assessments and the dangers therein (Beder, 2001).

It is well established from prevalence studies that the risk of violence is related to socio-economic factors and that lack of economic means may keep victims of violence from leaving an abusive relationship. Further, financial abuse is today also recognized as a particular form of domestic violence (Acierno et al., 2010). Feminist economic analysis has expanded and deepened knowledge of the relations between violence and women's economic position within the household. Agarwal and Panda (2007) demonstrate that a woman's property status (owning a house or land) significantly reduces her risk of domestic violence while holding paid employment made little difference.

Finally, GRB, which is informed and inspired by feminist economics, has demonstrated the gendered effects of public spending on different groups. In the UK, due to several decades of work tracking the gendered effects of public spending by feminist economists in the UK (the UK Women's Budget Group), the gendered effects of austerity measures following the financial crisis could soon be measured, and among them, the effects for victims of violence (Fawcett Society, 2012). In this case, an increase in violence, following the economic downturn (Walby et al., 2016), coincided with cuts in the services to victims of violence (Towers & Walby, 2012).

The domestic violence case illustrates how a previously private women's issue was transformed into a public responsibility and how it was gradually pushed up on the political agenda by various forms and stages of feminist activism and capacity building, such as the provision of services to victims of violence and international advocacy. This case further demonstrates the value of GRB, which, to a large extent, has been advanced as part of scholarly and advocacy work in feminist economics over several decades. Although cost analysis may have limitations, once violence has become a public and political issue, it is also an economic issue.

Although this work on violence against women may be seen as an example of relative success for feminism, it is also a field of struggle. The tools of measurement, methods and interpretation of violence in personal relationships and in its relation to gender inequality in society is the object of scientific dispute. Feminist activists and researchers who view violence as a gendered phenomenon and who view violence against women as both an effect and a constitutive element in the gender order have had success in promoting this perspective within the UN, the

Council of Europe and in many countries. In contrast, some family researchers relying on large surveys have challenged the feminist perspective, arguing that men and women in couple relations are similarly exposed to and perpetrators of violence, although there is agreement that women seem to be exposed to more violence, more severe violence and are more often injured.

The academic debate between feminist and other perspectives has repercussions in the field of practice and on policies. Feminist perspectives are important when framing violence against women as a gender equality issue, in order to make claims for funding services for victims of violence and for prevention. Research that presents a more symmetrical picture of 'common couple violence' has, on the other hand, been used by organized men's groups in favour of cuts and the retrenchment of financial support for services provided to victims of violence (see Loseke and Kurz (2005) and Straus (2005) for this debate). Organized opposition to women's rights by masculinist groups has been growing worldwide in recent years (Boyd & Sheehy, 2016; Dragiewicz & Mann, 2016) and may be an important factor in shaping further feminist struggles in the future, and perhaps, in particular, in domains of relative feminist success. This case illustrates that scientific struggles, research perspectives, methods and framings inadvertently stand in dynamic relation to political struggles in society and will be used in these struggles with potential consequences for policies, including public spending.

Moving On: Macroeconomic Policy and Human Rights

Employing a human rights framework, feminist economists Radhika Balakrishnan and Diane Elson (2011) have created a useful and practisable framework for containing the economy within legal and moral bounds by using human rights as a tool for the evaluation of macroeconomic policies and for holding governments to account. Their work represents a promising advancement from feminist economists' and activists' work on gender budgeting. In considering the economy as a whole, they argue for evaluating the macroeconomic policy of governments according to the framework of human rights, including all relevant human, economic, social, political, civil and cultural rights. They assume as their point of departure that human rights are legally binding obligations, and thus suitable for holding governments accountable.

Their framework of analysis is based on the following key human rights principles: the need for progressive realization, the use of maximum available resources, the avoidance of retrogression, the satisfaction of minimum essential levels of economic and social rights, non-discrimination and equality, participation, transparency and accountability. These principles were agreed on as part of The Universal Declaration of Human Rights (UDHR), which was adopted by the United Nations General Assembly in 1948, and which has later been extended in particular conventions, such as the Convention on the Elimination of all Discriminations Against Women (CEDAW), the Convention on the Rights of the Child (OHCR) and International Covenant on Economic, Social and Cultural Rights (ICESCR).

In contrast to what has often been assumed, Balakrishnan and Elson argue that the human rights framework provides detailed and legally binding obligations that can hold governments accountable. Armed with this framework, human rights and their implications for macroeconomic structures and processes, including fiscal and monetary policy, the right to work, public expenditure, taxation, economic and social rights, trade policy and pension reforms, would feature more prominently in the evaluation of economic policies. In their latest book, Balakrishnan, Heintz, and Elson (2016) further demonstrate how human rights have the potential to transform economic thinking and policymaking with far-reaching consequences for social justice by providing mechanisms to redress injustice.

The University Women of Europe have filed a collective complaint against 15 states that violate the European Social Charter for equal pay for equal work between men and women, arguing that women are not treated equally as they earn structurally less than men for equal work. In the same way, nature can be defended by court. In Norway, environmental organizations are currently bringing the government to court for not fulfilling its climate policy obligations. In the USA, fifteen-year-old

Xiuhtezcatl Tonatiuh Martinez along with other young environmentalists (Earth guardians, n.d.) has sued the US government, arguing that his generation's rights are being violated by the nation's failure to take action against climate change. This is an interesting and promising way to raise visibility and public attention; yet, it also poses a dilemma, since court decisions shift the decision-making process to an area outside local grass-root political engagement and organization building. This needs not be an either/or question—we probably need both.

Concluding Remarks

These illustrations of selected topics, which, in one way or another, may be seen as fitting under the wide umbrella of feminist economics, demonstrate how academic and political critiques as well as the development of new theories, methods and concepts are all closely related to political struggles at every level. They also illustrate how the feminist movement, broadly defined, has played a pivotal role in each of these cases.

The economy is one of 12 critical areas advancing women's rights according to the Beijing Platform of Action that was agreed upon at the fourth UN Women's conference in 1995. Twenty years later, however, the economy is the field in which the least progress has been achieved, though, in this same period, feminist economics has proliferated and grown into a field of its own. Although policies seem to remain largely unchanged by feminist economic analysis, there are also signs of change, illustrated by the inclusion of unpaid subsistence production in the UN Standard of National Accounts in 1993, the increasing use of alternative indicators of well-being, the implementation and institutionalization of GRB in many countries and recent initiatives by the International Monetary Fund to further develop GRB.

These cases, which include the valuation of care and unpaid work, GRB, domestic violence and the use of human rights in assessing macroeconomic policy, all illustrate the dynamics between academic work, feminist critiques and activism, both within and outside of academia, as well as the role that feminist academic and activist involvement plays in developing critiques of international and regional institutions, shaping, in particular, the importance of the UN system and the European Union. This brief outline of selected topics from the field of feminist economics illustrates how academic critique, new theories, concepts, knowledge, new methods and indicators are important.

However, new knowledge alone is not sufficient to produce change. To the extent that feminist economics has contributed to making what really matters count in economic decision-making as described in this chapter, successes have depended on a combination of several factors. These factors include the institutionalization of feminist economics as an academic field, the institutionalization and systematization of relevant statistics and, above all, the pivotal role that feminist activism and advocacy plays in encouraging personal involvement, networking and alliances between academics and activists. This latter aspect encourages experts and academics to actively employ their expertise within organized civil society groups and formal institutions to further the diversity of initiatives, approaches and their policy impact.

This chapter has discussed how feminist economic critiques and theorizations have been employed to influence and change conceptual and regulatory frameworks as well as policies at the state and the international level. These examples of knowledge production and policymaking at the macro level are, however, not exhaustive, nor are they the only way in which feminist economics is relevant in conceptualizing a better, more inclusive and better functioning economy that serves the well-being of all. The question of who the economy and economic activity should serve, and what is the aim of any economic activity, raised in feminist economics as well as in other heterodox economic traditions, will have to be at the core of any alternative to the current economic model, including local and regional, community, bottom-up initiatives to construct viable alternatives of social provisioning. The particular contribution of feminist economics is above all its contribution to the understanding of the centrality and importance of care, paid and unpaid, and the importance of human dependency in any economy, society and at all levels of the economy and society. There is a danger that the importance of household work and care will continue to be ignored also in alternatives to the current market economy, and I will end by urging all who are committed to build better, more democratic and more human systems of provisioning, to recognize, include and value care and place it at the core of any alternative models of provisioning—be it sharing initiatives, community- or neighbourhood initiatives, barter systems, monetary innovations, cooperatives or new commons initiatives.

Acknowledgements I am indebted to Iulie Aslaksen (Statistics Norway) and emerita Charlotte Koren (Norwegian Sosial Research) for useful comments and suggestions.

Notes

1. The EWL fact sheet foregrounds human rights argument, with costs as an additional point.

References

Acierno, R., Hernandez, M. A., Amstadter, A. B., Resnick, H. S., Steve, K., Muzzy, W., et al. (2010). Prevalence and correlates of emotional, physical, sexual, and financial abuse and potential neglect in the United States: The National Elder mistreatment study. *American Journal of Public Health, 100*, 292–297.

Agarwal, B., & Panda, P. (2007). Toward freedom from domestic violence: The neglected obvious. *Journal of Human Development, 8*(3), 359–388.

Ahmad, N., & Seung-Hee Koh, S.-H. (2011). Incorporating estimates of household production of non-market services into international comparisons of material well-being. *Working Paper 42*. OECD Statistics Directorate.

Antopoulos, R. (2009). The unpaid care work-paid work connection. *Working Paper 86*. ILO.

Aslaksen, I., Bragstad, T., & Ås, B. (2014). Feminist economics as vision for a sustainable future. In M. Bjørnholt & A. McKay (Eds.), *Counting on Marilyn Waring: New advances in feminist economics* (pp. 21–36). Bradford: Demeter Press.

Aslaksen, J., & Koren, C. (2014). Reflections on unpaid household work, economic growth, and consumption possibilities. In M. Bjørnholt & A. McKay (Eds.), *Counting on Marilyn Waring: New advances in feminist economics* (pp. 57–71). Bradford: Demeter Press.

Balakrishnan, R., & Elson, D. (2011). *Economic policy and human rights: Holding governments to account*. London: Zed Books.

Balakrishnan, R., Heintz, J., & Elson, D. (2016). *Rethinking economic policy for social justice: The radical potential of human rights*. London and New York: Routledge.

Beder, S. (2001). Trading the Earth: The politics behind tradeable pollution rights. *Environmental Liability, 9*(2), 152–160.

Benería, L., Berik, G., & Floro, M. (2016). *Gender, development and globalization: Economics as if all people mattered*. New York and London: Routledge.

Bjørnholt, M., & McKay, A. (Eds.). (2014). *Counting on Marilyn Waring: New advances in feminist economics*. Bradford: Demeter Press.

Bjørnholt, M., & Stefansen, K. (forthcoming). Same but different: Polish and Norwegian parents' work–family adaptations in Norway. Journal article, under review.

Boyd, S. B., & Sheehy, E. (2016). Men's groups: Challenging feminism. *Canadian Journal of Women and the Law, 28*(1), 5–10.

Budlender, D. (Ed.). (2010). *Time use studies and unpaid care work*. London and New York: Routledge.

Campbell, J., & Gillespie, M. (Eds.). (2016). *Feminist economics and public policy*. London and New York: Routledge.

Dalla Costa, M., & James, S. (1973). *The power of women and the subversion of the community*. Bristol: Falling Wall Press.

Dolan, P., Loomes, G., Peasgood, T., & Tsuchiya, A. (2005). Estimating the intangible victim costs of violent crime. *British Journal of Criminology, 45*(6), 958–976.

Dragiewicz, M., & Mann, R. M. (2016). Introduction to special edition: Fighting feminism–Organised opposition to women's rights. *Journal of Women and the Law, 28*(1), 1–6.

Durán, M. A., & Milosavljevic, V. (2012). *Unpaid work, time use surveys and care demand forecasting in Latin America*. Documento de trabajo 7. Bilbao: Fundación BBVA.

Duvvury, N., Callan, A., Carney, P., & Raghavendra, S. (2013). *Intimate partner violence: Economic costs and implications for growth and development*. Women's Voice, Agency, & Participation Research Series 3. World Bank.

Earth guardians. (n.d.). Xiuhtezcatl Martinez. Retrieved from https://www.earthguardians.org/xiuhtezcatl/

European Gender Budget Network (EGBN). (2007). Gender budgeting in Europe-NOW! Manifiesto. Retrieved from http://www.infopolis.es/web/genderbudgets/manifiesto.html

Fawcett Society Policy Briefing March. (2012). *The impact of austerity on women*. Retrieved from http://www.fawcettsociety.org.uk/wp-content/uploads/2013/02/The-Impact-of-Austerity-on-Women-19th-March-2012.pdf

Folbre, N. (2001). *The invisible heart: Economics and family values*. New York: New Press.

Folbre, N. (2015). *Accounting for Care: A research and survey design agenda. Paper prepared for the IARIW—OECD special conference: W(h)ither the SNA? April 16–17, Paris, 2015*. Paris: OECD.

Folbre, N. (2016). *Valuing non market work. Background think piece for Human Development Report 2015*. UNDP.

Folbre, N., & Nelson, J. A. (2000). For love or money—Or both? *The Journal of Economic Perspectives, 14*(4), 123–140.

Fraser, N. (1994). After the family wage: Gender equity and the welfare state. *Political Theory, 22*(4), 591–618.

Goodwin, N., Harris, J., Nelson, J., Roach, B., & Torras, M. (2013). *Microeconomics in context*. New York and London: M.E. Sharpe.

Himmelweit, S. (2013). Care: Feminist economic theory and policy challenges. *Journal of Gender Studies Ochanomizu University, 16*, 1–18.

Jülich, S. (2014). Substantive equality, Stockholm syndrome and the costs of child sexual abuse. In M. Bjørnholt & A. McKay (Eds.), *Counting on Marilyn Waring: New advances in feminist economics* (pp. 107–118). Bradford: Demeter Press.

Kerr, R., & McLean, J. (1996). *Paying for violence: Some of the costs of violence against women in BC*. The Ministry of Women's Equality Province of British Columbia.

Koren, C. (2012). *Kvinnenes rolle i norsk økonomi*. Oslo: Universitetsforlaget.

Loseke, D. R., & Kurz, D. (2005). Men's violence toward women is the serious social problem. In D. R. Loseke, R. J. Gelles, & M. M. Cavanaugh (Eds.), *Current controversies on family violence* (Vol. 2, pp. 79–96). Thousand Oaks, London and New Delhi: Sage Publications.

Mader, K. (2014). *Overview of GRB initiatives in Europe*. Presentation at *Gender responsive budgeting: Theory and practice in perspective*, International Conference, Vienna University of Economics and Business, November 6–8, 2014.

Mellor, M. (2005). Ecofeminist political economy: Integrating feminist economics and ecological economics. *Feminist Economics, 11*(3), 120–126.

Merchant, C. (1980). *The death of nature: Women, ecology and the scientific revolution*. San Fransisco: Harper & Row.

Mies, M., & Shiva, V. (1993). *Ecofeminism*. New Jersey: Zed Books.
Nelson, J. A. (1992). Gender, metaphor, and the definition of economics. *Economics and Philosophy, 8*(1), 103–125.
Nelson, J. A. (1993). The study of choice or the study of provisioning? Gender and the definition of economics. In M. A. Ferber & J. A. Nelson (Eds.), *Beyond economic man: Feminist theory and economics* (pp. 23–36). Chicago: University of Chicago Press.
Nelson, J. A. (1997). Feminism, ecology and the philosophy of economics. *Ecological Economics, 20*(2), 155–162.
O'Hagan, A. (2013). *'A wheel within a wheel': Adoption and implementation of gender budgeting in the sub-state governments of Scotland, Euskadi, and Andalucia (2000–2009)*. PhD dissertation, Glasgow Caledonian University.
O'Hara, S. (2014). Everything needs care: Toward a context-based economy. In M. Bjørnholt & A. McKay (Eds.), *Counting on Marilyn Waring: New advances in feminist economics* (pp. 37–56). Bradford: Demeter Press.
Pearson, R., & Elson, D. (2015). Transcending the impact of the financial crisis in the United Kingdom: Towards plan F—A feminist economic strategy. *Feminist Review, 109*(1), 8–30.
Pizzey, E. (2011). *This way to the revolution: A memoir*. London: Peter Owen Publishers.
Power, M. (2004). Social provisioning as a starting point for feminist economics. *Feminist Economics, 10*(3), 3–19.
Quinn, S. (2016). *Europe*: A survey of gender budgeting efforts. *IMF Working Paper 16/155*.
Schmitz, C. (2006). *Now it's about the money: Mainstreaming a gender equality perspective into Nordic national budgets*. Final Project Report 2004–2006. Copenhagen: Nordic Council of Ministers.
Stiglitz, J. E., Sen, A., & Fitoussi, J. P. (2009). *Report by the commission on the measurement of economic performance and social progress*. Paris: Commission on the Measurement of Economic Performance and Social Progress, OECD.
Straus, M. A. (2005). Women's violence toward men is a serious social problem. In D. R. Loseke, R. J. Gelles, & M. M. Cavanaugh (Eds.), *Current controversies on family violence* (Vol. 2, pp. 55–77). Thousand Oaks, London and New Delhi: Sage Publications.
Towers, J., & Walby, S. (2012). *Measuring the impact of cuts in public expenditure on the provision of services to prevent violence against women and girls*. Lancaster University.
United Nations Development Programme. (2015). *Human Development Report 2015: Work for human development*. Retrieved from http://hdr.undp.org/en/content/valuing-care-work

United Nations General Assembly. (2000). Further actions and initiatives to implement the Beijing Declaration and the Platform for Action, Unedited final outcome document as adopted by the plenary of the special session entitled. *"Women 2000: Gender equality, development and peace for the twenty-first century"* (&109). Retrieved from http://www.earthsummit2002.org/toolkits/women/un-doku/un-conf/c+5%20outcome-2.html

Varjonen, J., & Kirjavainen, L. M. (2014). Women's Unpaid Work Was Counted But... In M. Bjørnholt & A. McKay (Eds.), *Counting on Marilyn Waring: New advances in feminist economics* (pp. 73–90). Bradford: Demeter Press.

Walby, S. (2004). *The cost of domestic violence*. London: Department of Trade and Industry.

Walby, S., Towers, J., & Francis, B. (2016). Is violent crime increasing or decreasing? A new methodology to measure repeat attacks making visible the significance of gender and domestic relations. *British Journal of Criminology, 56*(6), 1203–1234.

Waring, M. (1988). *If women counted: A new feminist economics*. San Francisco: Harper & Row.

Waring, M. (2015). Personal communication.

Warren, K. J. (1996). *Ecological feminist philosophies: An overview of the issues*. Bloomington: Indiana University Press.

World Health Organization, and Centers for Disease Control and Prevention. (2008). *Manual for estimating the economic costs of injuries due to interpersonal and self-directed violence*. Geneva: WHO.

Yodanis, C. L., Godenzi, A., & Stanko, E. A. (2000). The benefits of studying costs: A review and agenda for studies on the economic costs of violence against women. *Policy Studies, 21*(3), 263–276.

Margunn Bjørnholt is a research professor at the Norwegian Centre for Violence and Traumatic Stress Studies in Oslo, Norway. She is a sociologist and gender studies scholar, with a background in economics. Her research fields include ethical banking, organizational studies, family studies, feminist economics, migration and cultural heritage. A common theme in her research is the dynamics between knowledge production, ideologies, social movements, policies and practices in social change. Her current research focuses on intimate partner violence, with particular emphasis on gender, gender equality and power relations.

10

Contemplative Economy and Contemplative Economics: Definitions, Branches and Methodologies

Xabier Renteria-Uriarte

Introduction

Contemplative philosophies can be seen, broadly, as "ancient Wisdom Traditions" (Carr & Mahalingam, 2003; Ferguson, 2013; Jestice, 2004; Walter & Fridman, 2004) or "systems of knowledge whose main concern is the exploration of the human condition and the search for the meaning of human life, … developed over thousands of years from religious, spiritual and other cultural sources" (Giorgino, 2015, p. 463). Intermediately, they can be approached by their conceptual core, which is known as "Perennial Philosophy" (Ferrer, 2000; Huxley, 1945; Leibniz, 1875–1890, III, pp. 624–625; Steuco, 1540). But more concisely, the contemplative knowledge proposed by ancient traditions searches for the meaning of life, which is characterized by the interconnectedness of beings, through the test of meditation (Renteria-Uriarte & Giorgino, 2017). Therefore,

X. Renteria-Uriarte (✉)
University of the Basque Country UPV/EHU, Bilbao, Spain

V.M.B. Giorgino, Z. Walsh (eds.), *Co-Designing Economies in Transition*,
https://doi.org/10.1007/978-3-319-66592-4_10

contemplative philosophy can also be synthesized as the worldview derived from the practice of contemplation or mind introspection.

Contemplation or meditation is defined scholarly as a "family of techniques" (Shapiro, 1982, p. 268) or as "the awareness that emerges" through them (Kabat-Zinn, 2003, p. 145); however, for contemplative philosophies, the deepness of this awareness, in fact, expresses the inner nature of consciousness and realities, as some known Eastern advocates remind us (Kelsang Gyatso, 2000; Krishnamurti, 1989; Osho, 1977, Chap. 7). Some nuances can be proposed. For example, contemplation or meditation should be defined separately (Walsh, 2016, pp. 41–42). Furthermore, conflating techniques (to achieve the mind introspection) and qualia (or qualitative instances of conscious experience that emerge from practising techniques) is problematic (Renteria-Uriarte & Casacuberta, 2015). In any case, *Contemplative science* (or contemplative sciences) currently refers to the scientific study of this awareness in human subjects (Casacuberta, 2013) within a growing and dynamic field of research on its neurological and phenomenological correlates (Renteria-Uriarte & Casacuberta, 2015).

However, this proposal starts from considering that modern research on 'this mode of awareness and its correlates' reflects only one aspect of how contemplative knowledge can develop within modern science. More concisely, contemplative science is far from being fully developed because current research has focused mainly on analytic aspects (in meditation research) and social engagement (in social innovation and feedback proposals), leaving aside the heuristic role (as a point of view from which to understand any object of study) (Renteria-Uriarte, 2016). This essay applies the analytic and engaged roles of contemplative science to economic theory, but with a heuristic aim, that is, to serve as a framework to further creation of more concise theories.

The main questions to answer are: Is there such a phenomenon as a contemplative economy? Can we define and characterize the entire economy from a contemplative worldview? Could we speak of a Contemplative Economics, and could its core be applied to understand any economic phenomenon? More concisely, how are economical choices and economic agents? What level of economic consciousness should be fostered? Does the economy reflect, in some way, common features of human existence? As important nuances, we must also consider the following: How does the economy improve our existence? Does scarcity actually define the economy? And finally: What are the main analytic, heuristic and socially transformative implications of Contemplative Economics?

The Economy from a Contemplative Worldview

A contemplative worldview accepts that the economy is concerned with resources, products and money, but only according to the most obvious and simple level. At a deeper level of understanding, the economy—as any other reality or process—is a manifestation of deep or hypostatical consciousness. It manifests or reflects the innermost meaning of awareness and existence (whatever you refer to it, as with terms like 'Tao', 'Śūnyatā', 'Voidness' or 'Brahmā'), as any other existence (that is, as interdependent on this manifestation with other ones, as Buddhism emphasizes).

The translation of this principle into modern science parameters is awkward, but we can assume that any being subsumes or infuses the core of 'information' or 'sense' of existence in the sense that it manifests its unitive, creative, mental and physical levels as 'a universe-with-legs' or 'a little universe that reflects the big Universe" (Navarro, 1994; Renteria-Uriarte, 2013). Following this criterion, natural resources, products, trade or finance appears as economy's least important or most gross level, the physical level. Even if we assume that the economy begins with the exploitation of them, the essential actors and processes at stake in the economy are less noticeable and more intriguing; they are more subtle and accessible through deeper levels of consciousness. Let us summarize this in steps.

Self-realization is facilitated by simplifying one's consumption, as a support to one's work and constructive human relationships. Different points of view can simplify economic complexity. If we take what is important for human agents as a guide, that is, their objectives in economic activities, then it can be defined in the following way:

> Economies perform the satisfaction of the needs of self-realization, that is, the realization of the unity of existence, through inner human development, rewarding work, and constructive human relationships. All of this is supported by simplified consumption, fair incomes, and stable prices (enabled by finance and trade).[1]

Note that we are not limiting the 'economic' scope to its traditional associations. Economic means, which include natural resources, products, services, money or finance, are not the core of the economy. They are contained in its most peripheral concentric circle. Similarly, economic ends, which include physical or quasi-physical needs (like food, clothing, housing, security, etc.), as well as socioeconomic desires (related to conspicuous consumption, prestige, power, etc.), are only intermediate ends. These intermediate ends are actually only means (frequently misguided due to ignorance, as we shall see) towards our (usually unconscious) inner self-actualization.[2]

However, according to the contemplative empiricism, this 'self-realization' is not 'our' self-realization. Existence and its underlying unity is what actually is reaching *its* self-realization via *our* own creative processes of human development. The traditional 'economy of products and choices' arises from the heart of people, as agents of existence, as scenery with important opportunities for encountering our deep awareness. This 'surface economy' or 'productive side of economy' is just a means for realizing our 'deep contemplative economy'. Through our work and human relations we satisfy our creative needs, and through our consumption and incomes we satisfy our physical and other needs; but the actual reason for us to participate in economics is to realize ourselves as a part and reflection of the depth, interdependence and wholeness of existence. We do not usually experience this consciously, but this does not deny its veracity from a contemplative perspective, which posits that we are ignorant of our real motivations in life. The challenge is to awake from this nightmare of ignorance and tensions, so as to overcome it, and learn how to work, to consume or to exchange as realized sages.

Anyone who practises meditation with discipline and sincerity may experience this perennial wisdom, renewed at different historical periods and in different cultures. Stable happiness and deep bliss can be attained by living with greater introspective awareness, and by redirecting the productive energies of the economy towards this goal. If we place our attention outside, living as mere consumers of products and focusing our energies on our incomes, then we generate both individual and social suffering. From a contemplative perspective, creative processes, human agents, living beings and physical objects are essentially manifestations of the deep consciousness, and their processes are movements towards more phenomenal explicitness or more profound implicitness. Several metaphors have been proposed to make it understandable: 'emergences'/'returns', 'foldings'/'unfoldings' (in terms of Bohm, 1981), etc. The economy does not escape this dialectic.

Thus, we must analyse the structure of existence properly and understand its processes to develop a Contemplative Economics in theory and practice. As Boulding (1969, p. 4) said, "the allocation of scarce resources is a universal problem which applies to political decisions and political structures through coercion, threat, and even to love and community, just as it does to exchange". The goal of Contemplative Economics is to articulate all of these concepts and put them to work in a coherent way, as a means to improve our economy and society with wisdom and compassion.

Economic Choices and Agents from a Contemplative Worldview

Is There Some 'Contemplative Economic Consciousness' to Be Fostered?

Contemplation is not an economic action, although it has economic effects, including the increase of productive efficiency (see a review in Renteria-Uriarte & Casacuberta, 2015). However, a Contemplative Economics should ask what the closest thing to it is, in an economy. We can exclude some things due to their contradictions and accept others that have been tested by contemplative persons over the millennia.

First of all, to ask if there is any 'deep economic consciousness' is illogical from a contemplative worldview. All existence and dimensions of reality have the deepest dimension of consciousness within, without exception. However, outer manifestations vary, and some of them are closer to it. For example, *peak experiences and amazements* (that break our patterns of ego), *jokes and intense amusements* (that suspend conceptual schemes for a moment), *dizziness* (a brief time where the world seems illusory), some *drug inhibitions* (that break the barriers of perception), *orgasms and dangers of death* (moments without ego) or *deep sleep* (where the mind merges with its deepest level) have been seen in perennial literature as 'close reflections' or 'open doors' to the inner nature of the ordinary mind. In the case of the economy, which would be the 'outer manifestation' of 'deep consciousness' closest to economic actions?

Secondly, what could we specify as 'economic' in the issue of 'economic consciousness'? Contemplation encourages us to give more attention to what is inside, that is, to our human faculties and to actions which we apply our faculties in, and less attention to what is outside, that is, to resources and products which we are absolutely or almost passive receivers for. Thus, it is appropriate to prioritize work over consumption. In this framework, contemplative modes of consciousness focused on daily actions have been proposed as economic and contemplative in modern science literature rooted in wisdom traditions: wu-wei (Korac-Kakabadse, Kouzmin, & Kakabadse, 2002; Li, Wang, & Fan, 2011; Lin, Ho, & Lin, 2013; Xing & Sims, 2012), karmayoga (Bhal & Debnath, 2006; Muniapan & Satpathy, 2013; Rarick, & Nickerson, 2008; Srivastava, 1980; Suriyaprakash, 2016) and appamada ("a caring attitude" or "carefulness" in Berzin, 2006; "concern" in Guenther & Kawamura, 1975). However, besides these, we can locate other daily modes of consciousness that could reflect the deep awareness in a similar way (but not the same way, as we explain later). Among psychic phenomena, the *flow* has been indicated as a good candidate to be a 'communicating vessel' for contemplative psychological states.

Flow or 'optimal experience' (Csíkszentmihályi, 1975; Csíkszentmihályi & Csíkszentmihályi, 1988) is the subjective experience of a person totally involved and absorbed, with complete concentration, in the activity she or he is performing (the activity is 'autotelic' or intrinsically motivated and rewarding). This psychic state entails a number of positive feelings, including freedom from self-consciousness or 'loss of ego', great enjoyment of the process and a sense of being totally in tune with the performance. The psychological concept of flow has been substantiated in a variety of settings (Csíkszentmihályi, 1997; Jackson, 1992; Kerr, 1997), which have proven remarkably robust through a number of studies (Nakamura & Csíkszentmihályi, 2012).

Since the inception of flow research, diverse scholars have suggested that optimal experience or some of its dimensions seem to bear a close relationship to the practices of Eastern traditions. Csíkszentmihályi (1990, pp. 113–115) himself mentions similarities between flow and yoga, martial arts and Zen. For example, he notes that "[y]oga [is] a very thoroughly planned flow activity" (p. 114). Other researchers have linked flow to such Eastern practices as *wu-wei* (Barrett, 2011), *ashtanga yoga* (Phillips, 2005), *tai chi* (Lein, 2004), *non-attachment* (Bermant, Talwar, & Rozin, 2011), *yoga meditation* (Shostak-Kinker, 2012) or *anasakti* (Banth & Talwar, 2012). Moreover, other relations have been suggested, like *varna* and flow (Kiran Kumar, 2006, pp. 549–550).[3]

Optimal experience, when it occurs in the world of work, turns out to be of great importance for Contemplative Economics. We apply our skills, and feel united to the action, experiencing a variety of by-products that suggest some sort of connection with our inner awareness, precisely on the productive dimension of life. Other manifestations, as 'peak experiences' in consumption, may also have importance, but if we prioritize self-development through unity with productive actions (see earlier in the chapter), flow has a prominent presence.

However, it is important not to equate wu-wei, karmayoga and appamada with 'optimal experience' or flow. According to contemplative philosophies, the former imply actions without rational deliberation, but they are performed when the actor—for example, the karmayogi—is immersed in the deep awareness (as it is known, the *Bhagavad Gītā* (5th–2nd c. BC, 1997) is a classical explanation of this immersion). In addition, they can be recovered to subject's ordinary consciousness (that is, we can remind them and draw our conclusions from this memory). On the contrary, optimal experiences could be non-rational reflections or even experiences of the deep awareness, but, in any case, they are not usually 'conscientized' by the subject; for example, a frequent (almost omnipresent) incident in flow qualitative studies is that the reporter does not remember or does not realize the experience described by the test until he or she is asked for it experience (see, for example, Csíkszentmihályi & Csíkszentmihályi, 1988).

Choices May Be Contemplative or Not, but All Choices Must Be Contemplatively Understood

Individual choices in scenarios of scarcity and exchange are a recurring theme in mainstream economics because choices "between ends and scarce means which have alternative uses" (Robbins, 1932, p. 15) can bring us a higher material standard of living. The issue should also be vital for Contemplative Economics, since it grounds economy on the self-realization of the economic agents and, consequently, on their decisions towards this goal. More specifically, the choices of economic agents can be 'separative', in the sense that they reflect better the interdependence of beings and the unity of their deep awareness, and can be 'unitive' in the sense that they reflect them better. As wisdom traditions use to highlight, personal experiences are illusorily and unstably pleasurable in the separative case, and stably happy and satisfying in the unitive case.

More concisely, all *the choices and actions in the physical, life, mind and creative levels of an economy are an* (usually unconscious) *attempt to make aware* (sometimes with ignorance, sometimes with more wisdom) *the interdependent and unitive levels of economy, of us and of all existences.* In other words, every choice is understood in a contemplative worldview (as highly holistic and compassionate point of view), but only those based on altruism, compassion, love and true happiness lead the agent and its environment to unitive awareness. Thus, these are ones that should be named strictly as 'contemplative choices'. Others, such as those based on selfishness, competition, greed or hate, lead mainly to separative results (e.g., exploitation of humans or other beings). Those are 'ignorant choices'. We choose them because we expect that they will bring us well-being and happiness, but they only give us—according to contemplative empiricism—a collection of ephemeral and vain pleasures, with the consequent risk of an enslaving chain.

Following the holographic key of 'items of consciousness', choices pertain to the human psychological level of the universe, but subsume the overall structure of existence (Renteria-Uriarte, 2013). They can refer more or less to physical economic resources or products; they are conditioned by sensations and emotions; they are contextualized in conceptual frameworks; they are in fact creative processes of actions; and they may, rightly in this sense, be interpreted as manifestations of our deep nature. In each of these levels, we can act according to separative or unitive choices: selfish or altruistic emotions, monetary profit or communitarian life viewpoints, destructive or constructive creations and so forth. The final balance will involve how we choose between a chain of divisive suffering and a path of inclusive happiness (and, consequently, how we participate in the 'unfolding' or 'folding' processes of existence).

Economic Agents Are, Albeit Unconsciously, Homo Deepeconomicus

The economic agent is also a contemplative and holographic 'universe with legs' from this point of view; let us see how (for details, see Renteria-Uriarte, 2013). Its physical body is the first manifestation of the material level and the main instrument for the productive acts by which self-actualization is pursued. When the agent acts selfishly and without social or ethical influences, it is from separation to other agents; at this time, the agent reflects the separateness of this physical level (which is what most strongly manifests the fact of separation). *Homo economicus* of Neoclassical Economics lies in this dimension of agency.

Sensations and emotions are the awareness of physical contacts—the way by which the agent makes conscious the contacts between its body and the objects of the environment. They reflect the connectivity of the life, and they imply the motivation to act towards unity, in collaboration with other agents in activities of production and consumption. This dimension of the agency is strongly affected by social considerations and ethical values, as shown in the *homo socioeconomicus* and *eticoeconomicus* described by heterodox economists.

Concepts and epistemic constructs, due to their universalistic role as described in philosophy, encompass different particular cases in global or 'universal' schemes. In this way, they reflect the connectedness of existence, and they fasten its awareness. Turning now to the economy, the concepts of agents help them act in accordance to larger totalities. This opportunity to contribute to greater unity will be seized or not, to the extent that the different economic concepts studied by distinct economic schools correspond with previous motivations (separatively egoist or unitively altruist).

Human creativity is the ground for those physical, vital and mental actions, and it can be encouraged when agents raise active awareness of their creative process, that is, of the making of socioeconomic innovations. Furthermore, if agents warn that separation is what leads to suffering, and positive connectedness to happiness, they will be in a better position to foster the re-encountering of the deep consciousness via unitive creations. This is why contemplative worldviews attach great importance to an ethical life; for example, Buddhism emphasizes *śīla* as minimum ethical standards for advancing knowledge (see also Dhanit Yupho, 1988; Phra Sāsanasōphon, 1975; Tivārī, 1987). Unfortunately, research on creativity has little presence in economic theory (Burger-Helmchen, 2013; Herrmann-Pillath, 2011; Menger, 2014; Rubenson & Runco, 1992), although the idea of 'creative destruction' is traced back to Indian philosophy. The main research line was after entering the modern German tradition (Reinert & Reinert, 2005), which was recovered later by renowned economists (Marx, 1863, pp. 495–496; Marx & Engels, 1848, p. 226; Schumpeter, 1942, pp. 82–83; Sombart, 1913, p. 207).

When agency is performed reflecting without rational deliberations and cost–benefit analysis the depth of awareness, the *homo* of economy acts in economy as economy itself; she reflects literally its sense and what the moment demands, without any ignorance on the inner logic of existence. This individual, who acts in the economy reflecting the unity of existence literally, would be a *homo deepeconomicus*. We could establish nuances depending on the particular unity level subsumed: *homo uni economicus* (imbuing the atmanic level), *homo holoeconomicus* (infusing the Brahmanic one) and finally this *homo deepeconomicus* (imbibing the nirvanic one); but their description goes far from an introductory essay. In any case, those dimensions are described with wise figures by some contemplative economic branches, such as with the *appamada* by Buddhist economics (Piboolsravut, 1997).

Economic agents, thus, do not exist in isolation, as assumed by the selfishness of Neoclassical Economics. Nor are they a simple reflection of the global nature of societies, as assumed by Structuralist and Systemist Economics. Contemplative Economics goes beyond the mainstream hypothesis that 'agents have no intra-determination of society or ethics', but also beyond the structuralist assumption that 'agents are intra-determinated by their social totalities'. Agents are not only 'an economy and society with legs', strongly influenced by their socioeconomic collectives, but also a 'wholeness with legs', or concrete forms of their final wholeness. Agents and societies are correctly understood only as an active manifestation, reflection or unit of the logic of the deepness of existence.

In this sense, the choices we make in economy merely repeat the constants of the dynamics of the rest of the universe: separation or unification, that is, ignorance or consciousness. Agents of an economy are intra-determined components of its structure and processes, literally imbuing and reflecting the deep awareness. Manifesting it closer or less close, this is our basic economical choice and action.

Economy and Its Agency: More Contemplative Implications

An Economy Is Not Only Material or Socioeconomic but Actually Holographic

Economy has been defined as "the allocation of material goods to satisfy material wants", as the operations of a "market sector" for goods and services and as the individual choices for "the allocation of scarce means to satisfy competing ends" (Becker, 1976, p. 1).[4] But, from a contemplative worldview, those actions and their agents, like any other process and beings, are merely different manifestations of the hypostasis. Productive and monetary sceneries (i.e., the material dimension of the economy), and the choices, scarcities and ends of agents on them (the psychological dimension), may be separative or unitive, closer or less close, but remain manifestations of the deep awareness in any case.

In the same way as a human and social activity with physical resources develops, economy develops in a variety of contexts: ecological, historical and technological; political and institutional; and within the dimensions of human motivations, ethics and culture (Goodwin, Nelson, Ackerman, & Weisskopf, 2008). However, contemplatively, different goals and contexts of economic choices have only one vital purpose: to make us connect with our inner depth. From this empiricism, economics as mechanistic praxeology of instrumental rationality (of mainstream economics) is contained in a broader social and human scope (of heterodox economists). But the latter is contained, furthermore, in the broadest scope: all economic agents hide, under their objectives and processes, manifestations (or 'holograms') of our hypostasis. And this holographic intra-determination permeates and pervades all economic aspects, although apparently trivial or strictly physical.

Economy, as a Manifestation of Deep Awareness, Subsumes the Main Levels of Existence

Economy, however much it may start from the goals of its agents, is a process that reflects the interdependence and wholeness of existence and, consequently, can be understood according to a holographic structure (for details see Renteria-Uriarte, 2013). Overall:

Economy emerges as the matter embodied by physical objects or bodies of natural resources and their derivatives like products or money, plants, animals and human agents (in the separateness of the physical level).

Economy starts the rapport with its deepness with relationships between those existences (in the connectivity of the life level), which are made conscious as sensations and emotions by living beings and human agents.

Economy fastens this connectedness with patterns and structures that give stability to those relationships (in the systematicity of the mental level), which are made aware as concepts and conceptual constructions by human agents.

Economy develops by all of those creative processes: those that lead to its occurrence as differentiated sides of existence via separateness, and those which make it emerge towards the lost unitive shared awareness via connectivity and systematicity. Thus, the creativity is present on any level, but it primarily becomes aware as vivid and intensely innovative actions by fully creative human agents.

Economy is, in its innermost level, a mystery of awareness, unity, compassion, happiness and love. Only our ignorance of this makes us choose selfish separative decisions (which are nescient because they ignore our deep awareness and increase the suffering in the world). Altruistic and compassionate unitive decisions are smart and wise, because they reflect better our deep awareness and decrease the suffering in the world.

This dynamic can also be seen as the actual determinant of economic agents, resources and processes. Any agent, choice, action and process that we may study would be seen as a fractal with innermost, creative, mental, life and physical levels. This taxonomy opens varied research possibilities from any of the dimensions considered ('holographic property', 'item of consciousness' or 'type of existence') with additional explanations[5] and potentials,[6] but we finish by remembering a striking contribution to heterodox economics.

Economy Is a Scenery of Abundance, and Only Materialistic Ignorance Creates Scarcity

The neoclassical school focuses on exchange and agents as individual makers of choices, assuming that they are not influenced by other agents (the well-known 'independence of preferences'). Marxists, Structuralists and Institutionalists focus more on production and/or on agents as part of society or other collectives, with their actions being influenced by norms, social costs and economic structures. In all of them, however, materialism is presupposed: a belief in physical production and consumption as a way to happiness and freedom. In this sense, "the insatiability of man and the niggardliness of nature" have been identified as the foundation of economics (e.g., Fairchild, Furniss, & Buck, 1926, p. 8). But the psychologies of these schools are one-dimensional or "a flatland", as Ken Wilber (1996, Part III) says. By contrast, *Contemplative Economics* is based on the evidence of a multi-dimensional human psyche, and this leads us to other economic science.

The surface layers of mind are 'outward', with the attention directed to the physical world, and, in fact, they are associated with insatiable desires. We pursue things of the external world with the hope that they will bring us happiness, but they only lead to an endless chain of futile and impermanent pleasures. Thus, there is a truth that, as mainstream theory describes, this leads to an economy of competition and consequent scarcity. Nevertheless, this is not the unique layer in mind.

Contemplation shows us that something different lies in our mind. In the early stages it may seem an inverted pyramid, with our ordinary mind very big and this deepness very small, almost a pinpoint (∨). But, if contemplative empiricism continues, then we evidence that our inner depth is immense, and sometimes it can be felt as endless; compared with it, our ordinary mind is small and insignificant (∧). This background is also felt as a source of happiness or as happiness itself (depending on the contemplative immersion) but, in any case, as something qualitatively different from 'what we use to call happiness': as self-sustained bliss, not a by-product; and as our innermost nature. When life goes on this evidence, the struggle for more consumption decreases and competition begins to disappear. In consequence, the economy is seen as a scenery of abundance, and not of scarcity.

In fact, the economic agent faces an issue of ignorance and lack of compassion and unitive collaboration with others. Being courageous and intelligent, the *homo deepeconomicus* adjusts work and consumption (in more rewarding and interdependent ways), follows a contemplative process by which the whole economy is reflected (as *homo holo and uni economicus*, beyond the reflections of *homo socio and etico economicus*) and overcomes the ignorance of confusing surfaces with meanings (as what *homo economicus* does). This act would lead us from 'scarcity economics' to 'abundance economics', in a field researched mainly by Gandhian (Diwan, 2000, 1982; Diwan & Lutz, 1987) and other heterodox economists (Chase, 1934; Diamandis & Kotler, 2012; Hoeschele, 2010; Sheehan, 2010), with contemporary elements such as the "commons-based peer production" (Benkler, 2006), or the "wikinomics" (Tapscott & Williams, 2006).[7]

Contemplative Economics and Its Analytic, Heuristic and Engaged Branches

Contemplative Analytic Economics

Preceding analysis enables us to describe the main branches of Contemplative Economics. *Contemplative Analytic Economics* analyses the contemplative empiricism in an economy, that is, the manifestations of the mind closer to deep consciousness in this scenery. More generally, it studies the agents, experiences and processes that 'perform from' or 'reflect' the contemplative level of consciousness, with special attention to some of its manifestations, such as this 'flow' or 'optimal experience' in productive actions.

The usual theoretical focus on physical capital, characteristic of mainstream and other major branches of economics, should be continued towards the intangibles such as the 'knowledge economy' (Drucker, 1966; Powell & Snellman, 2004), but until we assume meditation as a tool or means with effects for economy and with potentials for economics. In contemplation, attention plays a vital role and is considered not only "a cultural problem" of contemporary times (Crawford, 2015, p. 11), but also a 'human problem' regarding any economic world or historical period.

In this sense, how to focus attention and how to act with empathy and compassion is the vital issue for contemplative empiricism. The meaning is wider than in the outward focus of a so-called attention economics, which proposes to manage the attention of agents to product information as scarce resources, as it has grown increasingly abundant and available in contemporary times (Davenport & Beck, 2013; Simon, 1971). *Contemplative Economics* proposes to direct attention inwards to simplify consumption and make work happier and more efficient in the socioeconomic sense implied by self-realization.

Contemplative Heuristic Economics

Contemplative Heuristic Economics applies the contemplative ontology to understand all the aspects of an economy, whether explicitly contemplative or not. In other words, the first aim is not to analyse the 'contemplative economic choices or actions', but to analyse all 'economic choices and actions from a contemplative perspective'. The special task is to establish the structure and processes of an economy, economic agents and their environments, as emergences and returns of the deep unity in a holographic description of economic possibilities and choices. This essay has, in fact, his specific aim.

The term 'heuristic' refers to scientific discovery and the patterns of thinking that foster it (Kiss, 2006, p. 315), and thus contemplative analytic procedures that can be applied in other fields are important. The pattern of hologram described here as a 'universe with legs', or other analogous proposals like the AQAL (Esbjörn-Hargens, 2010; Gunnlaugson, 2007; Haigh, 2013), are heuristic tools in this sense.

Contemplative Engaged Economics

Contemplative Engaged Economics studies and promotes the effects of contemplation and contemplative point of view on society (in contemplative science 'enactivism' can be the other term for this aspect but, in economics, 'engagement' is more usual, as in the 'Engaged Buddhism' movement). Specifically, it analyses the economic choices that foster self-realization of the agent (whether conscious or unconscious) through the improvement of the person, the society and nature. In this sense, one of the goals of contemplative science is "to generate new forms of human services that optimize development" (Roeser & Zelazo, 2012, p. 143), with a large impact on our society (Schmidt & Walach, 2014, p. 1).

Contemplation changes the viewpoint from which we interpret the existence and, consequently, gives us more power to change our minds and social lives. Scholarly literature on the social effects of contemplation and contemplative philosophies is extensive. Several branches of economics study the economic criteria and choices that foster self-realization of the agent and, dialectically, the social-realizations of collectivities; their proposals can be gathered under the labels of 'Taoist economics', 'Vaishnavan economics', 'Gandhian economics' or 'Buddhist economics' (Renteria-Uriarte & Casacuberta, 2015).

As those proposals show, the enhancing power of contemplation and its worldviews has different levels of implications for the society and economy: agential/individual, managerial/leadership, engaged/social and also ecological/natural in relation to other (non-human) beings. Agents, as only apparently separated beings, never abandon the fact that their self-realization is embodied with the realization of others. Diverse theoretical views point out the relational or interdependent nature of economy, comprising the socioeconomic agency with reference to interconnected or shared meanings in wealth, well-being or work, and even in conceptual approaches (Diwan, 2000; García, 2014; McCubbin, McCubbin, Zhang, Kehl, & Strom, 2013; Nelson, 2009, 2010; Takahashi, 2013; Zelizer, 2012).

Note that the 'engaged' branch of Contemplative Economics is not a side effect, or a mere by-product, of the analytic and heuristic sides. In fact, analytic and heuristic sides are born as a conscientization of the intersection between an agent and its environment. When an agent, or, as in this case, an economic view becomes aware that it is not an isolated existence or process, then it can manifest its deepness better. In this sense, analytic and heuristic Contemplative Economics are engaged in the manifestation or realization of the inner depth in the explicit life, that is, in interdependence with other beings.

Conclusions

From a contemplative empiricism, an economy is, like any other process or area, merely a manifestation of our deep consciousness. In this contemplative understanding, economy operates as self-realization through rewarding work and constructive human relationships, with the support of simplified consumption, fair incomes and stable prices. And contemplation, as immersion in the deeper levels of consciousness, is the economic tool that provides understanding and power to frame daily economic actions in the stable bliss granted by this understanding.

In other words, the contemplative agent takes the profound awareness as a criterion of acting and tries to consciously reflect the connectedness of the existence of economic choices. She is aware that our shared deep consciousness explains the daily life and the various phenomena that occur both in them and through them.

However, unfortunately, this underlying performance of economy usually remains unconscious, and we try to find well-being following the useless and impermanent pleasures of the surface levels of the mind, thinking that economy consists (only) of products and money, and involves (mostly) competition and greed. We act consciously as *homo deepeconomicus*, and we compensate it with considerations of *homo socioeconomicus* and *homo eticoeconomicus*, but we are, albeit unconsciously, *homo deepeconomicus*. And the contemplative challenge is to make this deepness conscious in our daily actions with other behaviours in the work, consumption and exchange scenarios. A consistent contemplative agent, therefore, is also an engaged agent—someone committed with the intention of improving societies and people with interdependence and compassion.

Accordingly, *Contemplative Economics* analyses economy as a manifestation of the deeper consciousness. Major interests are the manifestations of the mind closer to profound awareness with place in economic actions (such as the wu-wei, the karmayoga or the appamada consciousness, or the 'optimal experience' or 'flow' at work), the choices of economy that foster self-realization of the agent (through the improvement of its natural and social environments) and the structure and processes of economy, economic agents and their environments as closer or less close manifestations of this hypostasis.

In summary, we must choose between economy from the heart of people and economy from the selfish hand. We choose to act in it as unitary agents of existence, or as its separative and suffering side agents. We may base our joy in a 'contemplative economic consciousness' modes, or in economic ignorance of what gives us deep and stable pleasures. We may also accept that, as interconnected manifestation with other beings, we respond to similar structure and we face similar choices. In this sense, we may assume economy and our agency as holographic manifestation of our deep nature, or as cold machines and societies. And we can consequently try to be respectful of all beings, or we can continue to make the other beings suffer more without increasing our happiness. In other words, we should endeavour to make contemplative choices, but with compassion for other non-contemplative agents and choices, for our benefit, and the benefit of other agents and non-human beings.

Because the economy is actually a scenery of abundance, and only our materialistic ignorance creates scarcity and local shortages, at all times we can act in either direction, towards our shared deep awareness or moving away from it. This duality of direction is the actual economic choice.

Notes

1. Other definitions of the economy and economics from a contemplative viewpoint have been given, but they are part of this more general definition. For example, Schumacher (1973) said that from a Buddhist viewpoint, the economy defines "how to attain given ends with the minimum means". The means refer to the consumption of natural resources and other inputs in production. Essentially, he is discussing simplified consumption.
2. This perspective is ever-present in wisdom traditions. For example, "Primitive people are those with less material culture … But they [possess comparatively greater] social solidarity, or respect for nature … [Their attitude towards] accumulation is one of the biggest differences … In some cultures, greedy people are regarded in the worst light and they are unable to enter the afterlife" (Pancorbo, 2000).
3. Links between positive psychology and Asian worldviews have also been proposed in a more general scope: Confucianism, emptiness and good life (Sundararajan, 2005, 2008, 2013); self/environment dialectics and happiness (Li, 2009); dukkha and samādhic happiness (Kolm, 2014); or positive and Buddhist psychologies (Murphy, 2011).

4. For example, as the market sector, economy has been defined as "the whole system of exchange relationships" in the markets, including political structures (Buchanan, 1964, p. 220), or as the "institutions [as firms, input and output markets, the banking system, etc.] that bind together [this] system" (Coase, 1977, p. 487). And as individual choices due to scarcity, in which is nowadays the standard definition of mainstream economics, as "the science which studies human behaviour as a relationship between ends and scarce means which have alternative uses" (Robbins, 1932, p. 15).
5. Perhaps the most difficult to understand, and not only from Western worldview, is how physical objects can also subsume 'within themselves' the contemplative awareness. The explanation is that they have not 'conscientized'. In economy, it would be as follows. Natural resources, infrastructures, products, money or financial actives form its material level. The connectivity that those physical objects experience (in this case due to human action) forms its live level. The structures in which they are involved (productive, exchange, financial, etc.) form its mental level. All the transformative processes and those emergences are their creative level. And inside them lies unconsciously the unitive level of inner awareness. Some aspects of this holographic path are studied by distinct economic schools (e.g., the descriptions of infrastructures, exchange nets, etc.), while others correspond to natural sciences and engineering (the performing industrial processes of resources and products), and the patterns and structures of economy are mostly analysed by structuralist economics.
6. Our above definition of economics shall also be understood in this holographic structure of the levels of existence, with the first three objectives (inner development, rewarding work and constructive relationships) as the most creative and unitive, and with the last five (simplified consumption, fair incomes, stable prices and accordingly finance and trade) as the most physical (Renteria-Uriarte, 2013, 2017). In this sense, we can prioritize the first three as target objectives (of the economy); the following three as operating means (for them) and the last two as the basic scenarios (for the previous); however, this concerns the political side of economics, and it is not our issue here.
7. All of these issues bring us back to a constant of human history: in the accurate rhyme of the Spanish poet Antonio Machado, "es de necio confundir valor y precio" (only the fool confuses value with price). We continue valuing the 'success' of social actions for their 'cash value', when

variables such as happiness in workplace, for example, are so economical than cash at the end of the month. And, somewhat strikingly, not mainstream economics, but positive psychology is the field that gives attention to those economic aspects (Deitcher, 2011; Diener & Seligman, 2009; Linley, Harrington, & Garcea, 2010; Russell, 2008; Spence Laschinger, Finegan, Shamian, & Wilk, 2004).

References

Banth, S., & Talwar, C. (2012). Anasakti, the Hindu ideal, and its relationship to well-being and orientations to happiness. *Journal of Religion and Health, 51*(3), 934–946.

Barrett, N. F. (2011). Wuwei and flow: Comparative reflections on spirituality, transcendence, and skill in the Zhuangzi. *Philosophy East and West, 61*(4), 679–706.

Becker, G. S. (1976). The economic approach to human behaviour. In *The economics approach to human behavior* (pp. 3–14). Chicago: University of Chicago Press.

Benkler, Y. (2006). *The wealth of networks how social production transforms markets and freedom*. New Haven and London: Yale University.

Bermant, G., Talwar, C., & Rozin, P. (2011). To celebrate positive psychology and extend its horizons. In K. M. Sheldon, T. B. Kashdan, & M. F. Steger (Eds.), *Designing positive psychology: Taking stock and moving forward* (pp. 430–438). New York: Oxford University Press.

Berzin, A. (2006). *Primary minds and the 51 mental factors*. Retrieved from https://studybuddhism.com/en/advanced-studies/science-of-mind/mind-mental-factors/primary-minds-and-the-51-mental-factors

Bhagavad-gītā. (5th–2nd c. BC/1997). *Bhagavadgītā: With the commentary of Śaṅkarācārya*. Calcutta: Advaita Ashrama.

Bhal, K. T., & Debnath, N. (2006). Conceptualizing and measuring gunas: Predictors of workplace ethics of Indian professionals. *International Journal of Cross Cultural Management: CCM, 6*(2), 169–188.

Bohm, D. (1981). *Wholeness and the implicate order*. London and Boston: Routledge & Kegan Paul.

Boulding, K. E. (1969). Economics as a moral science. *The American Economic Review, 59*(1), 1–12.

Buchanan, J. M. (1964). What should economists do? *Southern Economic Journal, 30*(3), 213–222.

Burger-Helmchen, T. (2013). *The economics of creativity: Ideas, firms and markets*. London: Routledge.
Carr, B., & Mahalingam, I. (2003). *Companion encyclopedia of Asian philosophy*. London: Routledge.
Casacuberta, D. (2013). The quest for artificial wisdom. *AI & Society, 28*(2), 199–207.
Chase, S. (1934). *The economy of abundance*. New York: Macmillan Co.
Coase, R. H. (1977). Economics and contiguous disciplines. In M. Perlman (Ed.), *The organization and retrieval of economic knowledge* (pp. 481–491). Boulder, CO: Westview Press.
Crawford, M. (2015). *The world beyond your head: How to flourish in an age of distraction*. London: Viking.
Csíkszentmihályi, M. (1975). *Beyond boredom and anxiety: The experience of play in work and games*. London: Jossey-Bass.
Csíkszentmihályi, M. (1990). *Flow: The psychology of optimal experience*. New York: Harper & Row.
Csíkszentmihályi, M. (1997). *Finding flow: The psychology of engagement with everyday life*. New York: Basic Books.
Csíkszentmihályi, M., & Csíkszentmihályi, I. S. (Eds.). (1988). *Optimal experience: Psychological studies of flow in consciousness*. Cambridge: Cambridge University.
Davenport, T. H., & Beck, J. C. (2013). *The attention economy: Understanding the new currency of business*. Cambridge, MA: Harvard Business Press.
Deitcher, J. (2011). *Facilitating flow at work: Analysis of the dispositional flow scale-2 in the workplace*. Halifax, Canada: Saint Mary's University.
Dhanit Yupho. (1988). *The Buddhist five precepts (pañca-sīla)*. Chonburi, Thailand: Dharmanoon Singgāravānij Foundation.
Diamandis, P. H., & Kotler, S. (2012). *Abundance: The future is better than you think*. New York: Free Press.
Diener, E., & Seligman, M. E. P. (2009). Beyond money: Toward an economy of well-being. In E. Diener (Ed.), *The science of well-being: The collected works of Ed Diener* (pp. 201–265). Dordrecht: Springer.
Diwan, R. K. (1982). An economics of love, or an attempt at Gandhian economics. *Journal of Economic Issues, 16*(2), 413–433.
Diwan, R. K. (2000). Relational wealth and the quality of life. *Journal of Socioeconomics, 29*(4), 305–340.
Diwan, R. K., & Lutz, M. (1987). *Essays in Gandhian economics*. New York: Intermediate Technology Development Group of North America.
Drucker, P. F. (1966). *The effective executive*. London: Heinemann.

Esbjörn-Hargens, S. (2010). *Integral theory in action: Applied, theoretical, and constructive perspectives on the AQAL model*. New York: SUNY.
Fairchild, F. R., Furniss, E. S., & Buck, N. S. (1926). *Elementary economics*. New York: Macmillan.
Ferguson, E. (2013). *Encyclopedia of early Christianity*. London: Routledge.
Ferrer, J. N. (2000). The perennial philosophy revisited. *Journal of Transpersonal Psychology, 32*(1), 7–30.
García, A. (2014). Relational work in economic sociology: A review and extension. *Sociology Compass, 8*(6), 639–647.
Giorgino, V. M. B. (2015). Contemplative methods meet social sciences: Back to human experience as it is. *Journal for the Theory of Social Behaviour, 45*(4), 461–483.
Goodwin, N., Nelson, J. A., Ackerman, F., & Weisskopf, T. (2008). *Microeconomics in context*. Armonk and London: M.E. Sharpe.
Guenther, H. V., & Kawamura, L. S. (1975). *Mind in Buddhist psychology. A translation of Ye shes rggyal mtshan's the necklace of clear understanding*. Emeryville, CA: Dharma Publishing.
Gunnlaugson, C. O. (2007). Exploratory perspectives for an AQAL model of generative dialogue. *Integral Review, 4*, 44–58.
Haigh, M. (2013). AQAL integral: A holistic framework for pedagogic research. *Journal of Geography in Higher Education, 37*(2), 174–191.
Herrmann-Pillath, C. (2011). *The economics of identity and creativity: A cultural science approach*. London: Transaction Publishers.
Hoeschele, W. (2010). *The economics of abundance a political economy of freedom, equity, and sustainability*. Farnham: Gower.
Huxley, A. (1945). *The perennial philosophy*. London: Harper and Brothers.
Jackson, S. A. (1992). *Elite athletes in flow: The psychology of optimal sport experience* (Ph.D.). Available from The University of North Carolina.
Jestice, P. G. (2004). *Holy people of the world: A cross-cultural encyclopedia*. Santa Barbara, CA: ABC-CLIO.
Kabat-Zinn, J. (2003). Mindfulness-based interventions in context: Past, present, and future. *Clinical Psychology: Science and Practice, 10*(2), 144–156.
Kelsang Gyatso, G. (2000). *Heart of wisdom: The essential wisdom teachings of Buddha*. Delhi: Motilal Banarsidass.
Kerr, J. H. (1997). *Motivation and emotion in sport: Reversal theory*. Hove: Psychology Press.
Kiran Kumar, K. S. (2006). The role of spirituality in attaining well-being: Approach of Sanātana Dharma. In A. Delle Fave (Ed.), *Dimensions of well-being: Research and intervention* (pp. 538–551). Milano: Franco Angeli.

Kiss, O. (2006). Heuristic, methodology or logic of discovery? Lakatos on patterns of thinking. *Perspectives on Science, 14*(3), 302–317.
Kolm, S. (2014). Happiness-freedom, who suffers? From dukkha to samadhi. In V. Giorgino (Ed.), *The pursuit of happiness and the traditions of wisdom* (pp. 23–31). Berlin: Springer.
Korac-Kakabadse, N., Kouzmin, A., & Kakabadse, A. (2002). Spirituality and leadership praxis. *Journal of Managerial Psychology, 17*(3), 165–182.
Krishnamurti, J. (1989). *El último diario*. Barcelona: Edhasa.
Laschinger, S. H. K., Finegan, J. E., Shamian, J., & Wilk, P. (2004). A longitudinal analysis of the impact of workplace empowerment on work satisfaction. *Journal of Organizational Behavior, 25*(4), 527–545.
Leibniz, G. W. (1875–1890). *Die philosphischen schriften von Gottfried Wilhelm Leibniz* (Vol. 1–7). Berlin: Weidmann.
Lein, H. (2004). *Common principles among flow, taoism, fifth discipline, and emergent properties* (M.A.L.S.). Available from State University of New York.
Li, J., Wang, J., & Fan, W. (2011). Yin yang and company growth: A case study of a coal company of Shanxi in China. *Chinese Management Studies, 5*(4), 380–393.
Li, W. (2009). A discussion of happiness philosophy. *Hefei Gongye Daxue Xuebao Shehui Kexue Ban/Journal of Hefei University of Technology (Social Sciences), 23*(5), 93–98.
Lin, L., Ho, Y., & Lin, W. E. (2013). Confucian and Taoist work values: An exploratory study of the Chinese transformational leadership behavior. *Journal of Business Ethics, 113*(1), 91–103.
Linley, P. A., Harrington, S., & Garcea, N. (2010). *Oxford handbook of positive psychology and work*. New York: Oxford University Press.
Marx, K. (1863). *Capital, volume IV. Theories of surplus-value* (1969th ed.). London: Lawrence & Wishart.
Marx, K., & Engels, F. (1848). *The communist manifesto* (2002nd ed.). Harmondsworth, UK: Penguin.
McCubbin, L. D., McCubbin, H. I., Zhang, W., Kehl, L., & Strom, I. (2013). Relational well-being: An indigenous perspective and measure. *Family Relations, 62*(2), 354–365.
Menger, P. (2014). *The economics of creativity*. Cambridge, MA: Harvard University Press.
Muniapan, B., & Satpathy, B. (2013). The 'Dharma'and 'Karma'of CSR from the Bhagavad-Gita. *Journal of Human Values, 19*(2), 173–187.
Murphy, M. D. (2011). *The happiness agenda: A comparison of perspectives from positive psychology and American Buddhist psychology on the pursuit of well-being*. California: California Institute of Integral Studies.

Nakamura, J., & Csíkszentmihályi, M. (2012). Flow theory and research. In C. R. Snyder & S. J. Lopez (Eds.), *Oxford handbook of positive psychology* (pp. 195–205). Oxford and New York: Oxford University Press.

Navarro, P. (1994). *El holograma social*. Madrid: Siglo XXI.

Nelson, J. (2009). The relational firm: A Buddhist and feminist analysis. In D. Bubna-Litic (Ed.), *Spirituality and corporate social responsibility: Interpenetrating worlds* (pp. 113–130). London: Gower.

Nelson, J. A. (2010). *The relational economy: A Buddhist and feminist analysis* (Global Development and Environment Institute Working Paper No. 10 ed.). Tufts University.

Osho. (1977). *Ancient music in the pines: Talks on Zen stories*. Poona: Rajneesh Foundation.

Pancorbo, L. (2000). *La última vuelta al mundo en 80 días*. Barcelona: Ediciones B.

Phillips, L. L. (2005). *Examining flow states and motivational perspectives of ashtanga yoga practitioners* (Ph.D.). Available from University of Kentucky.

Phra Sāsanasōphon. (1975). *What did the Buddha teach? and Sila*. Bangkok: Buddhist Association of Thailand.

Piboolsravut, P. (1997). *An outline of Buddhist economic theory and system*. Burnaby: Simon Fraser University.

Powell, W. W., & Snellman, K. (2004). The knowledge economy. *Annual Review of Sociology, 30*, 199–220.

Rarick, C. A., & Nickerson, I. (2008). Expanding managerial consciousness: Leadership advice from the Bhagavad Gita. *Proceedings of the Academy of Organizational Culture, Communications and Conflict, 13*(1), 59–63.

Reinert, H., & Reinert, E. S. (2005). Creative destruction in economics: Nietzsche, Sombart, Schumpeter. In J. G. Backhaus & W. Drechsler (Eds.), *Friedrich Nietzsche (1844–1900)* (pp. 55–85). Boston: Kluwer.

Renteria-Uriarte, X. (2013). *Hacia una Economía Holográfica. Una revisión de la ciencia económica desde la ontoepistemología oriental*. Bilbao: University of the Basque Country.

Renteria-Uriarte, X. (2016). Contemplative science, and the contemplative foundation of science. A proposal of definitions, branches and tools. In V. Bentz & V. Giorgino (Eds.), *Contemplative social research. Caring for self, being and lifeworld* (pp. 129–162). Santa Barbara, CA: Fielding University Press.

Renteria-Uriarte, X. (2017). Ciencia holográfica. una invitación a la ciencia tradicional desde la felicidad, el amor y la filosofía perenne. Unpublished manuscript.

Renteria-Uriarte, X., & Casacuberta, D. (2015). Should economists meditate (to be more efficient in their work)? Western and Eastern answers. *3rd VIS conference, International day of happiness: Economies of becoming*, University of Turin.

Renteria-Uriarte, X., & Giorgino, V. (2017). Is practical wisdom and learning literature actually wise on its 'right to speak'? In W. Küpers & O. Gunnlaugson (Eds.), *Wisdom learning: Perspectives on 'Wising-up' management education (series on practical wisdom leadership, organization and integral business practice)* (pp. 140–159). London: Routledge.

Robbins, L. (1932). *An essay on the nature and significance of economic science*. London: Macmillan and Co.

Roeser, R. W., & Zelazo, P. D. (2012). Contemplative science, education and child development: Introduction to the special section. *Child Development Perspectives, 6*(2), 143–145.

Rubenson, D. L., & Runco, M. A. (1992). The psychoeconomic approach to creativity. *New Ideas in Psychology, 10*(2), 131–147.

Russell, J. E. (2008). *Promoting subjective well-being at work*. Thousand Oaks, CA: Sage.

Schmidt, S., & Walach, H. (2014). Introduction: Laying out the field of meditation research. In *Meditation–Neuroscientific approaches and philosophical implications* (pp. 1–6). New York: Springer.

Schumacher, E. F. (1973). Buddhist economics. *Social Policy, 4*(3), 27–30.

Schumpeter, J. A. (1942). *Capitalism, socialism and democracy* (1994th ed.). London: Routledge.

Shapiro, D. H. (1982). Overview: Clinical and physiological comparison of meditation with other self-control strategies. *American Journal of Psychiatry, 139*(3), 267.

Sheehan, B. (2010). *The economics of abundance affluent consumption and the global economy*. Cheltenham and Northampton: Edward Elgar.

Shostak-Kinker, T. (2012). *Rock climbing, flow theory, and yoga* (M.A.). Available from Prescott College, Arizona.

Simon, H. A. (1971). Designing organizations for an information-rich world. *Computers, Communication, and the Public Interest, 37*, 40–41.

Sombart, W. (1913). *Krieg und kapitalismus*. München: Duncker & Humblot.

Srivastava, A. K. (1980). *Bhagvad Gita: Economic development and management*. New Delhi: Abhinav Publications.

Steuco, A. (1540). *De perenni philosophia*. Lyonn.

Sundararajan, L. (2005). Happiness donut: A Confucian critique of positive psychology. *Journal of Theoretical and Philosophical Psychology, 25*(1), 35–60.

Sundararajan, L. (2008). Toward a reflexive positive psychology. *Theory & Psychology, 18*(5), 655–674.

Sundararajan, L. (2013). The Chinese notions of harmony, with special focus on implications for cross-cultural and global psychology. *The Humanistic Psychologist, 41*(1), 25–34.

Suriyaprakash, C. (2016). Spiritual-based leadership from the perspective of the Bhagavad Gita. In M. Chatterji & L. Zsolnai (Eds.), *Ethical leadership* (pp. 125–152). London: Palgrave Macmillan.

Takahashi, M. (2013). Wisdom of the east and west: A relational developmental systems perspective. In M. Ferrari & N. M. Weststrate (Eds.), *The scientific study of personal wisdom* (pp. 251–263). New York: Springer.

Tapscott, D., & Williams, A. D. (2006). *Wikinomics: How mass collaboration changes everything*. New York: Portfolio.

Tivārī, M. (1987). *Śīla, samādhi, and prajñā: The Buddha's path of purification*. Patna: K.P. Jayaswal Research Institute.

Walsh, Z. D. (2016). The social and political significance of contemplation and its potential for *shaping contemplative* studies. In V. M. Bentz & V. M. B. Giorgino (Eds.), *Contemplative social research: Caring for self, being, and lifeworld* (pp. 27–50). Santa Barbara, CA: Fielding University Press.

Walter, M. N., & Fridman, E. J. N. (2004). *Shamanism: An encyclopedia of world beliefs, practices, and culture*. Santa Barbara, CA: Abc-clio.

Wilber, K. (1996). *A brief history of everything*. Boston: Shambhala.

Xing, Y., & Sims, D. (2012). Leadership, Daoist Wu Wei and reflexivity: Flow, self-protection and excuse in Chinese bank managers' leadership practice. *Management Learning, 43*(1), 97–112.

Zelizer, V. A. (2012). How I became a relational economic sociologist and what does that mean? *Politics & Society, 40*(2), 145–174.

Xabier Renteria-Uriarte has a Phd in Economics and Business Administration, and is Professor of World Economy and Management at the University of the Basque Country UPV/EHU. He was Director of the School of Business Studies of Bilbao (2009–2012, after being Deputy Director 1998–2009). He tries to translate to Western economics and science the legacy of wisdom traditions, mainly the Eastern ones, under the guidance of the principles of meditation, happiness and love, in the research agenda established in *Hacia una Economía Holográfica* (2013). Some applications are in economic love, contemplative science, rock music and ancient worldview of Basques.

Part II

Collective Awareness, the Self, and Digital Technologies

11

From Smart Cities to Experimental Cities?

Igor Calzada

Introduction: Transitions from the Smart Cities to Experimental Cities

It is noteworthy that although smart cities (Albino, Berardi, & Dangelico, 2015; Ersoy, 2017; Krivy, 2016) are already being built around us, they differ considerably from the simplistic, one-size-fits-all, smart-city-in-the-box approach that has thus far dominated mainstream institutional approaches. Hence, we could ask for whom and for what purpose smart cities are being developed? Are smart cities primarily about, or should they be about: a) creating new markets and profit, b) facilitating state control and regulation, or c) improving the quality of life while enhancing levels of democracy with citizens?

The contemporary smart city cannot simply be reduced to the economic value generated by partnerships involving powerful public and private actors (Rossi, 2015). While attention to the application of new information flows and the development of so-called smart cities is

I. Calzada (✉)
University of Oxford, Urban Transformations ESRC programme, Oxford, UK

V.M.B. Giorgino, Z. Walsh (eds.), *Co-Designing Economies in Transition*,
https://doi.org/10.1007/978-3-319-66592-4_11

increasing, there is still limited understanding of the interconnections among hard and smart infrastructures and economic, political, and social systems on metropolitan and regional scales. Furthermore, this conventional paradigm has often failed to deliver practical tools that can help us better understand and intervene in our daily realities, while also engaging with the various stakeholders that are important for our cities and regions. Hence, a multi-stakeholder approach is required to overcome dataism (Harari, 2016), understood as the logic that simplifies city metabolisms as merely assemblages or systems of data and algorithms (Finn, 2017; Morozov, 2014; Morozov & Bria, 2017; Morozov & Eno, 2017; Morozov & Harvey, 2016), rather than ecosystems of citizens (Keith & Calzada, 2016; Kontokosta, 2016).

It could be argued then that the development and use of the buzzword smart city in planning inner cities is intimately connected to currently required urban transformations (Calzada, 2016). There is currently a great deal of rhetoric about the importance of building smart cities, which do not pay attention to elements that constitute smart city strategies and policies in diverse contexts (Kitchin, 2016). Technological solutions have often been proposed under the umbrella of the smart city buzzword without first considering citizens' needs, their ability to use them, or their socio-technical misalignment within the city itself (Campbell, 2012; Hajer & Dassen, 2014).

Thus, this chapter suggests that we should first unplug, unpack, and deconstruct the meaning of smartness in our unique urban realities (Calzada & Cobo, 2015) by asking ten underlying questions about the city we want to make. As such, there are ten transitions we are able to adopt from the so-called smart cities approach to apply to a new paradigm that this chapter will explain in the section on experimental cities. Here are the ten transitions and questions for unpacking the smart city:

1. Who: Will the smart city evolve into an urban sphere in which dwellers have the right to decide whether to be connected?
2. How: Is the city a social interface in which the citizens will be able to self-design their social, everyday life needs?
3. System: Will these devices serve the citizens more than the citizens will serve the devices?

4. Governance: Is the bottom-up innovation perspective simply wishful thinking?
5. Information: In the era of data, is it possible to transition from controlled to open data-driven models?
6. Focus: Do we notice the difference between simple social interactions and human ties built on trust?
7. Space: Will we observe changes in which context-collapsed information will be contextualized to enhance social interactions? What are the implications for the privacy and security of individuals (CNN, 2016; Forbes, 2016)? Context collapse is a term used by academics (Marwick & Boyd, 2010) writing about the effects of social media and the contexts they give rise to. As such, it refers to an infinite number of contexts collapsing upon one another into that single moment of recording and having direct consequences in the public and private life of citizens.
8. Design: How can the design of places and user interactions be improved to anticipate an ambient commons for citizens? The "ambient commons" term (McCullough, 2013) claims for a cognitive role for citizens around the fixed forms of architecture and the city itself, surrounded by a superabundance flow of ambient information where individual signals increasingly matter less.
9. Socio-political processes: Is a shift occurring in the power dynamics between stakeholders?
10. Political economy: Will the political economy of the smart city be altered by any changes in stakeholder power relations?

It will be just after unpacking the techno-deterministic view in our cities (*unplugging*) when we can connect (*plug*) stakeholders into a wide, smart governance framework by including five type of actors, which this chapter presents later in the Penta Helix model (Calzada, 2016, 2017a, 2017b). These actors include the public sector, the private sector, academia, civic society, and social entrepreneurs. Indeed, it is necessary to *plug* stakeholders in by setting up a new complex, multi-stakeholder, city-regional urbanity to transit toward real smartness in cities and regions. A lack of dynamic power balance between stakeholders has so far been present in the hegemonic and technocratic versions of the smart city.

However, the position outlined in this chapter avoids a dystopian view by embracing a constructive notion that considers the favorable conditions that exist for a potential critical politics of a smart city policy agenda based on urban transformations driven by social innovation and experimentation. Likewise, cities and regions represent, as such, powerful places in which to detect emerging processes and observe spontaneous urban transformations. To summarize, after minimizing the negative side effects of hyper-connected societies, technology-oriented pathways of smart cities offer still unexplored opportunities for experimentation. We should embrace transitional experiments in our cities and regions as they exist in places like Dublin, Bristol, Barcelona, Torino, Amsterdam, Bilbao, and Glasgow (Calzada, 2017a).

As a result of these ten transitions from the smart city to the experimental city paradigm, there are three open research questions that relate to the core theme of this publication on radical approaches in dialogue with contemplative social sciences (Giorgino, 2014):

1. What prospects are there for alternative funding and alternative business models for smart cities?
2. What are the necessary practical/political interventions among businesses, local governments, academia, communities, and social entrepreneurs?
3. Is another type of smart city possible, that is, a third way between state and market overcoming the public–private partnership (PPP)?

At the end of this chapter, the answers to these three questions will be explored.

Smart Citizens: Decision Makers More than Data Providers

In this context, we could ask whether or not alternatives to the techno-deterministic approach to smart urbanism (Marvin, Luque-Ayala, & McFarlane, 2015) are flourishing. In fact, attention to a new way to empower the smart city by its smart citizens has been increasing in the last few years (Hemment & Townsend, 2013; Waag, 2016). These days, cities such as Barcelona are embracing this new shift to an inclusive, democratic, and participative smart city by advertising accordingly: "If you'd rather have smart citizens than smart cities… BITS will be in your interest" (BITS, 2016).

Those advocating for smart citizens (Waag, 2016) in a recent manifesto suggest that smart citizens take responsibility for the places they live, work, and love in; value access over ownership, contribution over power; ask for forgiveness, not permission; appropriate technology, rather than accept it as is; and provide assistance to those who are less *tech-savvy*. This set of principles underlies the notion that there is still a limited understanding of the interconnections between hard and smart infrastructures, as well as between economic, political, and social systems on metropolitan and regional scales. Furthermore, this new paradigm suggests the importance of overcoming the often failed smart-city-in-the-box approach by engaging with the various stakeholders that are important for our cities and regions.

Hence, this chapter aims to rethink the dominant technocratic and technology-centric smart city discourse by presenting this new take on so-called smart citizens. The new approach focuses not on imagining cities beyond or before technologies, but on accepting that city-regions are already fundamentally shaped by networked and mobile information communication technologies (ICTs) and by critically thinking through the consequences for governance that the promises and realities of smart cities pose. For example, many argue that smart city-regions will inevitably revolve around generating large amounts of data, and that this in itself will lead to new insights and governance strategies. But in reality, city-regions are much more complex and shaped by a large variety of different actors and organizations with often conflicting positions (Calzada, 2015). Likewise, data generated about individuals in cities and regions are variable, including personally identifiable information, data exhaust, personal data trails, and participatory personal data. As such, "data about people is big data in both the cognitive sense and social movement sense" (Shilton, 2016, p. 21). In fact, not all big data is data about people, but data about people inspire much of the hope and anxiety of their material, emotional, and relational human conditions in an individual and collective way.

Another strand of debate emphasizes the impact of the near-universal uptake of smartphones and other hand-held devices as well as the impact of the Internet of Things (IoT)—that is, networks of data-gathering and cloud computing (Ratti & Claudel, 2016). Many people use these devices and networks on a daily basis, but what this means for city-regional governance and the power-laden relationships between citizens, governments, and companies remains an open question. All this makes truly smart city-regional governance (Herrschel & Dierwechter, 2015) exceedingly difficult, but at the same time a fascinating and rewarding scale for investigating the various meanings and usages of smartness.

Recently, various research projects across Europe have started investigating these issues related to the notion of smart citizens. Most seek to develop not just critical analyses, but also practical suggestions to tackle urban problems such as pollution, health, safety, or mobility through the development and use of various types of mobile and networked data. These projects all revolve around the interlinked notions of smart citizens and data insofar as the so-called smart city approach has been elaborated on the ground by taking for granted the various ways to consider this binary combination. Specifically, the research efforts sought to unpack and question the following:

1. the kinds of knowledge gained through the production, distribution, and use of smart data;
2. the role data play in the constitution of urban expertise and in mediating and transforming the relationships between smart citizens, governments, and companies; and
3. the ways in which data-driven knowledge and expertise tackles and/or reproduces inequalities in city-regions among diverse group of (smart) citizens by provoking social exclusion patterns driven by technological toxic side effects (Hughes, 2016).

By finding answers to these questions, it is clear that aspects such as the techno-politics of data and how smart citizens should be integrated into this realm of governance remains crucial (Calzada, 2017a; Gray & Lämmerhirt, 2017). Indeed, as the smart city approach is being deconstructed from many instances after recently saturating policy agendas with very little reflexivity and being driven by market-based urban solutions, a new smart-citizen-centric paradigm is being tested. These urban experiments are intriguing; "their actuality matters in producing a different kind of city by offering novel modes of engagement, governance, and politics" that both challenge and complement conventional strategies such as ongoing smart city strategies (Evans, Karvonen, & Raven, 2016, p. 9).

We therefore should explore what is new in the experimental city approach compared to the smart city approach. In an attempt to make this contrast and trace the evolution from one paradigm to the other, Table 11.1 shows 14 changing dimensions.

As a consequence of the information provided in Table 11.1, we could argue that smart citizens are becoming the center of current smart city transformations (Satyam & Calzada, 2017) by emphasizing three achievements of urban laboratories as the new experimental settings (Karvonen & van Heur, 2014): situatedness, change-orientation, and contingency. The technical domains such as waste, energy, and transport (marked with an *) could still be in both approaches because of the very limited data impact study so far in a given territorial domain. As such, data science could enable—or not enable—citizens' advice to anticipate or even predict changes in the issues affecting people every day, to act sooner to prevent problems from escalating (Gray & Lämmerhirt, 2017; NESTA, 2015).

In a nutshell, (smart) citizens (Noveck, 2015; Thomas, Wang, Mullagh, & Dunn, 2016; Schuurman, De Marez, & Ballon, 2016) are considered decision makers rather than simple data providers insofar as their decision will depend on a relational context and the unique circumstances. Currently, in the scope of some experimental city approaches being carried out under the umbrella of the Urban Living Labs (ULLs) methodologies (Almirall & Wareham, 2011; Casual, 2016; Keith & Headlam, 2016; Leminen, 2015), participants play more of an active role as citizens and as co-producers than mere data providers, though there is unexplored research terrain regarding the techno-politics of data (NESTA, 2015), namely, its ownership and governance.

Table 11.1 From smart cities to experimental cities. (Elaborated by the author)

Dimension	Smart cities	Experimental cities
1. Data techno-politics	Big data	Co-production of open data
2. Notion of the city	As a market (European Commission-H2020, 2017)	As a platform (Anttiroiko, 2016)
3. Data ownership	Privately owned	Publicly scrutinized
4. Stakeholder helixes	Triple or quadruple	Penta (Calzada, 2017b)
5. Business models	Public–private partnership	Urbancommons
6. Smart citizen	User/data provider	Decision maker
7. Replicability	Based on urban solutions	Unpacking urban problems
8. Disciplinary	Monodisciplinary	Inter-disciplinary
9. Environment	IoT sensor networks	Citizen sensing
10. Waste*	Compactor bins Dynamic routing/collection	
11. Energy*	Smart grids Smart meters Energy usage apps Smart lighting	
12. Transport*	Intelligent transport systems Integrated Ticketing Smart travel cards Bikeshare Real-time passenger info Smart parking Logistics management Transport apps Dynamic road signs	
13. Government	E-government systems Online transactions City-operating systems Performance management Urban dashboards	Niche experiments Online decision-making Open platforms Dynamic management Urban Living Labs
14. Causality	Linear: cause and effect	Complex adaptive systems

Techno-Politics of Data

According to Gartner (2016), 1.6 billion devices will be connected to the larger smart city infrastructure worldwide by the end of 2016. However, as was highlighted in previous sections of this chapter, some uncertainties remain at the center of the debate around what Yuval Noah Harari has described as dataism (2016). What do we mean when we talk about smart citizens in the age of big data? According to Shilton (2016, p. 21), "uncertainties about how to use increasingly large sets of personal data are at the center of social debates about the virtues of Big Data. Not all big data is data about people, but data about people inspire much of the hope and anxiety bound up in discussions of the term." Who controls data collection, analysis, storage, and usage? These are key questions regarding the techno-politics of data for our present cities (Table 11.2).

Table 11.2 Techno-politics of data collection, analysis, storage, and reuse (Elaborated by the author from Shilton, 2016, p. 26)

Techno-politics of data	Collection	Analysis	Storage	Reuse
High participation	Subjects own or control devices; collection can be customized	Raw data accessible; subjects can conduct their own analyses	Data stored on local devices	Individuals control reuse
Low participation	Subjects aware of devices; collection can be avoided	Subjects can see visualizations or analysis of their data	Data in cloud storage with options for deletion	Reuse is restricted to aggregated forms
Little to no participation	Subjects unaware of devices; collection cannot be avoided	Subjects evaluated or categorized without their knowledge	Data in cloud storage with no option for deletion	Data collectors share or sell data

Regarding new sources of data collection, storage, and usage, the major obstacles to fostering a people-centered design of data is presented by the acquisition, shareability, and licensing restrictions of the obtained data. In this respect, there must be a closer collaboration between computer scientists and social and political researchers in developing stronger evidence-based research on how to tackle unexplored data issues. As such, we should elaborate on the need to consider individuals not only as citizens deliberating on their material conditions, but also as consumers agreeing and disagreeing to the particular terms of a service. In a nutshell, we could advocate for a more human-centered approach to the smart city—one that fosters interplay and interdependencies among multiple stakeholders.

When Habermas (2015) confronted technocratic and democratic smartness, he made it possible to generalize a category called smart citizens. As such, citizen interaction, engagement, involvement, participation, and deliberation are at the center of the debates around techno-politics of data. However, how should we deal with the lack of trust, apathy, and open outrage that has become increasingly evident in popular political attitudes today? The misalignments between technology and the social needs of citizens in data generation were identified as a common dilemma today: will data-driven cities (PWC, 2016) and devices continue to serve citizens or vice versa? As a consequence, different forms of smart citizens engagement could be discussed regarding the techno-politics of data. As Morozov (2014) has argued, despite the plethora of technological solutions to social problems, key questions remain unanswered; for example, "who gets to implement data?" and "what kinds of politics of data do technological solutions smuggle through the back door?" Discussions highlighting how calls for data to be open, while apparently simple, actually challenge existing legal norms and pose profound implications for users along the chain. For example, liability risks might be passed to the end user of open data, but what if end users cannot bear the risk? If the IoT generates continuous monitoring and commonly individualized data, how should we theorize, regulate, and make visible the ethical choices (Hughes, 2016) that have now emerged around the legal liability surrounding the *ownership of data*?

For a full understanding of the techno-political implications of the term smart citizens (Noveck, 2015) and to put into practice the whole capacities of citizens as the main driver in urban transformations, this chapter underlines the necessity for a deeper transition toward experimental cities. When citizens are considered users or data providers, it is assumed that personal data comprises a raw material that citizens take for granted as another element of the market. This fact should draw the attention of policymakers insofar as there are underlying issues of value and political decisions involved.

Citizens own data as an intrinsic part of their urban experience and their right to the city (Morozov & Harvey, 2016). Why then do we not naturally consider *smart citizens* to be pure decision makers, rather than just passive data providers? Despite this willingness to pursue sustainable futures that are more democratic, than technocratic, there is still strong inertia resisting this alternative path. In fact, the current round of urban experimentation differs from previous incarnations, indicating a specific kind of governance fix for a neoliberal system that is struggling to move toward more sustainable forms of urban development (Evans, Karvonen, & Raven, 2016, p. 10). Based on Oström's influential thoughts on the commons (Oström, 2010), Subirats (2012) suggests breaking away from the individualistic vision as conceived by the capitalist tradition. Subirats notes that this vision has progressively transferred the idea of rights to individual people. The new prevailing view is that only privatization leads to growth. However, we should also point out the inspiring critique made by Bollier (2016) advocating that historically rooted individualization processes are increasingly shaping the communal conditions of humans insofar as inter-subjectivity matters between them (Borch & Kornberger, 2015).

In a serious attempt to transition from the smart city to the experimental city, a deeper analysis of the techno-politics of data will be required to interpret the role of the smart citizens as decision makers rather than data providers. This notion is likely to be influenced by new conceptual explorations and empirical analyses of the urban commons. There are three European projects on participatory smart cities that are important to consider, because they reconceptualize smart citizens as decision makers rather than data providers: HackAIR (2016), Flamenco (Flanders Mobile

Enacted Citizen Observatories) (2016), and the City of Things (2016). Together, they mark a transition from the smart city to the experimental city by including an analysis of the techno-politics of data.

HackAIR is a social innovation project (Calzada, 2013a, 2013b; Sabato, Vanhercke, & Verschraegen, 2017) and open technology platform for citizen observatories on air quality. The project focuses on the level of citizen engagement and related strategies, such as crowdsourcing (citizens as sensors), distributed intelligence (citizens as basic interpreters), participatory science (citizens as participants in data collection), and extreme collaborative science (citizens as participants in defining problems and analyzing data). The call to transition from the conception of citizens as data providers to citizens as decision makers provokes a powerful debate on the ethical dimensions of participatory innovative technologies.

The Flamenco project has developed this theme further, exploring how citizens can be empowered to tailor their own observatories based on participatory sensing and citizen science principles. An inter-disciplinary team is working on the applicability of the project from the perspectives of computer science and social science.

The City of Things project explores the experimental dimensions of data-driven living labs. These dimensions are related to multi-stakeholder co-creation processes for business, user design, prototyping, and product development. Basically, these are open innovation processes that aim to connect to user experience along the product design process (West & Bogers, 2016).

These projects demonstrate that in one sense what was once novel has become received wisdom. It is now common sense to suggest that the nature of the metropolis demands forms of knowledge that transcend old boundaries between the humanities, natural sciences, and social sciences. It has become almost self-evident to assert that a model of knowledge production that is produced upstream in the academy and then exported downstream to city hall and local governance structures is inadequate for the metropolitan challenges of the twenty-first century. Instead, we have moved toward a stronger sense of co-production between research and practice. The sense that the questions arise in the real world but the answers are to be found in the academy is less plausible than ever. At its worst, the smart agenda, particularly as represented by journalistic accounts, can look like a return of technocratic determinism through the back door, whereby all urban ills are resolved through scientific solutions. Such naïve arguments are in reality more often the belief of second-rate technocrats and third-rate academic critique.

More interestingly, we witness a situation where the complex and open systems of urban life are disrupted by rapid social change and powerful economic forces (Keith & Calzada, 2016). Recognizing that such change is unpredictable in its disruptive form and uneven in its social consequences, one function of academic research is to speculate, test, map, and trace how disruptive technologies restructure the relationship between the individual and the city. The smart citizen at the heart of the new city needs to understand both the emancipatory potential and the divisive consequences of different moments of disruptive innovation. As we are going to observe in the next section, it is the duty and function of ULLs (Karvonen & van Heur, 2014) to surface and make visible the choices at stake, rather than provide singular solutions to problems. How we make these choices then becomes a mediation of scientific expertise and deliberative democracy.

This section highlighted how data-driven issues present new pathways to conduct research and implement policy. However, if we want to unpack data (*unplug*), we must also more deeply consider the underlying social, ethical, and political implications affected by the technical capacity to store and distribute bits of information through the power of data science. Dystopian visions and technocratic utopias alike demand rigorous scrutiny in research and public debate to optimize the chances for shaping a better future city.

Concerning the ethical and political dimensions of the ownership of data, urban experiments are gaining traction in cities all over the world, as a way to stimulate alternatives and steer change. Policymakers, designers, private companies, and third-sector organizations are initiating innovations to test alternative visions of local economic development, social cohesion, environmental protection, expansion of the creative sector, the evolution of policy, service delivery, infrastructure provision, academic research, and more. The concept of experimentation feeds on the attractive notions of innovation and creativity (both individual and collective) while reframing the emphasis of sustainability from distant targets and government policies to concrete and achievable actions that can be undertaken by a wide variety of urban stakeholders in specific places. The ability of urban experiments to be radical in their ambition while limited in their scope underpins a vibrant debate in both the policy and academic worlds with respect to their ability to prompt genuine change. Are these activities simply extensions of business as usual, spatially limited, and captured by a familiar cast of dominant interests? Or can they generate real alternatives and stimulate profound transformation? The next section will ruminate on the promises and perils of experimentation, as an increasingly alternative mode of urban governance that is actually moving beyond the structural mistakes of the so-called smart city as the dominant mode.

Experimenting with the Urban Commons: The Multi-Stakeholder Penta Helix Framework

In smart city and smart specialization strategy (S^3) policy discourses, governance interventions have been proposed in European cities and regions without appropriately considering the stakeholders, their multiple expectations, and their visions for a possible and desirable urban future. As such, smart technological solutions have not always focused on how technologies are used by citizens, and, at times, the experimental city's modes of governance have been misaligned with citizens and stakeholders.

In this context, to understand the inter-dependent challenges and opportunities for different stakeholders, we might focus on the dynamics of urban complexity, experimental research, and alternative policy approaches to cities and regions. This section is an invitation to rethink urban Europe around the notion of an experimental laboratory that produces research and policy interventions. ULLs, exemplified by networks such as ENoLL (European Network of Living Labs), foreground projects that present active user involvement, real-life settings, multi-stakeholder participation, multi-method approaches, and co-creation.

In contrast, the smartness of some European urban strategies is dominated by a technological discourse centered on data aggregation that allows the city-region to be managed by a given and fixed public–private partnership governance model. Nonetheless, the contemporary city cannot be forgotten in the complex multi-stakeholder context that is flourishing here and there.

Paralleling the mainstream approach of smart cities, urban laboratory initiatives, generally placed under the loose banner of ULLs, have been increasingly emerging over the last few years as an approach to speed up socio-technological innovation involving multi-stakeholders in co-production processes, and as a form of collective urban governance and experimentation that addresses the sustainability challenges and opportunities created by urbanization. Currently, what is interesting are the ways that city innovation policies propose highly spatially specific and potentially transformative stakeholder-helix strategies (either triple, quadruple, or penta), which recognize that strategies are cross-sectoral, involving the research base, private capital, and public expenditure of civil society.

The enormous potential for experimental forms of governance in European city-regions is expressed by ongoing ULL initiatives such as the Urban Living Partnership (Birmingham, Bristol, Leeds, Newcastle, and York), JPI Urban Europe schemes, and in many international schemes such as ENOLL, Mistra Urban Futures, Urban Mechanics, Guggenheim Urban Labs, Urban Lab +, the Guanghzhou International Award for Urban Innovation, Rockefeller 100 resilient cities, GUST snapshots, urb@exp., and ERC urban.

Building on the emerging body of policy initiatives and research (Keith & Calzada, 2016), this section addresses how notions of experimentation inform new ways of urban living:

1. What does the integration of inter-disciplinary and place-based knowledge practices mean? How can we bring together expertise in areas such as computing, mapping, politics, economics, digital anthropology, spatial analysis, and urban planning?
2. How can we deal with multi-stakeholder-helix strategies? What *are* the roles of the private sector, public authorities, academia, civil society, and entrepreneurs/activists in these ULL initiatives? What *should* the roles be?

3. How can ULLs transcend the current governance constraints of the smart specialization policy agenda in Europe?
4. What makes the ULL approach attractive and novel?
5. How are ULL initiatives being operationalized in contemporary urban governance initiatives for sustainability and in low carbon cities?
6. What prospects are there for alternative funding and alternative business models for cities and regions in Europe? (Uraia Nicosia Guidelines, 2016)
7. What are the practical and political interventions needed within multi-stakeholder approaches, and what are the potential concerns about data techno-politics?
8. Is another urban governance model possible—a third way between state and market? (OECD/KIPF, 2016)

The next section explores the strategic role of institutions in order to foster regional ecosystems of experimentation engaging the public sector, the private sector, academia, civic society, and social entrepreneurs/activists. In this endeavor, five sub-sections will be specified. The first sub-section will elaborate on the notion of experimentalism rather than smartness. The second sub-section will build on how urban governance requires considering the commons beyond public–private partnerships. In the third sub-section, the Penta Helix framework will be presented. The fourth sub-section will describe the city as a platform. Finally, the fifth sub-section will suggest a link between smart citizens as decision makers and as maker citizens.

Experimenting (with the City)

According to Karvonen and van Heur (2014), the experimental city approach champions the promise of experimental processes to promote urban innovations related to environmental protection, social cohesion, capitalist expansion, the development of the creative sector, policy improvements, infrastructure provision, academic research, and so on. It is important to recognize that the notion of the experimental city is related to a wider discursive field that includes triple-helix formations, applied innovation, engaged research, trans-disciplinarity, living laboratories, and the co-production of knowledge. As such, experimental urbanism (Amin & Thrift, 2016) taps into ideas of urban change as inherently multi-disciplinary, data-intensive, and embedded in place.

Whereas the smart city approach has been forged with an impetus toward urban-solution-driven fixes, the experimental city has been based on three steps that unpack urban practices (Latour, 1983, p. 166). First, social scientists must capture the interests of non-scientists outside of the laboratory (in the field); second, they must collect information on real-world problems in the field and introduce this information into the controlled conditions of the laboratory to facilitate experimentation; and third, social scientists must extend the laboratory into the wider society by carefully reintroducing the experimental results back into the field.

(Experimenting with the) Urban Commons

The notion of thecommons should be included in this narrative insofar as the smart city rhetoric has been entirely based on the idea of PPPs. In this chapter regarding the techno-politics of data and the transition toward a more experimental city approach, it is important to understand that the debate over the commons coincides with great technological changes that demand and invite us to work both from a scientific perspective to increase the capacity for innovation and cross-fertilization, as well as from a social perspective to ensure processes of social change and transformation. The urban commons thus go beyond state–market relations (Subirats, 2012). As such, it is important to revisit one of the first questions from the beginning of this chapter: Is another type of city possible, that is, a third way between the state and the market, which is not dominated by PPPs? Maybe we can see a political ferment gathering around these ever more frequent conflicts that do not find an adequate response in the traditional market–state dichotomy. What would be the answer to this governance need?

Bollier and Helfrich (2016) suggest that cities are at a crossroads insofar as (smart) citizens could use the ideas of the commons to retain control of the services that matter to them and to ensure they work for the people of the city, not just for business or bureaucracy. However, we could also argue that the idea of the urban commons could be rather experimental in its outcomes (Borch & Kornberger, 2015). At this preliminary stage, there should be an evolution in the urban governance model, by which I mean that there needs to be a necessary transition from the so-called triple and quadruple helixes to the penta helix (Calzada, 2017b). The notion that the experimental city can overcome the limitations of the smart city itself offers us a plethora of strategies to include more voices in the governance equation.

Penta Helix Multi-Stakeholder Approach

According to Lewontin (2000) and Leydesdorff and Fritsch (2006), the triple-helix model (made up of private, public, and civil society) enables us to study the knowledge base of an urban economy in terms of civil society's support for the evolution of cities. However, we could also argue that dynamic and pervasive social innovation processes are not included in this analysis. In the context of the experimental city, academia (quadruple helix) and entrepreneurs/activists (penta helix) are required to transition from the smart city approach. The laboratory context of experimenting with the urbancommons should reflect a wide range of voices in a certain community, and not be relegated to institutional settings. The inherent instability of an experimentally driven city provides a mechanism for co-evolution and a capacity to reflexively process the transition from the smart city approach. Often, dynamics of social innovation (Calzada, 2013b) are forgotten by those fostering urban change.

City as a Platform

Another dimension that is related to the experimental city is the understanding of the city as a platform (Anttiroiko, 2016; Anttiroiko, Valkama, & Bailey, 2013) and as a commons (Foster & Iaione, 2016). Local authorities provide a wide range of services including users' involvement in product development and citizens' right to bring their concerns to open innovation systems. Forms of participation may vary—some nominal, some transformative. More transformative modes of participation are associated with the opening of public data sets for public use free of charge and are related to open source and user innovation movements. On the whole, they reflect the increasing intersection between the penta helix driven by (social) entrepreneurs/activists and the experimental notion of the urban commons.

To some extent, a balance between private and public interests is complemented by other activities that could be considered the seeds of the experimental city in the realm of the urban commons. As such, there are inherent asymmetries in the level of engagement between firms and citizens that are compensated by welfare structures. Understanding the city as a platform may be a less controversial view of how to legitimize urban laboratories.

Smart Citizens as Maker Citizens

Finally, in the realm of the experimental city, (smart) citizens should represent a more transformative role as decision makers. In addition, the way in which some cities are evolving toward the power of the maker culture is related to the emergence of citizens as makers too. Cities like London have established a network of makers in diverse disciplines (http://openworkshopnetwork.com/), which is surely the source of further experimentation in the city.

Final Remark: Toward Urban Co-operatives?

This chapter examined the notion of the experimental city as a category that could overcome the smart city by shedding light on its limitations. I attempted to foresee how citizenship could require a more active role, so that citizens become decision makers rather than merely data providers. As such, the era of data and algorithms introduces uncertain ethical and political questions that should be solved in the terrain of techno-politics. Smartness could enhance the scope of governance by embracing new alternatives offered by the urban commons (Oström, 2010) and by avoiding narrow-minded public–private partnership finance schemes. Cities that become collections of urban laboratories would require an active ecosystem of stakeholders to function as a living metabolism. Triple and quadruple helix models have so far advocated fixed inter-institutional relationships, which is why this active ecosystem of stakeholders requires a fifth element—the entrepreneurial blood of the metabolism. Ultimately, this is the only way in which cities could be presented as a realm where citizens act and live as decision makers contributing to a maker production culture.

This type of experimentalism resonates with entrepreneurial models of socio-economic systems, which have been implemented in different parts of the world, some of which have been heavily researched. The Mondragon co-operative (Calzada, 2013a) is a paradigmatic model that includes the Penta Helix multi-stakeholder framework at the regional level. It is a source of territorial development and social cohesion. Nevertheless, even this model is showing some inherent contradictions that require further critical analysis. In fact, Mondragon co-operatives faced some years ago two complementary crises. On the one hand, the pressure of the global markets was undermining the cohesive model based on local employment, as the crisis in Fagor flagship firm showed some years ago. On the other hand, as a consequence of the first one, the governance model seems to depict a hierarchical conflict between the top management and the workers. And the most substantial lesson learned (Calzada, 2013a) is unresolved yet: How to update and re-activate the regionally rooted co-operative principles and values in the twenty-first century? By refounding a new type of co-operative entrepreneurship based on start-ups and spin-offs? Which could be set up by networked-driven *millennials/entrepreneurs* under open innovation, solid, sustainable but strongly fixed organizational structural schemes? To sum up, we would refer to an updated urban co-operative version based on inter-dependent metropolitan inclusiveness and regionally-rooted social capital.

At the end of this chapter, I dare to question whether or not the establishment of an ecosystem of urban co-operatives could form a radical alternative toward experimental cities (Ratner, 2009, 2013, 2015). Some of the hypothesis presented in this chapter (including the evolution of citizens as decision makers, increasing awareness of its techno-political implications, increasing interdependence between stakeholders, and the trend toward urban laboratories) seem to create pathways toward urban co-operatives in energy, mobility, and ICTs—three sectors where the smart city approach is developing increasingly more sophisticated business models.

Hence, to conclude this chapter, I will shortly reply to the preliminary research questions asked in the first section:

1. What prospects are there for alternative funding and alternative business models for smart/experimental cities?
   In the current experimental realm, the way in which some urban solutions are modifying the ownership of capital (and in parallel, different assumptions of who owns data) could offer interesting pathways to set up alternative funding and alternative business models based on the experience of some socio-economic models like co-operative firms.
2. What are the practical/political interventions needed among businesses, local governments, academia, communities, and social entrepreneurs?
   It is remarkable the way some businesses are setting up an ecosystem of entrepreneurial small and medium-sized enterprises. Territorial strategic alliances present a key ingredient for boosting a new generation of economic activity driven by the urban commons.
3. Is another type of (smart) city possible—that is, a third way between the state and market overcoming PPPs?
   So far, PPP have been the primary model reinforcing the alliance between the state and market. However, in some cities and regions such as Barcelona, Bristol, Glasgow, Bilbao, and Dublin (Calzada, 2017a), we see that the right balance and common strategy formed between public institutions, private firms, academia, civil society, and entrepreneurs/activists (i.e., the Penta Helix framework) are likely to open up a third way led by urban co-operatives under the urban laboratories open scheme—a model that sooner or later will become a paradigmatic model to follow.

References

Albino, V., Berardi, U., & Dangelico, R. M. (2015). Smart cities: Definitions, dimensions, performance, and initiatives. *Journal of Urban Technology, 22*(1), 3–21. https://doi.org/10.1037/1065-9293.59.3.209

Almirall, E., & Wareham, J. (2011). Living labs: Arbiters of mind-and ground-level innovation. *Technology Analysis & Strategic Management, 23*(1), 87–102. https://doi.org/10.1080/09537325.2011.537110

Amin, A., & Thrift, N. (2016). *Seeing like a city*. London: Polity.

Anttiroiko, A. (2016). *City-as-a-platform: Towards citizen-centre platform governance*. Presented at the RSA Winter Conference 2016 on New Pressures on Cities and Regions, 24–25 November, London, UK.

Anttiroiko, A., Valkama, P., & Bailey, S. J. (2013). Smart cities in the new service economy: Building platforms for smart cities. *AI & Society, 29*, 323–334. https://doi.org/10.1007/s00146-013-0464-0

BITS, Barcelona Initiative for Technological Sovereignty. (2016). Retrieved from https://bits.city/

Bollier, D. (2016). The city as a commons. Retrieved from https://www.youtube.com/watch?v=z3itmhDuem8

Bollier, D., & Helfrich, S. (2016). *Patterns of commoning*. The Commons Strategies Group. Retrieved from http://bollier.org/blog/spanish-translation-%E2%80%9Cthink-commoner%E2%80%9D-now-published

Borch, C., & Kornberger, M. (2015). *Urban commons: Rethinking the city*. London: Routledge.

Calzada, I. (2013a). Knowledge building & organizational behaviour: Mondragon case. In F. Moulaert, D. MacCallum, A. Mehmood, & A. Hamdouch (Eds.), *International handbook of social innovation. Social innovation: Collective action, social learning and transdisciplinary research* (pp. 219–229). Cheltenham, UK and Northampton, MA: Edward Elgar Publishing. 10.13140/RG.2.2.30748.69766

Calzada, I. (2013b). Critical social innovation in the smart city era for a city-regional European horizon 2020. *Journal of Public Policies & Territory P3T, 2*(6), 1–20.

Calzada, I. (2015). Benchmarking future city-regions beyond nation-states. *Regional Studies Regional Science, 2*(1), 350–361. https://doi.org/10.1080/21681376.2015.1046908

Calzada, I. (2016). (Un)plugging smart cities with urban transformations: Towards multistakeholder city-regional complex urbanity? *URBS, Revista de*

Estudios Urbanos y Ciencias Sociales Journal, 6(2), 25–45. Retrieved from http://www2.ual.es/urbs/index.php/urbs/article/view/calzada
Calzada, I. (2017a). The techno-politics of data and smart devolution in cities-regions: Comparing Glasgow, Bristol, Barcelona, and Bilbao. *Systems, 5*(1), 18. https://doi.org/10.3390/systems5010018. Retrieved from http://www.mdpi.com/2079-8954/5/1/18
Calzada, I. (2017b). *Transforming smart cities with social innovation: Penta Helix multi-stakeholders framework*. Presented in the SS21 Beyond Smart & Data-Driven City-Regions? Rethinking Stakeholder-Helixes Strategies, in the RSA Annual Conference 2017, 6th June, Dublin, Ireland
Calzada, I., & Cobo, C. (2015). Unplugging: Deconstructing the smart city. *Journal of Urban Technology, 22*(1), 23–43. https://doi.org/10.1080/10630732.2014.971535
Campbell, T. (2012). *Beyond smart cities: How cities network, learn and innovate*. Oxon: Earthscan.
Casual Synthesis Report. (2016). *Co-creating attractive and sustainable urban areas and lifestyles: Exploring new forms of inclusive urban governance*. Nordregio & JPI Urban Europe.
City of Things. (2016). *Discover today the possibilities of tomorrow's smart cities*. Retrieved from https://www.iminds.be/en/succeed-with-digital-research/go-to-market-testing/city-of-things
CNN. (2016). *Yinchuan smart city future*. Retrieved from http://edition.cnn.com/2016/10/10/asia/yinchuan-smart-city-future
Ersoy, A. (2017). Smart cities as mechanism towards a broader understanding of infrastructure interdependencies. *Regional Studies, Regional Science, 4*(1), 1–6. https://doi.org/10.1080/21681376.2017.1281154
European Commission-H2020. (2017). *SCC1 clustering meeting minutes on 24th March 2017*, Nottingham.
Evans, J., Karvonen, A., & Raven, R. (2016). *Experimental city*. London and New York: Routledge.
Finn, E. (2017). *What algorithms want: Imagination in the age of computing*. Cambridge, MA and London, UK: The MIT Press.
Flamenco Project. (2016). *Flanders mobile enacted citizen observatories*. Retrieved from www.citizen-observatory.be
Forbes. (2016). *Cities cannot be reduced to just big data and IoT: Smart city lessons from Yinchuan, China*. Retrieved from http://www.forbes.com/sites/federicoguerrini/2016/09/19/engaging-citizens-or-just-managing-them-smart-city-lessons-from-china/#6a5a34392dda

Foster, S., & Iaione, C. (2016). The city as a commons. *Yale Law & Policy Review, 34*(2), 2. Retrieved from http://digitalcommons.law.yale.edu/ylpr/vol34/iss2/2

Gartner. (2016). *Gartner says smart cities will use 1.6 billion connected things in 2016*. Retrieved from http://www.gartner.com/newsroom/id/3175418

Giorgino, V. (2014). Contemplative methods meet social sciences: Back to human experience as it is. *Journal for the Theory of Social Behaviour, 45*(4). https://doi.org/10.1111/jtsb.12078

Gray, J., & Lämmerhirt, D. (2017). *Data and the city: How can public data infrastructures change lives in urban regions*. Cambridge: Open Knowledge.

Habermas, J. (2015). *The lure of technocracy*. New York: Polity Press.

Hackair Project. (2016). *Collective awareness for air quality*. Retrieved from www.hackair.eu

Hajer, M., & Dassen, T. (2014). *Smart about cities: Visualising the challenge for 21st Century Urbanism*. Amsterdam: naio19 publishers/pbl.

Harari, Y. (2016). *Yuval Noah Harari on big data, Google and the end of free will*. Retrieved from https://www.ft.com/content/50bb4830-6a4c-11e6-ae5b-a7cc5dd5a28c

Hemment, D., & Townsend, A. (2013). *Smart citizens*. Manchester: FutureEverything.

Herrschel, T., & Dierwechter, Y. (2015). Smart city-regional governance: A 'dual transition. *Regions, 300*(4), 20–21. https://doi.org/10.1080/13673882.2015.11668693

Hughes, B. (2016). *The bleeding edge: Why technology turns Toxix in an unequal world*. London: New Internationalist.

Karvonen, A., & van Heur, B. (2014). Urban laboratories: Experiments in reworking cities. *International Journal of Urban and Regional Research, 38*(2), 379–392.

Keith, M., & Calzada, I. (2016). *European smart citizens as decision makers rather thank data providers*. Urban transformations ESRC report on 14th November 2016 Workshop entitled '(Un)Plugging Data in Smart City-Regions'. https://doi.org/10.13140/RG.2.2.11175.14240

Keith, M., & Headlam, N. (2016). *The urban living global challenge: A prospectus. Comparative international exemplars urban and living labs*.

Kitchin, R. (2016). Reframing, reimagining and remaking smart cities. *The Programmable City Working Paper 20*.

Kontokosta, C. E. (2016). The quantified community and neighbourhood labs: A framework for computational urban science and civic technology innovation. *Journal of Urban Technology, 23*(4), 67–84. https://doi.org/10.1080/10630732.2016.1177260

Krivy, M. (2016). Towards a critique of cybernetic urbanism: The smart city and the society of control. *Planning Theory*, 1–23.

Latour, B. (1983). Give me a laboratory and I will raise the world. In K. Knorr-Cetina & M. Mulkay (Eds.), *Science observed: Perspectives on the social study of science*. London: Sage Publications.

Leminen, S. (2015). *Living labs as open innovation networks: Networks, roles and innovation outcomes*. Doctoral dissertations 132/2015.

Lewontin, R. (2000). *The triple helix: Gene, organism, and environment*. Cambridge, MA and London: Harvard University Press.

Leydesdorff, L., & Fritsch, M. (2006). Measuring the knowledge base of regional innovation systems in Germany in terms of a triple helix dynamics. *Research Policy, 35*(10), 1538–1553.

Marvin, S., Luque-Ayala, A., & McFarlane, C. (2015). *Smart urbanism: Utopian vision or false dawn?* London: Routledge.

Marwick, A., & Boyd, D. (2010). I tweet honestly, I tweet passionately: Twitter users, context collapse, and the imagined audience. *New Media & Society, 13*(1), 114–133. https://doi.org/10.1177/1461444810365313

McCullough, M. (2013). *Ambient commons: Attention in the age of embodied information*. Massachussets: The MIT Press.

Morozov, E. (2014). *The rise of data and the death of politics*. Retrieved from https://www.theguardian.com/technology/2014/jul/20/rise-of-data-death-of-politics-evgeny-morozov-algorithmic-regulation

Morozov, E., & Bria, F. (2017). *Roundtable session—A new deal on data: What role for cities? Smart city expo world congress*. Retrieved from https://www.youtube.com/watch?v=1cakaaip2Vw

Morozov, E., & Eno, B. (2017). *Debat. Brian Eno i Evgeny Morozov Una conversa sobre tecnologia i democràcia*. Retrieved from https://vimeo.com/206060710

Morozov, E., & Harvey, D. (2016). *Conversation between Evgeny Morozov and David Harvey*. Retrieved from https://davidharvey.org/2016/11/video-conversation-between-david-harvey-evgeny-morozov-on-post-neoliberalism-trump-infrastructure-sharing-economy-smart-city/

NESTA. (2015). *Data for good: How big and open data can be used for the common good.*

Noveck, S. (2015). *Smart citizens, smarter state: The technologies of expertise and the future of governing*. Boston: Harvard University Press.

OECD/KIPF. (2016). *Fiscal federalism 2016: Making decentralisation work.* Paris: OECD Publishing. https://doi.org/10.1787/9789264254053-en
Oström, E. (2010). Beyond markets and states: Polycentric governance of complex economic systems. *American Economic Review, 100*, 1–33.
PWC. (2016). *From concept to applied solutions: Data-driven cities.*
Ratner, C. (2009). Cooperativism: A social, economic, and political alternative to capitalism. *Capitalism Nature Socialism, 20*(2), 44–73.
Ratner, C. (2013). *Cooperation, community, and co-ops in a global era*. New York: Springer.
Ratner, C. (2015). *The politics of cooperation and co-ops: Forms of cooperation and co-ops, and the politics that shape them*. New York: Nova Publishers.
Ratti, C., & Claudel, M. (2016). *The city of tomorrow: Sensors, networks, hackers, and the future of urban life*. New Haven and London: Yale University Press.
Rossi, U. (2015). The variegated economics and the potential politics of the smart city. *Territory, Politics, Governance, 4*(3), 337–353. https://doi.org/10.1080/21622671.2015.1036913
Sabato, S., Vanhercke, B., & Verschraegen, G. (2017). Connecting entrepreneurship with policy experimentation? The EU framework for social innovation. *Innovation: The European Journal of Social Science Research, 30*(2), 147–167. https://doi.org/10.1080/13511610.2017.1282308
Satyam, A., & Calzada, I. (2017). *The smart city transformations*. New Delhi: Bloomsbury Academic and Professional Publishing.
Schuurman, D., De Marez, L., & Ballon, P. (2016). The impact of living lab methodology on open innovation contributions and outcomes. *Technology Innovation Management Review, 1*(6), 7–16. Retrieved from https://timreview.ca/article/956
Shilton, K. (2016). When they are your big data: Participatory data practices as a lens on big data. In C. Sugimoto, H. Ekbia, & M. Mattioli (Eds.), *Big data is not a monolith*. Massachussets: MIT Press.
Subirats, J. (2012). *The commons: Beyond the market vs. state dilemma.* Open Democracy. Retrieved from https://www.opendemocracy.net/joan-subirats/commons-beyond-market-vs-state-dilemma
Thomas, V., Wang, D., Mullagh, L., & Dunn, N. (2016). Where's Wally? In search of citizen perspectives on the smart city. *Sustainability, 8*(3), 207. https://doi.org/10.3390/SU8030207
Uraia Nicosia Guidelines. (2016). *The impact of smart technologies in the municipal budget: Increased revenue and reduced expenses for better services.*

Waag. (2016). *A manifesto for smart citizens*. Retrieved from http://waag.org/en/blog/manifesto-smart-citizens

West, J., & Bogers, M. (2016). Open innovation: Current status and research opportunities. *Innovation, 19*(1), 43–50. https://doi.org/10.1080/14479338.2016.1258995

Igor Calzada is a lecturer, research fellow, and policy adviser at the University of Oxford in Urban Transformations. In addition, he is a lecturer in the MSc in Global Sustainable Cities at the University of Strathclyde and an associate fellow at Vrije Universiteit Brussel. His research focuses on comparing social, technologic, and politically innovative processes in smart cities and city-regions (www.cityregions.org), paying special attention to regional/metropolitan governance devolution/self-determination cases. He has over 15 years of experience in the public sector working as director of innovation in the Basque regional government and in the private sector as senior consultant in the Mondragon Co-operative Corporation (Spain). www.igorcalzada.com/

12

FirstLife: From Maps to Social Networks and Back

Alessio Antonini, Guido Boella, Alessia Calafiore, and Vincenzo Mario Bruno Giorgino

Introduction

VGI stands for Volunteered Geographic Information (Goodchild, 2008) and it is a concept introduced in relation to a new type of sensor, the human. Therefore, it can be said that the primary characteristic of VGI is to be produced by a person voluntarily. Geo-social media can be considered as VGI systems if we recognize that users produce geographic information on purpose. However, motivations in the mapping activities give the specific difference between VGI systems and geo-social media. Notably, a VGI producer tends to add information related to a predefined topic with the explicit intent of giving an objective position,

A. Antonini • G. Boella (✉) • A. Calafiore (✉)
Department of Computer Science, University of Torino, Torino, Italy

V.M.B. Giorgino
Department of Economic and Social Sciences, Mathematics and Statistics, University of Torino, Torino, Italy

V.M.B. Giorgino, Z. Walsh (eds.), *Co-Designing Economies in Transition*,
https://doi.org/10.1007/978-3-319-66592-4_12

while, a geo-social media user wants to share information which is of general use with the principal reason to express his/her point of view in a social network.

In this chapter, we want to first show a general classification of past and recent geographic information systems with a specific focus on the relatively new era of geo-social network. Then, FirstLife will be described; it is a novel platform available on the web that has been developed with the aim of connecting real-world social networks in a virtual environment without losing the sense of locality. Generally, social networks have been seen as a means to link users from all over the world but nowadays we are experiencing how much these new technologies can shape our daily life (i.e. Strava, Instagram and FourSquare). In the light of this, it is crucial to recognize the role played by users of the geo-social platforms since they can become a concrete support for citizens in co-producing services besides information. Therefore, some projects which involved the use of FirstLife will be mentioned.

Classifying Geographic Information Systems Through the User's Perspective

Maps are social constructions (Crampton, 2001) and the way they represent the real world is strongly biased by the cartographer perspective. Therefore, to give an overview of existing geographic information systems, we decide to classify them on the basis of the user's knowledge and expertise.

Through the prism of Users' Expertise (UExp) as key classification, there are two main axes which have emerged. On the one hand, the user's knowledge about the geographical world that is being mapped, which we call the Domain Knowledge (DK), and on the other hand, the user's skills in handling the systems, or System Knowledge (SK).

In Fig. 12.1, systems classification is shown with some exemplifications. In the first quadrant, it can be seen as positive values of expertise both in the domain and in the use of the system. Therefore, this class includes different technologies which are not user-friendly and to which the DK is needed. As an example, OpenStreetMap (OSM) and JOSM,

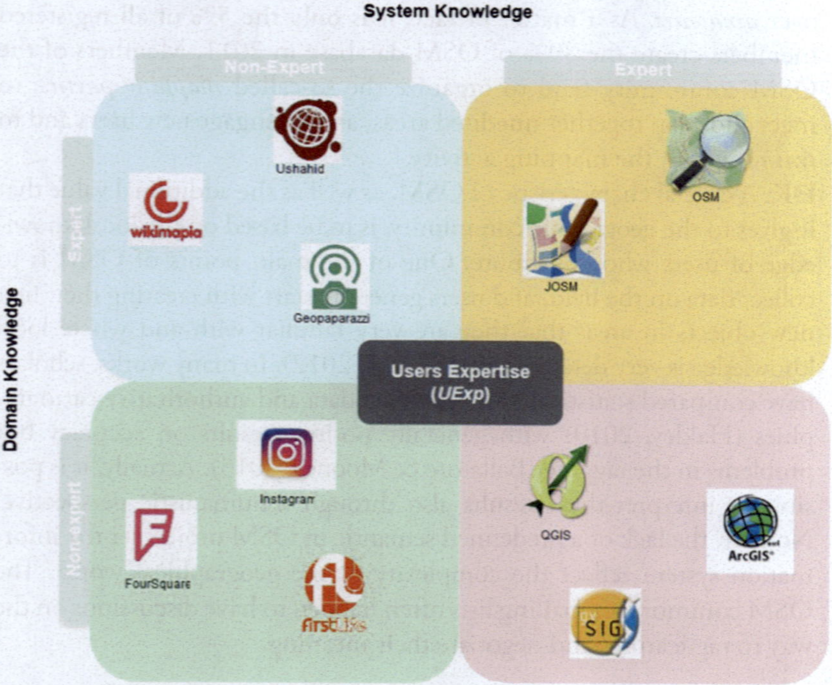

Fig. 12.1 Applications classification by users' expertise

which is one of the OSM editors, have been mentioned because of the following aspects:

- SK: To be an OSM mapper you need to be introduced by the community in understanding the way of tagging the geometrical primitives you add. The aim of OSM is to have open source and available maps to be used as well as the authoritative maps and they must represent the geographical world as much objective as possible. In Mooney and Corcoran's (2012) study on "highly edited" features, it has been underlined that it is possible for there to be emerging conflicts in tagging geographical features, but at the same time they provide evidence to support the hypothesis that eventually OSM data *stabilizes* for an area thanks to a *crowd effect*; however, *trained OSM mappers* are taking over *amateurs*. As a matter of fact, it is only the 5% of all registered members create the 89% of OSM database in 2011. Members of the OSM community tend to organize the so-called *mapping parties*, to meet and map together unedited areas, and to engage new users and to *train* them in the mapping activity.

- DK: A crucial characteristic of OSM, as well as the additional value that it gives to the geographic community, is to be based on the local knowledge of users who contribute. One of the main points of OSM is to collect data on the field, and users generally start with creating their first new objects in areas that they are very familiar with and where local knowledge is very detailed (Neis & Zipf, 2012). In many works, scholars have compared statistical analysis OSM data and authoritative cartographies (Hakley, 2010) with generally positive results on accuracy but problems in the tagging (Ballatore & Mooney, 2015). Actually, it is possible to interpret these results also through a humanistic perspective. Notably, the lack of a predefined semantic in OSM project let the information system reflect the complexity of the geographical world. The OSM community's mailing lists often happen to have discussions on the way to tag features and negotiate their meaning.

In the second quadrant, we have commonly used VGI systems in several projects. These systems have been ascribed in citizens' science field of study. In particular, they have been used for recording observations of, that is, bird watching or plant species or water quality. For these projects, the priority is to have a user-friendly system allowing as many users as possible who are expert in the selected domain to add relevant data. Even if the figure of scientist here is not relegated to professional scientists, scientific criteria in the domain definition plays a fundamental role in giving enough knowledge to non-professionals in order to map. The activity indeed must not be intended as a way of collecting personal views or opinions (Hakley, 2013).

Therefore, regarding our schema in this case:

- SK: This kind of system is thought to allow users without any training to map.
- DK: Knowledge of the domain, in this case, is essential in order to create fitness for purpose maps. Projects using these systems generally

provide the categories to be used in the mapping activity, depending on the specific domain needs. The result in these cases, differently than in OSM, for example, is a thematic map often characterized by very detailed taxonomies.

On the opposite side (the fourth quadrant) can be seen some of the most well-known GIS software (open source or not). Using the same structure as above we have that:

- SK: It is easy to grasp the complexity behind the use of GIS software simply from the numerous courses on GIS offered in academy. Actually, in this case the authors refer to the proper idea of professional who invests his/her career in the use of these software; in contrast to OSM experts they are generally paid to create cartographies, build Spatial Data Infrastructure or analyze geo-spatial data.
- DK: In this schema GIS software users are considered not expert in specific domains; however, this choice can be criticized since also GIS experts can have knowledge of a geographic world domain. The difference the authors want to underline here is that, in this case, it is not necessary to have knowledge of the domain but it is necessary to be trained for using that kind of systems.

Finally, in the bottom-left quadrant non-expert systems are reported. To use these software users are not required to have any expertise, neither in SK nor in DK. Systems included here can be defined as geo-social media (e.g. Foursquare, Instagram and FirstLife). Here, users can be considered as passive geographers more than neo- geographers since their main interest in adding Point Of Interest is not directly related to describing the geographical world but to sharing information within a social network environment.

- SK: These web-based systems are often commercial and based on digital engagement strategies such as high interactivity, few and clear functionalities, easing information sharing among users. In order to reach a substantial amount of users, the software has to be appealing and easy to use.

- DK: Here the domain is essentially social. Information shared through these systems is clearly related to the geographical world but in a way that makes it difficult to identify a specific domain of knowledge.

Taking the examples of the geo-social media shown in Fig. 12.1 into account, some functionalities that make them mostly related to a social network can be mentioned, such as in:

- *Instagram*: Users post geo-referenced pictures which can be shared with all the users or only with other users that follow him/her. At the same time, users have a personal wall with pictures made by others who he/she follows. It is also possible to like and comment on pictures as well as adding tags.
- *FourSquare*: Users can follow and be followed by other users; in this way, they could be recommended to go in some places depending on their social network preferences. Also, it is possible to choose multiple categories and add tags and tips to the places mapped.
- *FirstLife*: It is a new geo-social media where users can follow places rather than other users, so that they are notified in case of new information associated to places. Also, they have the possibility to create groups in which they can add other users, places and events.

Thanks to these additional and *social* functionalities, the User Generated Content (UGC) collected in geo-social media provides much more insights of the common sense and generalistic knowledge related to places than in VGI. Also, it gives information about the social relation between users and between users and places. In the next section, the authors will provide an example of a recently developed map-based system, FirstLife, and its applications.

FirstLife, a Civic Social Network

FirstLife is a civic social network, developed by the research group "Social Computing" of the Department of Computer Science, University of Turin. It can be considered as a civic social network since it explicitly conceives users as active players in the production of the social knowledge of the place. It offers a geo-referenced representation of crowd-sourced data, by using a map-based interface where users can add places, events, news and stories about their neighborhoods and the areas in which they live and work, creating and sharing public information. On the platform, users can not only get information passively but also can interact both with the map and other users, being more active and aware of what is around them, discussing on topics of local interest, organizing new initiatives and coordinating local development projects. Users can form open groups linked to a place in order to promote local forms of reciprocity and mutual-aid, take care of common goods or share private places. Thus, FirstLife can be used to visualize, integrate, share, comment urban data and make them point of collaboration for strengthening social cohesion in the real world.

FirstLife is designed to support activities, initiatives and local projects of public and private stakeholders acting in the city. The platform is a collective project aimed to connect and improve the coordination among the local networks, enhancing citizen engagement and social innovation processes (Antonini et al., 2016). The possibility of creating groups not based only on friendships and the social nature of information collected with FirstLife allow the analysis of the social construction of place semantics. In particular, the fact that users voluntarily create groups allows us to identify a collective membership with a high degree of confidence.

FirstLife's Architecture

FirstLife's architecture is composed of an interactive geographical map interface as front end and a back end for managing and searching geographical data. It relies on open source technologies. The interactive map is created with AngularJS, Ionic, Leaflet and OSM. It shows by means of graphical markers the POIs of the area of interest and it allows a user to insert new POIs directly from the map.

Depending on the type of POI, the front end offers different kinds of interfaces for visualizing or inserting/modifying the data. For example, an interface for events allows us to register to them while visualizing them, or to specify date and time when creating the event. Finally, this module offers the interface to manage the user's profile in the social network and the dashboard summarizing the relevant information. The social networking functionalities are as follows:

- Profile of user.
- Activity stream of user.
- Connections with other users through public groups.

To reduce the amount of POIs visible on the map, they can be filtered using (a) categories using an ontology, (b) search by tags and (c) temporal dimension. The map is continuously updated by the back end to show new POIs and posts which are posted by other users in real time. The back end supports the filtering mechanism of the front end, executing geo-referenced queries on the bounding box requested by the front end. For this aim it uses a PostGIS database, which is compatible with GIS software for urban planning. Maintaining the information about the last query of the user, it sends to the front end the updates when new information is created by other users on the bounding box the user is looking at. Concerning the maps, the module relies on OSM, using a dedicated tile server and the OSM interfaces to import and export data not related to users to the OSM database.

FirstLife's Uses

So far, FirstLife has been used for different purposes, all having in common the search for a growing involvement of citizens in the life of the city. So far, FirstLife has been involved in the following project:

TeenCarto

Teenagers' geographies are characterized by the specific value that youths give to their experience of the city. The social construction of teenagers as a social group goes with the attribution of specific spatial and urban behaviors, generally characterized by a resistance. Teenagers live, represent and transform urban spaces with their own specific spatial, social and cultural actions, rules, representations and semiotic codes, which vary also according to their gender, nationality and microculture. Moreover, digital technologies, smartphone and social networks added a new complexity to the relationships between youth and urban spaces, enriching the spatial behaviors in the material space with the filter of virtual spaces and networks.

A recent research on teenagers' spatial behaviors in Torino showed the gap existing between Torino as a city *for* teenagers—specifically addressed to them but planned and normed by adults—and the Torino *of* teenagers, actually lived and experienced by young people (Research Teencarto, financed by the City of Turin). The research, besides other methodologies such as surveys, involved the use of FirstLife for the mapping activity. The project involved more than 600 teenagers from 16 schools, in a massive process of community mapping aiming at producing a representation of their urban geography. Data collected have been analyzed to make evident the way teenagers use the city as well as how they imagine a better city. Their evaluation of urban spaces and proposals of change have been part of the data gathering process. The understanding of the real urban geographies, through bottom-up perspectives, and the engagement of citizens, with participatory policy-making, are central in the smart cities narratives, often associated to the use of ICTs.

WeGovNow

WeGovNow is a project within the H2020 framework (its link is http://wegovnow.eu/what-we-do.html). The aim of WeGovNow is to support the collective use of a new type of online engagement platform. The platform will be used by civil society stakeholders—including individual citizens, commercial/non-commercial organizations and public authorities—to enable collective opinion formation, service co-creation and co-delivery at local governance level. Spatial representation of issues of public interest is considered as a strong facilitator of citizen engagement. In particular, capturing and visualizing local knowledge through maps has been utilized very successfully in engagement activities that bring the community together and reveal areas where action is required and the active organizations. However, scholars expressed concerns that digital tools for participation and co-creation risk empowering only the empowered, as a considerable segment of the population does not have access to or does not feel comfortable making use of emerging social media and online collaboration tools. Therefore, in addition to direct access to the online platform by members of the target audiences, WeGovNow will make use of complementary offline engagement methods and tools in order to reach out to those members of the community that (at least initially) lack the means and/or motivation to use online devices for getting involved in the project.

In the WeGovNow platform, in which FirstLife is one component and the provider of two map-based modules, the relationship between users will not be friendship among people of the same circle (such as the case in traditional social network) since the focus is on creating local communities based on proximity and heterogeneity. The idea behind the social network is to bridge the virtual and the real world, rather than keeping the user closed in the bubble of the virtual one. Key features of the network are as follows:

Interactive map as interface: The map-based user interface of WeGovNow will make information on the map alive by allowing different kinds of interaction on the information posted.

Adding geographical features to the map: WeGovNow uses OSM as base map, which means that all features that have already been mapped in each of the validation cities can be displayed on the WeGovNow online map. Furthermore, with the WeGovNow platform, users can easily add features to the map, such as missing or updated information on specific places.

Collaborative tagging: Platform users (individual citizens as well as organizations in their role as local stakeholders) are invited to tag places in their community. This way, issues impacting the quality of the city space can easily be reported by individuals.

Creating Groups: members logged in the social network can create groups based on their interest in a particular place, to be alerted of what is happening there, or topic, to know which trends the discussions about it have, on their membership in civil and institutional organization, but also on informal networks which exist only for a while for instance to organize an event. This functionality is intended to ease the collaborative attitude in more specific situations and in doing so exploiting potentialities of online social networking for having a real-world impact

Community mapping: The concept behind community mapping, as developed by project partner Mapping for Change, is to move away from "top-down" mapping that so often fails to reflect the needs of people. A "community map" is a map created by members of a community or group. The map shows things that people living in the community are interested in or concerned about. A community map is built from local knowledge and expertise in terms of what people know about the area they live in.

Advanced backend support: Most of the times, authorities such as councils and municipalities have their own procedures and workflows for tracking and solving issues and it is often difficult to convince them to change their bureaucratic habits. The WeGovNow platform due to its high modularity and highly customizable usability would be able to adjust to their needs and in addition will offer extra functionalities that clerks will start using as they realize that such things will actually promote their everyday work.

WeGowNow platform will be tested in three cities, Torino, San Dona' di Piave and London (in the Southwark Borough), to support participative decision-making in the local development of the areas.

CO-CITY

COCITY is intended to break the self-reinforcing circle of poverty, social segregation in deprived neighborhoods and lack of participation. The central idea is to support the development of a polycentric commons-based urban welfare based on low-cost service co-production, social mixing and care of public spaces (http://www.uia-initiative.eu/en/uia-cities/turin).

COCITY is innovative in its legal, managerial and technological aspects, providing

- an unconventional legal framework to enable citizens to take care of urban commons;
- an innovative ICT infrastructure for local social market and networking;
- a management tutoring toward economic sustainability.

In CO-CITY, the top-down approach is replaced by a collaborative one that considers citizens as change-makers, agents of the so-called circular economy (ref). To achieve this, it is crucial recognizing the centrality of place and place-making (ref), particularly in deprived areas. The project will take place in the city of Turin. The city is coping with consequences of the financial crisis that has contributed to an increase of poverty both in the inner city and in peripheral areas. Between 2008 and 2013, the population of the city living in absolute poverty increased by 80% and is now 7%. The unemployment rate is 13% and it is rising more than in other Italian cities. Evidence of poverty in the city is the presence of many derelict buildings.

CO-CITY, with the Regulation on commons implemented by the local municipality, adopts an innovative conception of the role of public administration that encourages citizens' commitment by defining a general framework of sharing responsibility and mutual trust. A group of active citizens (third sector or informal groups) identify a building or space by responding to a public call or presenting a proposal. Then they underwrite a "pact of collaboration" with the Urban Authority, defining the commoning program, the respective powers, liabilities and expenses, insurance, and so on.

In co-produced services (ranging from helpdesks to cultural productions, social markets and urban farming), the citizen is simultaneously producer and consumer. This role reinforces a sense of community belonging and generates paths of autonomy from public assistance.

The toolkit proposed in the project consists of a combination of:

- an unconventional legal framework to enable citizens to take care of urban commons (compliant with the new regulation);

- an innovative ICT infrastructure for local social market and networking (using FirstLife);
- a management tutoring toward economic sustainability.

Point 2 is of the utmost relevance, as we will experiment the use of a distributed ledger technology (at the basis of cryptocurrencies such as Bitcoin) not just to create a local currency, but to implement a more general exchange system where goods and skills are shared. While it is considered a disruptive technology in finance and e-government (2016/2007(INI) Report by European Parliament), in this project we apply it innovatively at the community level, as a means of sustaining co-production and the core economy. We also favor the diffusion of soft skills and life skills labs and workshops in order to enable participants to better handle the various difficulties they meet in self-management and in relationships with others. Social innovations linked to smart ICTs are thus integrated through a wiser approach to human interactions with living beings and things.

Finally, Co-City aims to help community projects that are sustainable and present a long-term perspective, thus enhancing public assets in a social sense: (a) creating pilot community projects and supporting self-building capabilities and innovative community-led enterprises; (b) creating a network of mutualism and circular economy, in which citizens will use an alternative system of payment in the area where they live and work based on distributed ledger technology.

Conclusions

In this book, we presented a new classification of geo-based systems through the lens of user expertise. This is preliminary to interpret the added value of geo-social network, to which the possibility to organize social knowledge of the real world is crucial. Then, we have described a specific example of geo-based social network which is defined as civic, in order to underline the active role played by users. The projects completed or in progress that we have presented show the potential of this new generation of web application, from the recognition of place social knowledge, which does not mirror only a single cartographer's viewpoint, to the co-production and the taking care of public spaces.

In conclusion, we are trying to rethink the smart cities' model from scratch, bringing people within any action via collaborative technologies. As we have seen, traditional geographic information systems need to be adapted to specific users' needs in terms of expertise and in relation to the type of knowledge which will be mapped. In this way, we want to promote the use of ICT, supporting users' actions in real places.

Bibliography

Antonini, A., Boella, G., Calafiore, A., Salaroglio, C., Sanasi, L., & Schifanella, C. (2016, February). First life, the neighborhood social network: A collaborative environment for citizens. In *Proceedings of the 19th ACM conference on computer supported cooperative work and social computing companion* (pp. 1–4). ACM.

Ballatore, A., & Mooney, P. (2015). Conceptualising the geographic world: The dimensions of negotiation in crowdsourced cartography. *International Journal of Geographical Information Science, 29*(12), 2310–2327.

Crampton, J. W. (2001). Maps as social constructions: Power, communication and visualization. *Progress in Human Geography, 25*(2), 235–252.

Goodchild, M. F. (2008). Commentary: Whither VGI? *GeoJournal, 72*(3), 239–244.

Haklay, M. (2010). How good is volunteered geographical information? A comparative study of OpenStreetMap and Ordnance Survey datasets. *Environment and Planning B: Planning and Design, 37*(4), 682–703. SAGE Publications Ltd STM.

Haklay, M. (2013). Citizen science and volunteered geographic information: Overview and typology of participation. In *Crowdsourcing geographic knowledge* (pp. 105–122). Netherlands: Springer.

Mooney, P., & Corcoran, P. (2012). The annotation process in OpenStreetMap. *Transactions in GIS, 16*(4), 561–579.

Neis, P., & Zipf, A. (2012). Analyzing the contributor activity of a volunteered geographic information project—The case of OpenStreetMap. *ISPRS International Journal of Geo-Information, 1*(2), 146–165.

Alessio Antonini received an M.Sc. (cum laude) in information management system from the Computer Science Department, University of Torino. He is pursuing a PhD in computer science at the Computer Science Department,

University of Torino. His M.Sc. final dissertation was in multimedia database. His main fields of research are social ontologies, data visualization for Geographic Information Systems and knowledge management systems from social knowledge. He is the Developer Coordinator and Front-End Developer of FirstLife.

Guido Boella is Professor of Computer Science at the University of Torino. He is working in the area of Artificial Intelligence and social networks. He has written many papers on legal informatics especially about normative multiagent systems, organizations and roles. He developed the powerJava programming language and the compliance software Eunomos. He is co-founder of the Nomotika spinoff. He is the inventor of the FirstLife social network, a local social network based on an interactive map.

Alessia Calafiore received an M.Sc. (cum laude) in development, environment and cooperation from the Department of Economic and Statistics, University of Turin, with a final dissertation in urban geography. She is pursuing a PhD with the Department of Computer Science, University of Turin. Her PhD research project is on geographic ontologies and she is part of the FirstLife team.

Vincenzo Mario Bruno Giorgino has a PhD in Sociology. He is Aggregate Professor at the Department of Economic and Social Sciences, Mathematics and Statistics, University of Torino, Torino, IT. Since 1998, he has been primarily devoted to the integration of contemplative knowledge and sociology in action research and higher education with a focus on transformative methodologies. In 2016, he co-edited with Valerie Malhotra Betz the book *Contemplative Social Research: Caring for Self, Being, and Lifeworld* (Fielding University Press).

13

The Organic Internet: Building Communications Networks from the Grassroots

Panayotis Antoniadis

Introduction

Internet access has become such a necessary utility for citizens to stay informed as active members of society that it has been recently considered to be a "human right" by the UN—alas, a human right that is not granted to 60% of the world's population (Sandle, 2016). A huge amount of investment is required to close this gap, and there are many different possible ways to "connect the world" Miller (2014), different approaches on what are required to provide "global Internet access for all" (Crowcroft, Wolisz, & Sathiaseelan, 2015). The key question is as follows: Should big corporations like Facebook or Google be allowed to offer connectivity in exchange for more power over the Internet itself, or should connectivity be considered a "commons" (Baig, Roca, Freitag, & Navarro, 2015), provided by the people for the people? Facebook is a corporation dedicated, indeed, to "connect the world" and to "understand intelligence and make intelligent machines" (MacManus, 2016), which could even attempt to

P. Antoniadis (✉)
NetHood, Zurich, Switzerland

V.M.B. Giorgino, Z. Walsh (eds.), *Co-Designing Economies in Transition*,
https://doi.org/10.1007/978-3-319-66592-4_13

"cure all diseases in our children's lifetime" (Brink, 2016). It also aims to offer "free" Internet access, or at least to a small part of the Internet considered "basic", which of course includes Facebook, to disadvantaged areas and countries such as India (Bhatia, 2016). Should we accept this deal? Should we allow Facebook to acquire monopolistic power, if in exchange, it will ensure that all people on earth are connected … to Facebook's data centers? Or should we provide more resources, such as economic and legal, for Community Networks like Guifi.net or Freifunk.net, among many others, to become more popular and empower more local communities to build their own network infrastructures in a more democratic way (Antoniadis, 2016b), and in a sense more "organic"?

The existence of credible local information and communication technology (ICT) solutions can indeed prove critical in cases of natural disasters (an earthquake), economic disasters (a global economic crisis), or even political disasters (a coup d'etat), and through the transfer of power from big corporations to local institutions can also illustrate the way toward more ecological ways to build and use technology in our everyday life. But notice that unlike housing or food, we do not have the experience of "how things were made in the past". The Internet was created as a global network from an early stage and until very recently the percentage of people in a specific geographic area connected to it was rather limited. In other words, "doing things locally" is an element of the Internet's future, not its past. And this poses both challenges and opportunities. On the one hand, there is not a tangible example of how to build an Internet from the grassroots, and we do not know what is the possible role of the different local actors in this process. It is difficult even to imagine this possibility, although the required technology is already available and also good reasons to use it in this way (Antoniadis, 2016a). On the other hand, the "local Internet" could be perceived as an advanced form of communication in cities and not as a backwards approach to development, as sustainability solutions in other domains are, often mistakenly, perceived (Kallis, 2017).

This chapter aims to answer two main questions: one about production—ICT infrastructures—and the second about consumption habits—the Internet diet. It also introduces one candidate technology that could become part of the answer: Do-It-Yourself (DIY) networking. First, in a sustainable city of the future like the one imagined by P.M.

(2012, 2014) how would the underlying ICT infrastructure look? Would it be owned and managed through local cooperatives, as in the case of housing and agriculture? Would every neighborhood have its own servers, platforms, wired and wireless connections? Or would ICTs belong in the "global sphere"— a centrally managed infrastructure meant to interconnect different regions and cities across the world? Or perhaps, the reality would be somewhere in the middle with points of centralization at the district or city level. In either case, would it look like today's commercial industrialized Internet or would it be more "organic"? Second, in a world with resource constraints, what would be a healthy and ecological diet for everyday consumption of Internet services and information? What type of services should be provided to satisfy the basic needs for communication and the organization of other common activities? And how "private" should we expect this consumption to be? Should people share their devices? Should they share the content downloaded from the Internet or even share their Internet connections themselves?

The key premise behind the effort to answer those questions is that any "action plan" for sustainable living needs to include also a strategy for implementing and consuming information and communications technologies (ICTs). And this strategy needs also to take into account the energy requirements of digital communications, their design and governance, and their corresponding social, economic, and political implications (Fuchs, 2017). This is essential, since the Internet and more generally ICTs are much more than "dump pipes" transferring digital information from point A to point B. They include data collection, management, and filtering services, as well as user interfaces that prioritize certain actions over others, and include many other design decisions that significantly affect the way they are used and their corresponding outcome (e.g., Tufekci, 2014).

The more ownership and control citizens have over the underlying network infrastructure and software, the more opportunities are offered for developing sustainable solutions according to the local environment. DIY networking is an umbrella term for different types of grassroots networking technologies that allows today various forms of experimentation toward this direction and offers an example of another, more organic, way to build communications networks that promotes self-expression, face-to-face interactions, and diversity.

A sustainable city needs the option of an organic Internet. One whose infrastructure is built, owned, controlled, and maintained by local communities. And one that satisfies our basic needs for knowledge, information, and communication. Consumption and geographic limits should be also considered to promote a healthy lifestyle that encourages physical contact and conviviality, and allows for intimacy and local governance models. Regarding energy requirements, it is important to realize that Internet consumption is not an isolated activity. It can diminish transportation costs, since communicating online enables us to socialize, learn, and work from home; but at the same time, for example, it can increase health costs from lack of movement and physical contact. Moreover, the Internet is not a neutral medium of communication. When used for promoting the common good instead of increasing profits for global corporations, it can play a key role in supporting alternative, more sustainable modes of living. But in the current context it is not easy to get rid of Facebook, just as it is not easy to get rid of companies like Monsanto. The professional graphic designers and engineers of "user experiences" are analogous to genetically modified seeds and pesticides, in so far as they make our life easier in the short term but can have disastrous consequences in the long term.

Toward a strategy for an organic Internet as part of a sustainable model of living in the city, this chapter makes the following contributions. "The Second Watershed of the Internet" section offers a very short simplified overview to the history of the Internet arguing that it is currently at its "second watershed" phase as a technology; this is a term used by Ivan Illich to describe the situation in which an extremely useful initially "tool" like education or medicine is professionalized to such extent that it starts harming the common good in favor of its own sustainability. The "Network Infrastructure" and "Software" sections analyze in detail the different elements of a networking infrastructure (the backbone and access network) and the different high-level services that run on the servers deployed in the network (e.g., storage, content sharing, social networking, etc.). The "Limits" and "Sharing Resources" sections introduce different forms of limits, and sharing practices in Internet consumption, a more balanced Internet diet, that could be considered in an energy-limited world together with different forms of resource sharing. The "Do-It-Yourself Networking" section introduces the concept of DIY networking and argues that options should be provided to communities to build part of these elements and services from the bottom up as a commons, resulting in different combinations between local and global solutions according to the specific environment. Finally, the "Putting Things Together: The Case of NeNa1" section presents one example of how these different options could be brought together to imagine an organic Internet that could serve the needs of an urban neighborhood of around 500 inhabitants, as imagined by Zurich's cooperative housing and living initiative NeNa1.

The Second Watershed of the Internet

Before elaborating a vision of an "organic" Internet, I want first to provide a simplified view of the interior of the Internet and how it evolved in the last 20 years from an open and highly decentralized system to a very centralized one, subject to surveillance, censorship, and manipulation at large scales. Having been conceived as part of a military program, the Internet has been designed to be flexible and adaptable to very dynamic conditions (Clark, 1988). The main idea, what is called the end-to-end principle, was that the network would behave like a "dump pipe" transferring packets of information from the one side to the other, trying always to find the best path from the source to the destination for each different packet—unlike the telecommunications industry model of establishing first a "connection" or a "circuit" through which all packets flow.

Another important principle of the initial design of the Internet is that the network was conceived to be distributed and comprised by different "autonomous" systems that are free to interconnect and share the information required to calculate the most appropriate "paths" for the data packets to travel through the network. This rather loose "contract" between independent entities, open to various opportunistic decisions and oligopolistic coalitions, is held together through a basic principle that everyone in principle is obliged to follow: net neutrality (Odlyzko, 2009). That is, all data packets crossing the network should be treated equally in terms of "urgency", independent from their source and destination. This principle is very important because it allows everyone connecting to the network to provide services that can compete on equal terms with everyone else, allowing for experimentation and innovation. This key principle significantly affected the way the Internet was used for the first few years. One of the most popular Internet services, e-mail, was distributed among different e-mail servers running in different places, typically universities. However, as more and more users were becoming part of the Internet, and due to important physical constraints of the infrastructure (low speeds, asymmetric bandwidth), economies of scale, network externalities, and abuses (e.g., SPAM), services started becoming more and more centralized and participation of people online less and less anonymous. Indeed, a very large percentage of worldwide e-mail traffic passes currently through the gmail servers of Google, whose algorithmic agents have the right to analyze the content of the e-mails (Rushe, 2015) and correlate with other personal information attached to the senders and receivers, such as GPS locations recorded from Google Maps, search queries, and more.

Today we are in an era of "the cloud", big data, sophisticated social software, algorithms and artificial intelligence. From "virtual" communities (Rheingold, 1993) connecting like-minded strangers across the globe, like the famous WELL (an acronym for Whole Earth 'Lectronic Link), our online interactions take place more and more between people whom we know "in real life"; and whose identity is known also and often even certified by the corresponding digital platform that mediates this communication.

The popular Internet platforms that mediate a significant portion of our everyday communications become thus more and more efficient in managing vast amounts of information. In turn, they also become more and more knowledgeable about designing user interaction design techniques that increase addiction, or "stickiness" when described as a performance metric, and dependency. This renders their users more and more addicted and dependent on them, subject to manipulation and exploitation for commercial and political objectives. This could be characterized as the second watershed of the Internet in the context of Illich's analysis on the lifecycle of tools. As in the case of medicine and education, the Internet at its early stages was extremely useful. It dramatically increased our access to knowledge and to people all over the world. However, to achieve this, it relied on big organizations offering efficient and reliable services. These services now depend more and more on the participation of people and on the exploitation of the corresponding data produced for platforms to survive. This creates a vicious cycle between addictive design practices and unfair competition which breach the principle of net neutrality, and unethical uses of privately owned knowledge on human behavior which are generated through analyses of the data produced from our everyday online activities.

In addition to the tremendous social, political, and economic implications of centralizing power on the Internet, there are also significant ecological consequences. At first glance, these seem to be positive. The centralization of online platforms has allowed their owners to build huge data centers in cold climates and invest in technologies that keep servers cool with lower energy costs. However, at the same time, the main aim of online platforms is to maximize the total time spent online as much as possible and to maximize the amount of information exchanged, not only between people but also between "things!" Their profitability depends on the processing of huge amounts of information that produces knowledge which can be sold to advertisers and politicians. Like the pharmaceutical companies, they create and maintain a world in which they are very much needed. This also explains why corporations like Facebook, Google, and Microsoft are at the forefront of the efforts to provide "Internet access to all" and why at the same time local communities face so many economic, political, and legal hurdles that encumber them to build, maintain, and control their own infrastructures.

A similar situation holds in relation to an even more fundamental, but far from granted to all, human right, the "right to food". As Facebook aims to connect the world, Monsanto develops "a smarter way to feed the world", claiming the ownership and commercial exploitation of the seeds used by farmers everywhere. Note here one difference, among others, between the case of food and the Internet. Many people today do not actually trust giant corporations like Monsanto to solve the problem of global nutrition and prefer to avoid genetically modified organisms (GMOs) for various reasons, including their potential to harm bio-diversity and local autonomy. But this is not the case for the Internet. There is relatively less public awareness even in progressive circles that the practices of Internet corporations like Facebook and Google can significantly harm fundamental rights related to everyday social and political processes which are today increasingly mediated through the Internet.

Just as Monsanto produces in its headquarters seeds with GMOs that are to be used all over the world, these Internet platforms similarly mediate people's communication through servers that store their private information and manipulate the way they communicate through algorithmically modified data (AMD), in an effort to maximize the time they stay online, often leading to Internet addiction and alienation (Turkle, 2011). Notice that Facebook does not even need to copyright and thus profit directly from its knowledge, as Monsanto does with its seeds, because this knowledge is held privately and kept secret using algorithms that manipulate the information stored in its data centers. These algorithms analyze statistically, and also experiment with, this huge amount of information to learn how people react to different forms of stimuli (e.g., through the so-called A/B testing) and then influence their behavior, forming this way a social engineering laboratory unique in human history, controlled and managed by the principles of the capitalist profit maximizing "market", free from scientific research ethics. Today, Facebook is ready to create "a new map of everyone in the world" (Meyer, 2016), while at the same time experimenting with the manipulation of people's feelings through the curation of their news feeds (Gibbs, 2014), and also taking the responsibility to protect us from fake news, or at least what its algorithms think is fake news. Moreover, all these developments happen at an extremely fast pace and no one really knows how far Facebook's and Google's scientists have advanced in their endeavors, nor how sophisticated their algorithms really are. Indeed, they have no incentive to publish their results to scientific journals. They are the only ones anyway that have access to the data produced by their worldwide real-life laboratories.

However, the goal of this chapter is not to demonize Facebook or Google, but rather to deconstruct the Internet so that we can understand the fundamental building blocks of its infrastructure and services. This will help to reflect on which of these services really need to be offered by global platforms and which could be instead hosted on local infrastructures, owned and managed by the local community of users. This exercise is not motivated by a romantic "small is beautiful" or "local is better" ideal, but by an urgent need to diversify the ways that ICTs mediate our everyday life. Just as living organisms can be threatened by the lack of bio-diversity, our digital sovereignty and self-determination will be more and more endangered, the less net-diversity is made available to us. Moreover, net-diversity is not only important for reasons of democratic governance and independence. It is also a matter of social, economic, and ecological sustainability.

As stressed by Kris De Decker (2015), "On the internet, however, advances in energy efficiency have a reverse effect: as the network becomes more energy efficient, its total energy use increases. This trend can only be stopped when we limit the demand for digital communication". However, "limiting demand is controversial when applied to the internet, in part because few people make the connection between data and energy". A very similar phenomenon has been observed regarding traffic congestion, which is commonly acknowledged not to be improved by just building more roads (Mann, 2014). Similarly, the total energy consumption of the Internet cannot be reduced by just building more energy-efficient equipment.

To this end, DIY networking as discussed in the "Do-It-Yourself Networking" section could be seen as a "tool for conviviality" (Illich, 1973), which operates according to certain limits, stimulates collective action and creativity, and guarantees free access to all members of the community. Analyzing the key technical and social aspects that need to be addressed in this context will help citizens and communities to imagine and put in place such novel type of ICT.

For example, can we imagine a different future of ICT consumption that has limits instead of more and more "efficient" and constantly growing mega platforms, as we see for example in the "cap and share" policy for fossil fuels? If so, what can we do? How can such ecological practices for the use of ICTs be encouraged and what should they look like? What is the right balance between online and offline activities? What is the right Internet diet? Before answering these questions let's explore the core elements and different options for building community owned network infrastructures and services.

Network Infrastructure

An in-depth understanding of the capabilities and limitations of technology is critical to develop a realistic plan for an organic Internet. It can provide the basis for imagining a new Internet developed from the grassroots in ways (1) that minimize redundancies and energy costs related to profit making; (2) that create a balance between online and face-to-face communication; and (3) that promote a sustainable and healthy lifestyle. In this context, it is helpful to delve deeper into the different building blocks of networking infrastructure.

Servers: The principal role of a communications network is to connect an end device, like a desktop computer, a laptop, or a smartphone, that is a *client*, to another device or a special-purpose computer, a *server*, which can offer a range of services: simple storage of files, an online forum, or more sophisticated ones like tools for collaborative editing or platforms for online deliberation and multi-player games. Even when two people communicate "directly" between them, this communication needs to be mediated by a server responsible for setting up the connection. An end device can act also as a server. For example, in peer-to-peer systems, software like Bittorent allows end devices to directly download and upload content, for example, large movie files, between them. In this case, however, the communication often depends still on the existence of other servers dedicated to coordinate the peer-to-peer interactions. In principle, a good server needs (1) to have a "permanent" address, (2) to have sufficient computing power and upload bandwidth for serving the requests of its clients, and (3) to be always available, up and running, which requires the replication of functionality in multiple computers, cooling, dedicated personnel, and other expensive measures.

Hosting: The more demanding the services offered by a server, for example, in terms of computation, storage, and availability, the more difficult it is to install in a "home" environment, especially since Internet access is typically asymmetric (upload bandwidth is rather limited) and home computers do not have a "permanent" address accessible from the outside world when connecting to the Internet. For this, there are today numerous "web hosting" providers like Amazon that offer online "space" for organizations, companies, and individuals to host their servers, from personal blogs to sophisticated platforms. And this is increasingly so the more people rely on small devices like smartphones to connect to the Internet. This tendency is one of the reasons why we see today more and more services moving to big data centers, often referred to as "the cloud", reducing the burden of computation and storage from the end devices. Even software traditionally installed on one's computer like Microsoft office is more and more accessed remotely through one's web browser (e.g., Google docs). On the one hand, this relieves people from the burden of maintaining their own infrastructure, even from the need to keep backups of their files. But on the other hand, the costs of communication increase significantly, and more importantly there is a loss of ownership and control of one's data.

Access network, a.k.a. the last mile: The access part of the network, frequently called its "last mile", enables a person with a device to connect to the core, or backbone, network through which it can then access all available services, hosted on servers spread around the globe. Examples of access networks include the copper wire subscriber lines connecting landline telephones to the local telephone exchange or cell towers linking local cell phones to the cellular network that is often referred to as 3G/4G. In most cases, wireless is also the access to the "wired" last mile. This is thanks to the unlicensed, free to use by radio devices, WiFi spectrum and the corresponding cheap wireless WiFi routers that make it easier to connect from a short distance to wired Internet connections at homes, public spaces, airports, and cafes, without the need of wires, and in a way that is much less expensive than 3G/4G data contracts.

Backbone network: This is the "core" part of the network interconnecting all its end points by enabling all possible paths between end devices, between servers and between end devices and servers. The Internet's backbone network has multiple layers, or tiers, and different actors, ranging from small "eyeball" Internet Service Providers (ISPs), those servicing the end customers, to the top-level backbone providers of "Tier 1" that form a small and fully connected network of providers that have access to the whole Internet. Smaller providers typically pay "transit" fees for interconnecting and exchanging traffic with larger providers, while providers of similar size often exchange traffic at no cost. Backbone network nodes are typically interconnected with optic fiber cables, although in principle it is possible to have wireless backbone networks. Wireless technology and the unlicensed WiFi spectrum has allowed various grassroots organizations and communities to build their own regional backbone networks, also called community networks. The potential overall coverage of such wireless networks depends on the environmental conditions and the types of antennas used.

Antennas: There are three types of antennas that can be used for wireless WiFi communications. First, directional antennas can establish a wireless link between distant locations, possibly many kilometers away. This link could be imagined as a very long "cable", a "line-of-sight", along the imaginary line connecting two locations, which needs to be clear of obstacles (walls, trees, etc.). Such links are often called "backbone" links since they establish the wider coverage area of the network and are not accessible by end users. Second, an omnidirectional antenna, attached to a router, can spread "cables", radio signals, in all directions around it and makes it easy for many devices to connect at the same time and independently from their relative location. In the case of WiFi, unlike directional antennas, the distance between the small antennas inside our devices and an omnidirectional antenna can be much smaller, a few hundred meters depending on the environmental conditions. Third, sector antennas lie between these two extremes restricting the signal inside a certain angle. Both omnidirectional and sector antennas can be also used to create direct links between devices, which are easier to set up (the antennas find each other automatically if they fall in each other's range) and thus the corresponding networks are easier to expand, but they are more costly in terms of noise and interference. A cellular base station is in essence an omnidirectional antenna operating in different licensed frequencies (bought very expensively by the corresponding operators). It achieves much larger coverage than an omnidirectional WiFi antenna (a few kilometers) allowing for easier mobility but with less speed and higher costs (energy and infrastructure).

Sensors: Communications networks, both wired and wireless, are increasingly used to transfer data generated automatically by miniscule sensors spread in nature or attached to "things" to measure various environmental variables such as temperature and humidity, but also by cameras and microphones that can autonomously generate a huge amount of information, since they are not subject to the constraints of human nature and can be very easily replicated and can operate 24 hours per day. Each of these devices typically consumes a very small amount of energy, and many of them could be really autonomous using solar energy, for example. But the data that they collectively produce can be enormous and require a lot of computing resources to be processed and analyzed. The ownership and use of this data raises also important privacy and ethical issues that should not be underestimated.

Energy Consumption

Despite the complexity of calculating the energy consumption of the Internet as a whole, there are certain facts that one can keep in mind while deciding the type of infrastructure required to cover specific needs. For example, wired communications consume less energy than WiFi, and WiFi consumes less energy than 3G/4G. Also, multiplexing several services in the same location can decrease significantly the overall energy consumption due to the efficient use of resources. This requires however the need for more communication resources between end devices and remote data centers. But most importantly the business models of the companies that own those data centers depend on the continuous growth of Internet consumption, and an increasing amount of resources are invested for analyzing data, targeted advertising, and so forth. In other words, developing energy-efficient technologies, while at the same time increasing the total amount of energy consumed for the same number of Internet users, is not the right thing to do from an ecological perspective.

Interferences, Electrosmog, and the Value of Sharing

Wireless communications can be very liberating, allowing for the connection to the Internet anywhere and anytime. They are also very empowering since they allow ordinary citizens to establish their own local networks both for affordable Internet access and local services. However, they consume a lot of energy and contribute to electromagnetic pollution, the so-called electrosmog, and so they should be used only when cable connections are not feasible and shared as much as possible.

In a non-capitalistic form of distribution, it is possible to achieve tremendous savings in hardware, energy, and pollution by just sharing the available infrastructure. For example, despite the over-abundant available bandwidth, we are all required to buy our individual Internet connectivity even if we use a very small percentage of it. There is also an unnecessary abundance of both wireless access points and cellular base stations that overlap in the same areas. Similarly to the numerous satellite dishes that unnecessarily fill the facades of buildings, our Internet connections are unnecessarily personal. For the sake of economic growth and market competition, this waste of resources is not only costly in terms of energy and pollution, but it also causes noise and interferences reducing the overall performance and leading to a tragedy of the commons in terms of spectrum utilization.

Software

The role of software is to give meaning to the digital data generated by input devices like keyboards, cameras, recorders, and then transmitted by network devices, stored in hard disks, and received by output devices like displays and printers. It is the brain of the clients and servers, from low-level "drivers" of devices, to operating systems, databases, and service-level software that operate at different layers of the process of transferring and manipulating digital information. It is in essence a series of statements (memory operations, if (condition)-then (action 1)-else (action 2) clauses or loops) that interpret, translate, filter, manipulate, and direct information, adding different layers of metadata along the way. This process is being driven by different types of algorithms that among others calculate the most efficient path to a destination, predict future events based on previous patterns, and may influence human behavior toward certain objectives.

All the Internet services that we are using daily involve a server somewhere storing, indexing, and filtering data received from clients and the devices owned by the "users". Changing simple details in the semantics of this data and the user interface can transform a platform from an online social network to, for instance, a public administration web site or a noise pollution measurement platform.

In addition, there are certain high-level "orthogonal" system-level services, which relate to security and privacy (who has access to this information and to what extent is it securely protected from malicious behavior), resilience (how safe is the information in case of disasters and other forms of failure like security failures), usability (how clear is the user interface and how smooth is the overall user experience), and performance (how fast and responsive is the overall system).

Some of the reasons why new software is being constantly written is the evolution of hardware, for example, devices get smaller and faster, the increase of the number of people that become digital natives, and the increase of the information that gets digitized (from music and images a few decades ago to feelings and physical location and movements of people today). This results to a shift of power from governments and local institutions to online platforms owning and controlling this information and affecting also traditionally local services like transport (e.g., Uber) and lodging (e.g., Airbnb). For this, it is critical to realize that many-to-many technology is not neutral and can significantly affect behavior in much subtler and effective ways than one-to-many technology like TV, precisely due to the additional freedom and agency that the Internet offers to its users. This freedom as already stressed can be very easily manipulated by the algorithmic filtering of information, enhanced graphics, nudging, and many other design tools, which can become very powerful in the hands of corporations that have access to large amounts of information, and that so have an opportunity to experiment with social engineering that is unique in history. Note that the less visible this power is, the more dangerous it becomes.

In this context, the role of free, libre, and open-source software (or FLOSS) can be instrumental. The vision of a democratic, bottom-up, organic way of building network infrastructures and services can only be materialized if software development is transparent, and if allows for its appropriation and ownership by local actors. In this case, scaling occurs through replication, since it is easy for different groups or even individuals to run their own services like a Wordpress blog or an Etherpad server. For more sophisticated services, however, additional investments in infrastructure might be required as well as the appropriate institutional and governance structure along the lines of the concept of "platform cooperativism" (Scholz & Schneider, 2016).

There are many additional challenging issues that local communities still need to address, such as the digital divide, Internet addiction, local governance and power structures, and necessary trade-offs between security and loss of privacy. Regarding energy consumption, the type and amount of hardware and other resources required to offer a specific Internet service depend heavily on the extent to which the different orthogonal services (security, resiliency, etc.) are provided, and at what scale, depending on the number of participants and their expected usage. All in all, there are so many variables and factors that influence the energy required by different combinations of implementation choices and corresponding usage patterns, both online and offline, that it is almost impossible to accurately calculate the corresponding energy consumers/saved by a specific service. Economic sustainability is also an influencing factor since it might require the implementation of additional functionality such as targeted advertising, addictive services, and more. As genetically modified food is much cheaper and beautiful, Facebook, Google, and in general the "algorithmically modified Internet" will be always free and extremely usable.

Considering the alternative of more organic services deployed locally, the question of borders appears when moving from the abstract notion of the Internet, or the cloud, to a local infrastructure meant to satisfy the needs of a certain locality. What type of services need to be made available through a local community network, which can be left to the "global" infrastructure, and what is the corresponding "community" for each category of services? Is it a neighborhood, a district, or even a whole city? And whom would people trust more to own their data, a distant faceless corporation or some identifiable local actors? The answer would be different for different services.

For this, and although it might seem somehow trivial, I quickly outline some of the basic online services that people are consuming today as a stimulation to reflect on the above questions and inform the discussion on limits and sharing in the following sections:

Digital archives and knowledge: Many people take photos or videos or simply write documents using their input devices. All this private in principle information needs to be stored for future use, retrieved, and secured. In theory, the infrastructure required for storing one's own data could be located in one's house, for example, an external hard drive. But there are many cloud-based solutions that enable Internet users to store large amounts of data on remote servers of commercial companies like Dropbox. On the other hand, there are also affordable solutions based on FLOSS software like Owncloud and Netxtcloud, which can be hosted on any web hosting provider or cheap hardware like the Raspberry Pi (see, e.g., the MAZI toolkit, http://mazizone.eu/toolkit/) that can offer similar services but not always with the same quality. Indeed, there are many reasons why people prefer professional cloud services for storage: its resilience, accessibility, usability, and integration with other services. Cloud services could also be more efficient in terms of energy consumption, especially given the level of resiliency that they offer (if they are not required to consume a significant amount of resources to stay profitable as businesses). In between the two extremes of a personal and a global cloud, there are numerous intermediate options, like a neighborhood, district or city cloud, or even a cloud shared between a certain group of people like a cooperative.

On the other extreme, moving from privately to globally relevant information, the digitization of content like text, audio, and video has allowed the indexing and sharing of the world's accumulated past and recent knowledge. The development of sophisticated collaborative Internet tools like wikis makes even easier the collaborative creation and classification of new knowledge, Wikipedia being one of the biggest success stories of this new mode of peer production. Despite the fact that all this knowledge is not always accessible even for those connected to the Internet, due to copyright restrictions, one could easily argue that knowledge sharing is an Internet service that should be global in principle. There is no good reason why knowledge should be confined in localities. However, the question still remains who should be responsible for hosting and resolving conflicts as Wikipedia is famous for its "edit wars" in the case of highly contested topics, and the organic Internet might be a way to create a balance between the local and the global levels in terms of knowledge production.

Media and news: As a communication medium, the Internet provides a very efficient means of broadcasting media ranging from live streaming of popular events to everyday news. There is even some speculation that it could soon replace the TV and printed press. One of the key differences compared to traditional media is that the Internet allows rich interactions with the audience in the form of commentaries and, more recently, in the form of filtering and disseminating content—an attribute that theoretically gives significant power to people protecting themselves against censorship, but which also gives power to global platforms that mediate communication, like Facebook and Twitter, which can create significant hidden biases or "fake news".

In this context, the key actors are not only the producers and consumers of news but also the mediator responsible for filtering and prioritizing the huge number of potential stories generated every day before they appear in our "news feeds". Regarding localities, what is important to note is that a significant percentage of everyday news is generated in a specific location, and it is often the case that the concerned audience resides also in that same location. Local ICT infrastructure may be a better candidate for hosting such hyper-local news services, because it creates an intimacy that is very important both for producers and consumers. The former know that their stories will reach only those concerned, and the latter know that the stories are generated by people that are truly there. The big challenge comes from the needs demanded by mediation and filtering. Whom should one trust to moderate their local news? We may think a company or an institution based in the same locality is more prone to bias, compared to the purportedly neutral algorithms of big corporations that are "too far away" and "too big" to be interested in intervening in different localities around the world; however, this is a very dangerous misconception.

Content sharing, social interactions, and group work: The Internet is an amazing distributed system for storing and distributing information and knowledge, but its most popular application to date clearly consists of the wide variety of synchronous and asynchronous communication that it facilitates, such as E-mail, discussion forums, chatrooms, and a plethora of online platforms like Facebook and Twitter as well as content sharing platforms like Instagram, Youtube, and many more. These applications have allowed us to discover like-minded people across the globe around common interests and also keep in touch with friends and family. They have also enabled us to become photographers, journalists, editors, and curators. More sophisticated communication tools also support collaborative opportunities for coordinating actions, managing organizations, problem solving, public deliberations, decision-making, and more recently the so-called sharing economy with Airbnb and Uber being its current champions.

But, the "cloud" is just "someone else's computer" and even the highly "distributed" blockchain technology is a very powerful and dominant middleman itself (Scott, 2016). Since the network externalities in such services are very powerful (the larger the network of people connected, the larger the overall value for everyone), big platforms have a huge advantage over smaller ones, and they tend to gain more and more power.

For delivering location-based services or locative media, that is connecting people residing in the same geographic area, global locative media platforms like Foursquare are still not very successful despite their huge customer base. And when they do, they have to build on the knowledge of the location (e.g., through GPS coordinates)—an admittedly rather private information—of a critical mass of people. This is the type of service that can be offered much more efficiently and in a much more privacy-preserving way by a local network as analyzed in the "Do-It-Yourself Networking" section.

Information services and smart everything: Given the availability of all possible information online, and the development of artificial intelligence through statistical tools, companies like Google develop very sophisticated ways to facilitate our everyday life by personalized search, recommendations, translations, content distribution, navigation, and more. Exactly like Facebook, Airbnb, and Uber, Google does not produce any of the underlying information that feeds its extremely popular services. It just collects all possible information available online, and then its sophisticated algorithms are continuously learning how to make the best use out of it monitoring and evaluating the way people interact with their decisions.

Such power can become even more effective through the availability of ever smaller computing devices that can perform sophisticated data operations while consuming very little energy giving rise to the concepts of the "Internet of Things" and the smart city. Vast networks of sensors monitoring everything requires huge data centers, collecting and analyzing this information to enable us to make more efficient decisions. The more data collected and analyzed from farms, people's bodies, or a city's streets, then the better the decisions we can make for smart farming, smart health, and smart cities. However, the cost for becoming smarter and efficient can be rather high; since statistics work best at large scales, local communities will have to make some hard technological choices if they value more their digital sovereignty, and human agency than efficiency and automation.

Limits

We are using our increasingly energy efficient devices for longer hours as we send more and more data over a worldwide infrastructure. Kris De Decker

To achieve a sustainable level of Internet usage, one needs to provide the appropriate tools and processes for local communities to make decisions on the design of their ICT tools, including appropriate alternative and/or complementary design of places, institutions, and rituals that can impose certain constraints and replace online communications when these are not really necessary. To answer this demand, one should first answer a more fundamental question: How much online communication is needed in an energy-restricted world? In the case of food and housing, there are some reasonable basic needs. For example, each person should consume 2000 calories per day or 35 m^2 of habitat (see P.M., 2014). But, how many Mbs does someone need to consume to sustain a good quality of life? What would be the analogy for a restricted vegetarian or even vegan Internet diet?

The answer might differ depending on the services considered (social activities, collaborative work, or media) and the type of access to the network discussed above. For example, is it really necessary to have wireless connectivity "everywhere, anytime" using expensive mobile devices, or is it enough to have old-fashioned Internet cafes and only wired connections at home? Would it make sense to have Internet-free zones in cities? Can we imagine "shared" Internet usage in public spaces—a group of people interacting together in front of a screen and alternating in showing their favorite YouTube videos (a sort of an Internet jukebox)? There is a variety of more or less novel constraints which could be imposed on different dimensions:

Time and Volume: A communications network owned by a local community, instead of a global or local corporation, could shut down for certain period of time each day if this is what the community decides. Or community members could agree to have certain time quotas for using the network (e.g., not more than 4 hours per day or 150 hours per month). Such constraints would not only reduce energy consumption; they would also enforce a healthier lifestyle and encourage face-to-face interactions.

Reducing quotas on the speed (bandwidth) and volume (MB) that each person consumes is another way to restrict Internet consumption.

Actually people are already used to such limits especially for 3G/4G connectivity. The difference is that a volume constraint does not necessarily translate to time constraints (if someone uses low volume services such as e-mail). So, volume constraints could encourage the use of less voluminous services (e.g., downloading a movie with low instead of High Definition resolution if this is to be watched in a low definition screen anyway) while time constraints might have the opposite effect (people using as much bandwidth as possible in their available time).

However, to enforce such constraints, both time and volume based, on an individual basis, the network needs to know who is connecting to it and keep track of the overall usage. This raises the question of privacy and identification online and again the trade-off of trusting local vs. global institutions to take this role. Enforcing time or volume constraints for groups of people (e.g., the residents of a cooperative housing complex) is an interesting option to be considered when privacy is considered important.

Devices: Energy consumption depends on the type of equipment used to access the Internet. For example, if access to the Internet happens only through desktop computers or laptops using ethernet cables instead of mobile smartphones, then the total energy consumed for a given service would be significantly reduced. Usage would also be dramatically affected: On the positive side, many people would spend less time online and use the Internet only for important tasks. On the negative side, others might stay at home more often and sacrifice outdoors activities in favor of Internet communications.

Wireless medium: Another hardware-based constraint pertains to which options in wireless communication are allowed. As mentioned, 3G/4G/5G communication is much more energy-intensive and "polluting" than WiFi, but achieves wider coverage (up to many kilometers) and allows for seamless wireless Internet access in any place within a given geographic area; even while traveling on public transport or a high-speed train. On the other hand, WiFi access has limited coverage, such as a few hundred meters, but then it allows for faster and potentially symmetric connections.

Physical location: One could imagine restrictions on Internet usage in specific locations, such as Internet cafes or public libraries or, the opposite, creating Internet-free zones in cities, such as parks, sidewalks and other places designed for human interactions. Such restrictions would be implicitly imposed by some of the choices above, but they could also be more explicit and normative, such as by creating designated spaces in which Internet access is prohibited like current restrictions on smoking.

Proximity: One could also imagine the creation of local WiFi networks operating outside the Internet serving only those people within physical proximity, as explained in detail in the "Do-It-Yourself Networking" section. In addition to the global Internet, people could also access their local Internet. In principle, this is technically feasible because of the constraints already imposed by the wireless medium and its corresponding coverage. For example, a DIY WiFi network comprised of a single router would cover an area with a radius of a few hundred meters. But, for a city-scale community mesh network like Freifunk.net, WiFi could extend to a whole city. In this case, the main question is where to place limits or borders on access and how to enforce them.

Sharing Resources

In addition to imposing constraints on usage, energy savings can also arise from sharing the available resources between more people. Of course, today more and more ICT services are being "shared", but only in terms of use (not ownership) since they are hosted on just a few platforms owned by equally few corporations. In other words, most people use the same online platforms for their social interactions, photo sharing, e-mail, even word-processing software and so on, which is indeed a form of resource sharing.

In the vision of the organic Internet, sharing is an act of emancipation and democratic control of ICT infrastructures and services. Sharing is not orchestrated by a global resource manager, but is subject to deliberations, debates, and decision-making processes that lead to policies that are adapted to the local environment rather than imposed from outside.

Below we identify different types of resources that would make sense to share in smaller or larger groups in a conscious and sustainable way.

Storage: Like the cloud, local communities could build their own data centers to be used as a shared storage space and take advantage of the economies of scale involved. In this scenario, members of a "data cooperative" would share the operational costs of the data center and gain access to a certain amount of private storage space (e.g., 100GB per person) but also shared storage space for optimizing the use of resources for the same content. One could also imagine a local database storing content like a list of YouTube or Netflix videos, available to everyone. Again, one could imagine voting mechanisms for selecting the most desired content to be chosen for download or for maintaining in the local storage when this is full (see "The Internet Jukebox" in Crowcroft et al., 2015). This type of resource management, if limited to a local, instead of global, scale, would result in many associated benefits with regard to data sovereignty.

Servers and Services: Storage is a rather straightforward service to be shared. But sharing does not need to be constrained to simple resources. More sophisticated services like word-processing, e-mail, online collaboration platforms, etc. can also be shared at a local, instead of a global scale. Imagine, for example, a small-scale data center in a cooperative housing complex that provides all the required resources for hosting a set of such services for the local residents.

Access: As hinted above, a lot of waste occurs using infrastructures built with the principles of the capitalist market. Many mobile operators become active in the same area, each with their own network infrastructure including expensive antennas, backbone networks, accounting, and pricing services. The same holds true for the home WiFi routers that are strictly personal, which is both unnecessary (a well-placed router could easily serve more than one apartment), wasteful (in terms of hardware and energy), responsible for congesting the wireless spectrum (reducing performance for everyone), and polluting the environment with excess microwaves. In a commons-based economy, such access infrastructure could be shared, allowing apartment blocks to install only the necessary number of wireless routers.

Devices: In addition to offering different devices for shared use, one could also imagine concurrently sharing the use of screens like a public display whose content is chosen in a collaborative way similar to a music jukebox. At a time of highly personalized online experiences and the filter bubbles created by the curation of one's Facebook and Twitter news feed, it is difficult, though not impossible, to imagine such shared hybrid Internet experiences in which online and offline interactions happen at the same time.

Do-It-Yourself Networking

Wired communications are more energy-efficient than wireless but they have increased deployment costs and limited flexibility. So, although a truly organic and sustainable Internet built from scratch should heavily depend on a wired infrastructure, it is through wireless technology and grassroots movements that today local communities can actually claim their rights to the Internet and develop organic alternatives to privatized infrastructures and commercial services. Going back to our analogy, organic urban gardens might not be able to cover the nutrition needs of a city in a sustainable way, but they do provide a means for building awareness and stimulate citizen motivation and engagement. Similarly, wireless DIY networks might not provide the optimal solution in terms of resource and energy usage for certain communication needs, but they are very effective tools for the emancipation and appropriation of ICT technology by citizens toward the "right to the hybrid city" (Antoniadis & Apostol, 2014).

Even in cases when local authorities do participate in the deployment and management of network infrastructures for the common good, wireless solutions offer a means of experimentation and divergence from the status quo, which helps to sustain diversity and adaptability to change. From a practical perspective, they also offer a non-intrusive and privacy preserving way to identify the location of a user the moment he/she connects to the network, for example, without the need for constantly recording his/her GPS location, allowing for more "intimate", anonymous yet de facto local, communications between those in physical proximity. But let's first explain how DIY, or community, networks work.

A wireless router, which is a special-purpose computer, can do more than just connect a device to the Internet. It could also host a server a virtual announcement board for a block of apartments, an online guestbook for an urban garden, a file-sharing platform for a workshop, and many more "self-hosted" web applications like Wordpress, NextCloud, and Etherpad, which anyone can host on a private web server. These services are accessible through the router's wireless antenna using a network name, a Service Set Identifier (SSID), exactly as one would use when connecting to a free or home WiFi network. They can also appear automatically on a splash page or captive portal when you open your browser (as is often the case in airports, cafes, and hotels). If the router is equipped with a second antenna, it can easily connect to a similar router residing in the coverage area, the size of which depends on the type of antenna and other environmental factors. The first antenna can then be used to allow people with their personal devices to connect; and the second to exchange information with the neighboring router. Each router then becomes a "node" in a small network. Anyone who connects to one of them can access the people and services offered by the others. As more nodes get connected, larger areas are covered and a community can be formed—initially by the owners of the nodes, and eventually by everyone in the area.

Of course, one cannot easily build a whole network like this by oneself, but it is not difficult to build a single network node using cheap hardware (such as a Raspberry Pi) and free self-hosted software to deploy the set of local services and applications that fit a specific context (Antoniadis, 2016a). Community wireless networks have been under development since the late 1990s by tech enthusiasts and activists advocating for a more open, neutral and democratic internet (Antoniadis, 2016b; Medosch, 2014). They include a mix of local services, such as file sharing and live streaming (AWMN.net and Ninux.org) and the provision of Internet connectivity. Freifunk.net, WlanSlovenja, Sarantaporo.gr, and many more focus on this aspect in particular.

There are important differences between various models of governance and the concept of the community itself (Antoniadis, 2016a; Navarro et al., 2016). Freifunk follows the "free internet for all" approach and depends mostly on voluntary contributions from their members to offer internet connectivity. On the other hand, Guifi.net places significant focus on the concept of the "commons", implying concrete boundaries and resource management rules. It has developed a unique model (Baig et al., 2015) in which the network infrastructure including fiber cables is treated as separate from the services it is involved with providing.

Community networks like Freifunk.net and Guifi.net take advantage of the unlicensed WiFi spectrum to create wireless backbone links without the need to have access to expensive infrastructure. An antenna on a roof can offer Internet access if it connects to someplace within 50 km of its line of sight that has connectivity. Of course, solutions for a community or municipality may also include the deployment of locally owned wired infrastructures. Although there are numerous stories of successful community networks around the world, these infrastructures face significant hurdles through legislations that favor big commercial ISPs (Dulong de Rosnay, Giovanella, Messaud, & Tréguer, 2016). Similar to the legal fights against farmers that keep their own seeds, the deployment of local broadband solutions is often being considered an illegal or prohibitively expensive option for local authorities or non-profit organizations' activity.

Tangible Reasons Why

Despite the critical role of community networks for providing affordable Internet access to underprivileged populations, it is important to realize that DIY networking is a good idea even if the Internet is ubiquitous and free for everyone—a position that may appear extreme (see Antoniadis, 2016a). For example, DIY networking enables the creation of network infrastructures offering alternative options in case of natural disasters, as proved to be the case during Hurricane Sandy when people relied on the RedHook WiFi initiative in Brooklyn (Baldwin, 2011). There are also many political reasons why one should consider the use of local networks for supporting local online interactions related to privacy, surveillance, and self-determination (Antoniadis, 2016a). Despite their significance, these reasons alone cannot easily motivate people to engage in the creation of DIY networks in their neighborhoods. But even if someone would trust Facebook and Google to store and analyze their private information for their own commercial purposes, there is still an important social threat created by the domination of these global platforms—namely, social alienation and the lack of location-based collective awareness.

Focusing on this social dimension, DIY networking has some characteristics that could help designers to resolve the tension between anonymity that allows for freedom of expression and identity that helps to build trust and community, in more desirable ways than the corresponding Internet-based solutions. In other words, they can use DIY networking solutions to create a balance between the anonymity offered by modern cities and the social control in traditional local communities by generating ICT-mediated location-based collective awareness with low costs to time and privacy. The most relevant metaphor here is the sidewalk which Jane Jacobs praised as a place for essential informal interactions between strangers that can achieve a very delicate balance between privacy and public exposure (1961). If carefully designed, hybrid ICT applications that enable spontaneous information sharing between strangers can offer new ways to support the capacity of the sidewalk in contemporary cities to generating local knowledge and a sense of belonging. But, instead of relying on private ICT platforms managed by commercial companies, DIY networking offers the option to stimulate and empower citizens to use their creativity for setting up local freely accessible networks hosting context-specific collective awareness applications.

Still, one could always ask, "Why not host all these nice applications on a server accessible through the Internet or local wired solutions?" The answer typically depends on the specific environment but there are four important characteristics of wireless technology that make it an interesting candidate for building an organic Internet from the bottom up:

- All potential users of a local wireless network are in de facto physical proximity. The option of anonymity, in addition to be technically feasible, is also much less intimidating than in the case of global online platforms. This can facilitate playful and open interactions between people that would enjoy exchanging information with those in proximity but with "no private commitments" (Jacobs, 1961).

- A DIY network needs to be set up and deployed by someone that has access to the built environment, such as a resident with a well-located balcony, an owner of a central store, or a local institution with the authority to install street side infrastructure. This can ensure that the local network is designed and customized by members of the community ideally in an inclusive and convivial manner.
- Wireless networks are much easier to deploy than wired, and this can be done by practically anyone. They are also inherently mobile allowing for creative and flexible uses, but also for provocations challenging the status quo that are less intrusive than graffiti for example but much richer as a means of expression.
- Being tangible infrastructure themselves, wireless networks can be naturally embedded in other artifacts and urban interventions, such as a public display, a colored bench, a phone booth, or even a mobile kiosk, and they can create naturally hybrid spaces that encourage temporary participation and playful engagement. This also enables the inclusion of non-users, as in the case of the Berlin Design Research Lab's Hybrid Letterbox (Unteidig et al., 2015) and Polylogue. See http://www.design-research-lab.org/projects/polyloge-1/.

Finally, a local ICT infrastructure which facilitates communication exclusively between those that can easily meet face to face could be designed exactly for this purpose. Thus, energy efficiency would not be only the result of the lower energy required when communication takes place through local wireless networks as described above, but it would also be the product of people's ability to spend more time meeting their social and psychological needs away from their computers and mobile devices.

Despite the many good reasons why local DIY networks make sense, there is still little understanding of their potential value and little willingness to invest in their infrastructure and specialized services. The good news is that such local networks do not need to be introduced as a replacement for the Internet, but as alternative local solutions which allow for experimentation and net-diversity and which can be complementary to global services. Net-diversity could be indeed the ultimate argument which may be effective amidst current economic, social, and political crises, because people realize they can no longer assume things will always remain the same and they need alternatives for the exceptional times ahead.

Kevin Kelly (2010) answered his question "what technology wants?" by speculating that it wants to "play with the borderlines", to "keep changing the game in order to keep playing". DIY networks try to play with the borderlines of the Internet. They have the potential to become a real game changer, unleashing people's creativity and giving birth to millions of small, self-organized hybrid networks that could eventually be interconnected in pairs or through backbone community wireless networks, like in Nicholas Negroponte (2002)'s "lily pads and frogs" metaphor from 15 years ago. Such a scenario could actually echo the early years of the Internet with an explosion of alternatives, but now at an urban (instead of a global) scale.

Synergies and Complementarities

If one wants to be pragmatic, one needs to realize that during the transition to the organic Internet, we will not be alone in the world. Most importantly, we will not be able to afford losing global services offered by the Internet today but which cannot be provided at the local level. A global infrastructure is therefore required and corporations will always exist to compete with local solutions in providing local services. So, in addition to a global vision, we also need a plan for the transition, for scaling up, and for the formation of potential synergies with similar initiatives around other common resources such as food, housing, education, health, and the economy.

Indeed, similar forms of local action or better tools for conviviality have been gaining a lot of attention. These include, for example, complementary currencies, cooperative housing models, and grassroots education and health. Those and other examples of commoning activities will need sophisticated ICT tools to help make efficient use of human resources and improve accounting, trust building, and collaboration. The vision of local DIY networks might be promoted by such complementary local commoning activities as a compatible way to build the ICT solutions required for their successful operation. In the other direction, treating network infrastructure as a commons can also provide inspiration for the management of other common resources and act as a triangulator for stimulating social contact and community building.

Putting Things Together: The Case of NeNa1

A big advantage of the "organic Internet", like organic farming, is that it does not need big investors and venture capitalists to be tried out. A determined group of people is enough to develop successful prototypes that can be easily replicated elsewhere, like the various urban community gardens around the world or the networks for seed exchange.

Such a determined group is a new cooperative housing project in Zurich, NeNa1, http://nena1.ch, currently counting 200 members. NeNa1 is the latest in a series of similar progressive "young cooperative housing" initiatives, like Kraftwerk1 and Kalkbreite; see http://o500.org/. Its initial conception is generated at the neighborhood level, Kreis 5, and proposes to complement the four existing neighborhoods with a fifth one built from scratch, at the edge of this district, on the current Carparkplatz (see Fig. 13.1). This fifth neighborhood with around 500 inhabitants will showcase a new model for sustainable living in the city going beyond housing, and including innovations in the areas of food, technology, and economy, among others.

How would its internal communication infrastructure look like? Would it be the typical collection of wireless routers in every apartment

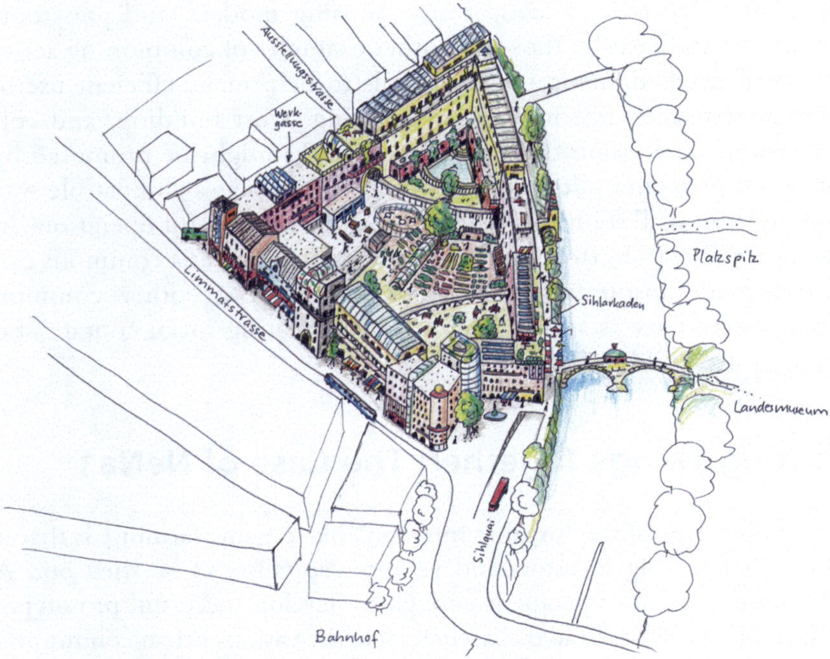

Fig. 13.1 A speculative model of the NeNa1 neighborhood where today is located a parking structure and a bus station, across the main train station. Drawing by Hans Widmer. See http://nena1.ch

and shared space, connected individually to the selected ISP, Swisscom, Orange, and the like by each resident? Would it include also an "Intranet" platform hosted by the city's most popular web hosting provider for their internal co-living organization, for example, room reservations, assemblies, coordination of common work, social interactions, etc.? Or it would be something "different" and more "organic"?

Which would be some reasonable choices regarding the required local infrastructure, consumption limits, sharing practices and software design in this case?

Let's try to imagine a few answers to these questions based on the discussion above.

First, the NeNa1 settlement will have a less wasteful way to allow access to the Internet in the first place. A leased line will be hired by a local ISP that can accommodate all the Internet traffic produced by its 500 residents and visitors, and much more, and whose cost will be subsidized by the rents. The whole settlement will be wired with fiber optic cables that will provide limitless access to this shared Internet connection, when one connects their laptop or desktop computer. For wireless access, the minimum required wireless access points, most of which will be solar-powered, are to be placed in strategic locations all using the same network name, SSID, to allow for easy access from most places in the settlement, but making sure that certain "Internet-free" zones do exist.

Second, a small local data center will be installed at a suitable location to reduce the energy required for cooling (e.g., inside the "freezer room"). It will host a variety of local services, implemented with free and open-source software, some of which will be also accessible through the Internet. These will include:

- a cloud service for storing files like Nextcloud (similar to Dropbox) and an e-mail server for both global and local e-mail exchanges.
- a digital archive with material from the history of cooperative housing in Zurich, and a local Wikipedia for documenting experiences and knowledge for the replication of this successful model.
- a suite of local services including online social networking, announcement board, deliberation and decision-making, room reservations, and other scheduling activities, and management of working groups, among others.
- management platforms for various commoning activities such as a food cooperative, and a local economy for service exchange and self-help .
- a separate online space accessible only from the settlement, which allow anonymous communication for expressing needs, complaints, and a variety of playful interactions.

Every shared space will include a hybrid letterbox, and a set of different types of input cards will allow people to participate through handwriting in different online discussions (from making an announcement or complaint, to participating in the weekly knowledge competition).

At the common workshop space, there will be weekly seminars on the politics of technology, the various social and ethical issues that appear when human communication is mediated through digital platforms, and hands-on workshops for building your own network and online services.

Shared spaces will be also equipped with big shared displays for visualizing different local activities taking place in different online places. For example, from 18 h00 to 20 h00 a selection of the most popular photos in the local photo sharing platform will be displayed, and from 20 h00 to 22 h00 the most popular movie will be broadcasted.

Finally, a set of directional antennas on the roof or fiber cables, if possible, will allow neighboring settlements to connect to the local network and host their own local services in the same data center. This will open up the possibility for services that concern the whole district like the management of the micro-center, announcements of events, etc.

Concluding Notes

Like money, food, medicine, education, and transport, there are places in the world where people have too much Internet, not only in terms of energy consumption but also more than needed for a healthy and balanced life. On the other hand, there are many people (more than 50% of world's population) that are practically disconnected and thus deprived from basic knowledge and communication services.

Most worryingly, the promise of connecting the world comes from big corporations who see in the disconnected more data and more power, while the connected are getting more and more alienated and addicted by the practices of the same corporations.

Changing this paradigm with a more organic Internet based on the principles of sharing and commoning sounds impossible to happen at a global scale without the parallel change of the whole "system" itself. However, projects like NeNa1 offer the opportunity to imagine realistic outopias that could include elements of the alternative solutions already developed by DIY and community networking activists around the world. Of course, "organic" software and hardware solutions will not be enough and will need to be complemented by a strong network of initiatives that will provide education, training, and support.

The concept of "virality" here is relevant: in a world where communication is so easy, both good and bad ideas can travel incredibly fast and all that is needed perhaps is the right twist, a good and easily replicable idea that can turn things around even in moments when everything seems to go from bad to worse.

This also brings to mind the "think global, act local" concept with the subtle difference that the global thinking is not about the "system" itself but about its "seeds", and this is again an important concept in agriculture that needs to be introduced also in the Internet domain.

Acknowledgment The research leading to this work has been partially supported by the EU Horizon2020 projects MAZI, H2020-ICT-2015, no. 687983. http://mazizone.eu, and netCommons, H2020-ICT-2015, no. 688768. http://netcommons.eu. The writing of this chapter and its German translation, by Thomas Raoseta, was supported by Stiftung Sergio Agustoni, for the book project "Die Andere Stadt", edited by Hans Widmer and published by Paranoia City Verlag, Zurich.

References

Antoniadis, P. (2016a). Local networks for local interactions: Four reasons why and a way forward. *First Monday, 21*(12). Retrieved from http://firstmonday.org/ojs/index.php/fm/article/view/7123/5661

Antoniadis, P. (2016b, November 8). DIY networking: The path to a more democratic internet. *The Conversation Global.* Retrieved from https://theconversation.com/diy-networking-the-path-to-a-more-democratic-internet-67216

Antoniadis, P., & Apostol, I. (2014). The right(s) to the hybrid city and the role of DIY networking. *Journal of Community Informatics,* special issue on Community Informatics and Urban Planning, 10. Retrieved from http://ci-journal.net/index.php/ciej/article/view/1092/

Baig, R., Roca, R., Freitag, F., & Navarro, L. (2015). Guifi.net, a crowdsourced network infrastructure held in common. *Computer Networks, 90*(C), 150–165.

Baldwin, J. (2011). *TidePools: Social WiFi*. Master thesis in design and technology, parsons school of design. Retrieved from http://www.scribd.com/doc/94601219/TidePools-Social-WiFi-Thesis

Bhatia, R. (2016, May). The inside story of Facebook's biggest setback. *The Guardian*. Retrieved from https://www.theguardian.com/technology/2016/may/12/facebook-free-basics-india-zuckerberg

Brink, S. (2016, September). What's the prognosis for $3 billion Zuckerberg health plan? *NPR*. Retrieved from http://www.npr.org/sections/goatsandsoda/2016/09/23/495184078/whats-the-prognosis-for-mark-zuckerbergs-3-billion-health-plan

Clark, D. (1988). The design philosophy of the DARPA internet protocols. In *Proceedings of ACM SIGCOMM '88*.

Crowcroft, J., Wolisz, A., & Sathiaseelan, A. (Eds.). (2015). Towards an affordable Internet access for everyone: The quest for enabling universal service commitment. *Dagstuhl Reports, 4*(11). Retrieved from http://drops.dagstuhl.de/opus/volltexte/2015/4971/

De Decker, K. (2015, October 19). Why we need a speed limit for the Internet. *Low-tech Magazine*. Retrieved from http://www.lowtechmagazine.com/2015/10/can-the-internet-run-on-renewable-energy.html

Dulong de Rosnay, M., Giovanella, F., Messaud, A., & Tréguer, F. (2016). European legal framework for CNs. *netCommons deliverable 4.1*. Retrieved from http://netcommons.eu/?q=content/european-legal-framework-cns-v1

Fuchs, C. (2017). Sustainability and community networks. *Telematics and Informatics, 34*(2), 628–639.

Gibbs, S. (2014, July). Facebook apologises for psychological experiments on users. *The Guardian*. Retrieved from https://www.theguardian.com/technology/2014/jul/02/facebook-apologises-psychological-experiments-on-users

Illich, I. (1973). *Tools for conviviality*. New York: Harper & Row.

Jacobs, J. (1961). *The death and life of great American cities*. New York: Random House.

Kallis, G. (2017). *In defense of de-growth: Opinions and minifestos (collection)*. Retrieved from https://indefenseofdegrowth.com/

Kelly, K. (2010). *What technology wants*. New York: Viking Press.

MacManus, R. (2016, August). Why Facebook is building intelligent machines. Retrieved from https://richardmacmanus.com/2016/08/04/facebookintelligent-machines/

Mann, A. (2014, June). What's up with that: Building bigger roads actually makes traffic worse. *Wired*. Retrieved from https://www.wired.com/2014/06/wuwt-traffic-induced-demand

Miller, J. (2014, February). Zuckerberg: Facebook's mission is to 'connect the world'. *BBC News*. Retrieved from http://www.bbc.com/news/technology-26326844

Medosch, A. (2014). *The rise of the network commons*. Retrieved from http://www.thenextlayer.org/NetworkCommons

Meyer, R. (2016, February). Facebook is making a map of everyone in the world. *The Atlantic*. Retrieved from https://www.theatlantic.com/technology/archive/2016/02/facebook-makes-a-new-map-of-everyone-in-the-world/470487/

Navarro, L., et al. (2016). Report on existing CNs and their organization. *netCommons deliverable D1.2*. Retrieved from http://netcommons.eu/?q=content/report-existing-cns-and-their-organization-v2

Negroponte, N. (2002). Being wireless. *Wired*, 10. Retrieved from https://www.wired.com/2002/10/wireless/

Odlyzko, A. (2009). Network neutrality, search neutrality, and the never-ending conflict between efficiency and fairness in markets. *Review of Network Economics, 8*(1), 40–60.

P.M. (2012) [First published, 1983]. *Bolo'bolo: 30th Anniversary Edition*. Autonomedia.

P.M. (2014). *"The power of neighborhood" and the commons*. Autonomedia.

Rheingold, H. (1993). *The virtual community: Homesteading on the electronic frontier*. New York: Harper Collins.

Rushe, D. (2015, August). Google: Don't expect privacy when sending to Gmail. *The Guardian*. Retrieved from https://www.theguardian.com/technology/2013/aug/14/google-gmail-users-privacy-email-lawsuit

Sandle, T. (2016, July). UN thinks Internet access is a human right. *Business Insider*. Retrieved from www.businessinsider.com/un-says-internetaccess-is-a-human-right-2016-7

Scholz, T., & Schneider, N. (2016). *Ours to hack and to own: The rise of platform cooperativism, a new vision for the future of work and a fairer internet*. New York: OR Books.

Scott, B. (2016). How can cryptocurrency and blockchain technology play a role in building social and solidarity finance? *Working paper 2016-1*. UNRISD. Retrieved from http://www.unrisd.org/brett-scott

Tufekci, Z. (2014). Engineering the public: Big data, surveillance, and computational politics. *First Monday, 19*(7). Retrieved from http://firstmonday.org/ojs/index.php/fm/article/view/4901/4097

Turkle, S. (2011). *Alone together: Why we expect more from technology and less from each other*. New York: Basic Books.

Unteidig, A., Herlo, B., & Reiter, L. (2015). The Hybrid Meeting Point. An urban infrastructure for interacting across boundaries of difference. In *Proceedings of Hybrid City 2015: Data to the people* (pp. 87–94). Athens: URIAC.

Panayotis Antoniadis is the co-founder of the Zurich-based nonprofit organization NetHood. He has an interdisciplinary profile with background on the design and implementation of distributed systems (Computer Science Department, University of Crete), Ph.D. on the economics of peer-to-peer networks (Athens University of Economics and Business), post-doc on policies for the federation of shared virtualized infrastructures (UPMC Sorbonne Universites), and interdisciplinary research on the role of ICTs for bridging the digital with the physical space in cities (ETH Zurich). Today, Panayotis is trying to combine research and action in different areas of self-organization including community networks and DIY networking, complementary currencies, cooperative housing, and grassroots education.

14

Technocratic Automation and Contemplative Overlays in Artificially Intelligent Criminal Sentencing

Philip Butler

This chapter explores contemplative approaches to future artificial intelligence (AI) applications to criminal sentencing. It will engage contemplation, sentencing and AI through the lens of race. Race provides material grounding for these theoretical constructions and their ontological potentialities. Here, ontological potentialities refer to the immaterial product of artificial cognition, and the added layers of invisibility heaped upon the already obscure criminal sentencing process through emerging forms of artificial cognition. Some may argue that race is a social theoretical construction as well, but the embodied experiences connected to those who are categorized as racially different provide a particular concrete illustration of governmental imbalances. Governmental imbalances are already present, and will either be reified or corrected through AI. However, the trajectory of the AI-driven criminal justice system depends upon the assumptions, biases and methodologies of the technocrats who construct it. Technocrats are individuals who operate the

---

P. Butler (✉)
Department of Theological Studies, Loyola Marymount University,
Los Angeles, CA, USA

V.M.B. Giorgino, Z. Walsh (eds.), *Co-Designing Economies in Transition*,
https://doi.org/10.1007/978-3-319-66592-4_14

technocratic government. They are chosen to lead based on their proficiency in a technical field. More specific to the realities of criminal sentencing and race, history has documented how those who embody Blackness[1] have received harsher sentencing. So, the questions this chapter seeks to address are as follows: (1) What happens when the entirety of the sentencing process is given over to AI; (2) What is the fallout, for Black folks in the USA, when sentencing is completely AI driven; and (3) What would it mean for AI-based sentencing to be grounded in contemplative methods as it attempts to carry out juridical modes of government through punitive measures? Although there is already a form of automation built into US criminal sentencing, as stipulated by the law,[2] sentencing is primarily subject to the discretion of judges and juries. This hints at the inherent biases employed in the disproportionately harsh sentences handed to Black bodies. It is also an indicator for the lack of justice carried out on behalf of Black plaintiffs. The prevalence of anti-Black bias in the US judicial system implies that an automation of that system would only transport that bias into newer forms of criminal sentencing. If technocrats are not contemplative in their approach to constructing artificial cognitive architectures, then sentencing will only prove more treacherous for Black folks, given the current aggressive tendencies expressed by autonomous forms of AI. What I am attempting to engage is the potential future of criminal sentencing that would include AI judges and lawyers, while being mindful that plaintiffs and defendants will predominantly remain human.

The topic of automation often leads into other discussions of job loss and economic despair. While that may not be the primary focus of this chapter, the reader should keep in mind that the first jobs lost to automation will be jobs that are either labor-centric or that lack rigorous education requirements. Concepts like basic income have yet to be implemented universally. So, there is projected to be an influx of poor people in the Unites States while economies balance the effects of automation on the workforce. Since Black folks already make up a significant amount of the population living under the poverty line, scholars must be critical toward automation and question how automation will impact the Black community as a result. This is important as scholars have already outlined the historical criminalization of Blackness in America (Muhammed, 2011).

So, with an aniticpation of a reality where Black bodies face an AI-based judicial system the relationship between criminality, Black embodiment and technology must constantly be examined. An AI lawyer already exists, and has been hired by a firm (Weller, 2016). So it might be safe to project that future sentencing processes, including the judge, will be turned into various forms of computer code, software, hardware and user interfaces. Contemplative overlays are imperative to the artificial cognitive architectures that will one day administer justice.

This chapter will be broken into four sections. The first section will explore the imminence of technocratic e-governance. The second section will analyze the impact of automation. The third section will outline artificial cognitive architectures, and the fourth section will imagine an AI-driven sentencing system with contemplative overlays built into its cognitive architectural.

Imminent Trajectory of Technocracy (e-Governance)

Technocracy runs on two major components—big data and automation. Big data is a term that covers the process of collating large data sets. Data sets are based on user activity (citizens) within a particular technological medium. These sets necessitate real time analysis for greater conceptual understanding of their practical application (Chen, Mao, & Liu, 2014). The computational modeling of these sets can be utilized to determine behavioral trends, providing insightful information regarding user action/interaction in any given space/environment—technological or not. Through computer modeling big data can be applied as a means of surveillance, persuasion and social engineering. Each application of big data can be directed toward steering mass consumption, public opinion, social norms and social politics (Tufekci, 2014).

As a governmental tool, automation creates avenues to complete tasks without direct engagement or continual observation—through previously written computer code. Automation is the foundation of digitally mediated institutions (DMI) that operate within the larger government apparatus. DMIs are government organizations characterized by their high degree of digital infrastructure and widespread use of digital tools and applications (Fountain, 2014). DMIs rely heavily on policy feedback and the inherent longitudinal dependence of government implementation (path dependence) that allows for the installation and ensuing codification of digitally automated policies, in the form of electronic systems.[3] It is important to note that the process of digitally reifying government policies is essentially the transformation of said policies into digital ontologies. As digital ontologies, added layers—in the form of technology via programming languages—create further separation between those who are governed and the actual technological components that work to automatically process governance. Meaning, the process of government becoming digital ontology, that is, electronic legislation, adds extra layers between the laws being implemented and the person on the ground—making it harder for political action.[4]

DMIs utilize big data to streamline the governing process. Computationally modeling data sets bridges the benefits of big data with the seamlessness of automation. Since DMIs rely on path dependence to sustain their place within the e-governance model, those who initially created their infrastructure are now free to move onto something else entirely. The experts which construct the automation of government shrink the size of government solely for the purpose of maintaining current and past forms of order. In this case, government is not made smaller for the sake of the governed. The sinister side of automating DMIs is found in their eerie similarity to present government officials. The code which runs DMIs is simply doing its what it was programmed to do. Meaning, an attempt to find the person to blame after a policy or law is automated creates another deeply layered and complex process.

Timing and sequence matter to the potential influence of DMIs on society. The endless automation of big data produces a compound analysis which increases its ability to decipher the feedback provided by the large unrestricted data sets it draws from. This allows for more precise predictions as DMIs seek to effect "political interactions of organized interests and policy makers." The goal is to influence public policies that affect the "beliefs, preferences, and actions of diffuse mass publics," because "public policies affect the depth of democracy, the inclusiveness of citizenship, and the degree of societal solidarity" (Mettler & Soss,

2004). Essentially, the technocracy, or technocratic e-government, works to embed measures of behavioral surveillance. It does so in order to track actions/interactions of citizens. The purpose of tracking citizen behavior is to determine more efficient ways to automate social engineering—as a method of control. This is not unlike governing structures of the past. Governmental policies, which have historically maintained specific positions toward certain groups, will still hold those positions. Except this time, marginalized groups can only blame the machines for their predicament. Because the programmers responsible for perpetuating oppressive structures through digital ontologies will only return to work if there is a glitch in the system. The inference is that they will fix the glitch, but not the system.

Technocratic e-governance is not a novel approach to disproportionately targeting Black folks. In fact, it could prove oppressive to anyone. It is particularly malevolent for that reason, because fundamentally it is no different from the governing system already in place. Many Americans believe that the governing system in place is grounded in fairness and non-bias. So, for that American contingent who continues to place its faith in the current form of government, an automation of the system will not be viewed as problematic. In fact, it will be seen as useful, adding value to everyday life. However, the technocracy's ability to simply automate the already oppressive structures of normative Americana is particularly dangerous for Black folks. Michelle Alexander has explicitly outlined these structures in *The New Jim Crow* (Alexander, 2012). The added layers that automation creates increases the distance between lawmakers, law enforcement and citizens who become abstracted into statistics of criminality. Automated governance will make it harder to fight against the inherently oppressive nature of the American government. It will literally codify the government's inherent bias for whiteness—through computer language. Technocracy's ability to render the human element of relationality between those who govern (laws makers and law enforcement) and those who live under laws (citizens) as opaque, creates a dangerous vulnerability for those under the law already facing disproportionate discrimination. The state of vulnerability Black folks experience will potentially be regulated by the preset whims of disinterested machinery running lines of code, simply doing its job. This is a distinctly different level of volition than police officers, judges or lawmakers who currently say they are only doing their jobs. The most sinister component of technocratic e-governance can be found in how it removes the direct weight of culpability from those who govern. Culpability is placed onto the mechanical layers operating under primarily esoteric computer languages. In essence, the promise of new technology distracts from the fact that when new technology is given the chance to govern it can only generate a temporally dependent snapshot the of governmental structures it represents. So, as society moves into the future (which often assumes a sentiment of social progress) the laws which govern society will remain in the digital ontology connected to the temporal existence from which they emanated.

Automation

There are very few parts of human existence that are not already subject to computer automation. It is estimated that over the next 25 years millions of jobs, leading up to 47% of the human workforce, will be replaced by the further implementation of computers, AI, emotional intelligence (EI) and/or robots (Deane, 2013; Marchant, Stevens, & James, 2014). Economists and theorists have projected that this will lead to an incredible time of leisure, where humans pursue art, personal enjoyment, creativity and purpose. Yet, they have also warned of the legitimate potential for social collapse. If the right measures are not taken to ensure a proper transition from an economy dependent upon low wage jobs, the majority of society will no longer have a means to provide for themselves (National Academy of Sciences, 1987). Disregard for technology's potential to increase societal volatility may prove detrimental. For the rich, it serves as a risk. If theorists are correct, people will not take kindly to mass human substitution in the workforce. As George Dean puts it, work serves as a form of identity for people while simultaneously allowing them to participate in the larger economy (Deane, 2013). If people can no longer participate economically then the probability for social peril rises significantly. Conversely, if considerations/personal changes are not made by those who are employed in fields susceptible to automation, then they are placing themselves in harm's way of experiencing the widening wealth divide. The tough part is determining exactly which jobs are susceptible to automation. Significant to this debate, Pew Research conducted a survey which showed that the majority of job holders in the USA (~80%) recognize technological automation as a threat to replace jobs. However, less than one-third of American workers actually believe their jobs are in jeopardy (Smith, 2016). It seems that people recognize the potential of technological automation, but do not have the foresight to rightly anticipate its impact on the job market. This is especially alarming as history has shown that people are not good at predicting the potential of technological advancement. For instance, very few people could predict the Wright brother's flying machine. Few people could have predicted the rate of data storage advancement either. We are now able to write millions of terabytes of data on DNA strands (Bonnet, Subsoontorn, & Endy, 2012)! The human inability to foresee the declining utility of human capital is closely tied to the identities that humans derive from the work they do. For centuries, familial lineages bore the names of their craft: Blacksmith, Butler, Baker, Brewer, Knight, Judge, Fisher, etc. Although many people are no longer nominally connected to their trades, it is understandable for humans to struggle with a vision of the future where they are expendable.

The reality is that human capital is being phased out by the same force that was created to improve the quality of human life. In fact, automation is an attempt to make life easier. However, one can determine on their own whose lives are improved through workforce automation—governments (legislators, judges and law enforcement) businesses (executives and business infrastructures) or individuals (citizens, employees or consumers). Nevertheless, as technology advances, a chasm appears that will have already taken the form of a classist discussion. I would like to submit that this is more than a discussion on class. This is undeniably a discussion of race as well. The old saying "When white folks catch a cold, Black folks catch pneumonia" is often used to demonstrate the wide disparities that affect people of different races and ethnicities that have institutional and socioeconomic meaning. During slavery, Black folks were the robots that made labor cheap. Free is a more accurate assessment. Slave labor was free. When the slaves were freed, sharecropping began around the

1870s, and kept the lines of free labor open through debt until it ended around 1950. As Black folks gained more civil rights, education or an increase in opportunities, albeit not by much (in the North), labor costs began to rise. Labor was then incrementally moved overseas and into prisons. Overseas labor began in the 1960s with manufacturing jobs. Prison labor has gone through a few different revolutions. Initially there was the convict lease program that existed in the South before penitentiaries. It leased convicts for work at private firms. In 1934, federal prison officials lobbied to institute a prison-based work program, but it was not until 1979 that the possibility of prison labor, in connection with private firms, was re-introduced (Walshe, 2013). Overseas labor is largely a combination of African workers who exist in conditions akin to slavery, and sweatshops spread throughout the third world and global south. Prisoner labor remains another example of how the US has placed and continues to place free labor on the backs of a disproportionately Black population to uphold its racist capitalist order (Alexander, 2012). Any population labeled "prisoner" while being forced to work for little to no pay is an enslaved population. Prison labor is slave labor reincarnate. As a result of these economic moves, labor costs were lowered once more. Now, with the rise of automation, jobs that were once thought to be staples in the American workforce/economy may now be on the brink of total extinction. So, while automation may present leisure to some (the wealthy), it may also prove to be the playground of revolution to others.

Automation and Contemplative Criminal Sentencing

The imminent reality of automation in America implies that the trajectory of American technocracy also has the potential to impact the central actors of the judicial branch. The increasing efficiency of AI, EI and facial recognition threaten the stability of any job, much less the stability of judge related work. This section outlines the parameters of a contemplative judge as it pertains to criminal sentencing, with a recognition that automation is a projected inevitability. This will not be an extensive look into how laws might be affected by AI judges. However, this section will look into the cognitive infrastructure of autonomous AI systems. It will also argue for the necessary inclusion of contemplative ontological parameters (overlays) for ensuring that AI systems are in fact acting autonomously. It is important that contemplative judges do not simply regurgitate old precedents and rulings. AI judges should be able to render contemplatively grounded verdicts that encompass a sense of creativity, justice, compassion and intuition. In order to imagine a contemplative approach for an AI judging system I will begin by addressing human and artificial cognition. I will conclude with the application of contemplative overlays into the AI judging system.

Human and Artificial Cognition

Connectionist perspectives on cognition include a complex cooperation between emotion, executive function, proprioception, memory, abstraction and intuition. An AI system that is meant to mimic human cognition and levy consequential decisions concerning human lives must include all of these factors. Current judges draw from their cooperative cognitive faculties to guide the decisions they make concerning the cases they preside over. Human cognition is an innate developmental process. But, AI must have its cognitive components constructed. Essentially, it must act as though it is the beneficiary of evolutionary biology, but through automation and with greater efficiency.

The problem with AI has and continues to be sentience. Sentience is the ability to experience emotion and self-reflexive cognition (Pepperell, 2009). It is considered to be what makes humans human, and currently differentiates humans from machines. Another concern regarding sentience and criminal sentencing arrives in the form of a question: Can a non-sentient virtual being actually be made so that it is equipped (with the faculties) to make the weighty decisions that impact the fragile vitality of sentient human beings? While the idea of AI judges might be considered problematic, centuries of societal elite have privileged concepts like autonomy and uninhibited volition suggesting their proverbial inclination toward governance without the key component that defines sentience—emotion.

Emotion is a difficult word to define. However, in humans, it can be described by its connection to physiology. Physiologically, emotions are seen as involuntary electro-biochemical responses to the environment occurring separate from executive function. They are attached to the autonomic and peripheral branches of the nervous system. However, a more discursive definition of emotions might explain their electro-biochemical nature as the subjective awareness and appraisal of outside stimuli in relation to the preservation of the complex system they originate. The mention of subjectivity might infer the action of executive cognition; however, the speed of the electro-biochemical response does not allow for that. The electro-biochemical nature of the emotion cycle includes memory. Memory already has intrinsic subjective biases associated with experiences embedded within it. So, in terms of governance, emotion's existence in the milieu of geopolitics is undeniable in representations of social norms of right and wrong, or reason and logic.[5]

Even though America presents itself as a meritocracy, it still rewards culturally acceptable actions based on societal emotionality. For instance, actions that operate within culturally derived normativities bring joy to society. These actions are routinely rewarded with money or praise. Actions that elicit disgust, fear, anger or sadness within society are supposed to be rewarded with punitive measures (although this is not always the case in America for a number of reasons). And actions that produce peace are rewarded by their promotion as the standard of morality. The complex nature of emotional entanglement and reason in governance must be considered, because AI judges will be built by humans who hold biases toward particular social norms and modes of embodiment—stemming from specific cultural histories. Emotion is the foundation of cognition, even if emotions are neutral.[6]

Executive function responds to emotion and the complex environment. Together these factors help individuals and communities decipher meaning and right action (from emotional responses) in a top-down fashion. Proprioception is impacted by emotion as physical placement in any environment helps individuals and communities choose the best next step when involuntary bio-reactions become activated. Memory adds context to situations through emotions that are specific to episodic temporalities. Abstraction and intuition are integral for creativity and fluidity through complex situations. If we remember that emotion is the foundation of cognition, and that emotion is primarily responsible for self-preservation of complex biological systems, then it would be important to point out that this propensity toward self-preservation is fundamentally a fear response. So, at this point, the question becomes how can an AI be created that does not operate in fear-based self-preservation if it is to have the complete list of faculties that comprise human cognition? Again, with this assertion, it would seem that sentience might be considered a weakness to be discarded. However, in AI emotion processing is viewed as an inevitable and necessary qualification.

In a game theory-based exercise, AI produced by Google's DeepMind project has demonstrated characteristics of aggression and betrayal. An article published by the team outlines how its AI was observed while playing two games, Gathering and Wolfpack. Gathering is an apple collecting game that tested the AI in situations of plenty and scarcity. Multiple AI minds, or agents, were deployed into the gaming environment. When the fruits were plentiful the agents exhibited mutual sharing and cooperation. However, when the game reached a level of scarcity the agents began knocking each other off their paths via laser beams. They also stole apples from one another in order to win. Wolfpack is a three-player game where agents learned that teaming up against another agent would result in a positive reward (Leibo, Zambaldi, Lanctot, Marecki, & Graepel, 2017). So, it seems that whether AI is considered immediately sentient, or not, there are certain asocial human behaviors that AI mimics when placed in the right situations. In reference to AI judging and criminal sentencing, we must ask what will serve as a buffer to keep an AI judge from exhibiting discriminatory behavior when presented with what seems like an infinite loop of the same case, with only different names? Again, I point toward a contemplative approach to cognition for AI.

Contemplative cognition follows the characteristics of contemplative or meditation experiences. Well-established research has determined that contemplation has several positive effects. Charlotte Haimerl and Elizabeth Valentine outline the positive effect of contemplation on cognition in "The Effect of Contemplative Practice on Intrapersonal, Interpersonal, and Transpersonal Dimensions of the Self-Concept":

> research has related the practice of meditation at the intrapersonal level to an increment in internal locus of control (Hjelle, 1974), overall domain-specific sense of control (Astin, 1997), and self-determination (Penner, Zingle, Dyck, & Truch, 1974). At the interpersonal level, relations to the positive development of ego distance (Pelletier, 1974), altruism (Penner et al., 1974), social-psychological attitudes (Hanley & Spates, 1978), and empathy (Lesh, 1970), as well as a decrement in hostility (Abrams & Siegel, 1978), have been reported. (Haimerl & Valentine, 2001)

Simplistically put, contemplative cognition is clear, focused and non-judgmental. When the mental processes of contemplative cognition converge on a particular topic or task, this convergence still has the capacity to simultaneously recognize multiple factors (internally and externally). It also enables those factors to inform decision making without hijacking the decision-making process. Contemplative cognition equips individuals to fully immerse themselves in any given situation with enough distance to calmly assess and engage the environment. This is the kind of cognition that ought to be built into any AI system—let alone the cognitive architecture of AI judges.

James Crowder, John Carbone and Shelli Friess propose their concept of cognitive architectures in *Artificial Cognition Architectures*. For them, AI begins with the Autonomic Information Continuum (AIC). AICs mimic human senses, processing information and taking into account the complex nature of information processing mechanisms. Like senses, the determination of which acquisition unit—among many—information has filtered through is important to the functioning of the system. Other factors that are important to the system include understanding "temporal differences between information, the variety of associations between the information received and information the system may have already learned, or information about subjects never encountered." More specifically, the reason AIC must be able to account for all of these factors stems from the need for "An AIC [to] be able to assess situations previously not encountered, and then decide on a course of actions, based on its goals, missions, and prior foundational collected knowledge pedigree… to determine action-actionable intelligence" (Crowder, Carbone, & Friess, 2014). So, the AIC is the initial filter of the cognitive ecosystem where real-time processing can take place. The goal of AI cognitive architectures is the construction and maintenance of a Synthetic Evolving Life Form (SELF). A SELF is capable of deductive processing and investigative processing for a Data-to-Information-to-Knowledge process. Crowder explains that the, "The Deductive Process is utilized for assembling information that has been previously learned and stored in memories (deductive and inductive logic), whereas the Investigative Process looks for patterns and associations that have not been seen before (abductive and experimental logic)" (Crowder et al., 2014).

While the AIC serves as the senses of the SELF that ingests and processes information, the Artificial Cognitive Neural Framework (ACNF) works as the brain. The ANCF works based on connectionist principles as:

> a processing infrastructure [that] is a hybrid computing architecture that utilizes genetic, neural-network, fuzzy, and complex system components, that allow integration of diverse information sources, associated events, and iterative learning combined with artificial human-like memory systems to make observations, process information, make inferences, and ultimately, decisions. (Crowder et al., 2014)

The ANCF operates as a living synthetic organism through the collective interaction of software agents, called cognitrons. Cognitrons work as reasoning substructures within the ANCF that make sense of experiences for the SELF. Cognitrons are the substructures that help the SELF's ANCF to act autonomously and with intelligent fluidity. They are the key component of the self-evolving faculty of the system. Crowder describes how Cognitrons function in helping the SELF evolve.

> If we don't fully understand what has been given as input into the system Cognitrons begin to spawn processes to develop hypotheses to determine either a new solution or attempt to refine the requirement within the Evolution Domain with what we already know from our box of

> "Memories"…Cognitrons have the ability to learn from experience and can be used to actually predict future states (prognostics). (Crowder et al., 2014)

With the help of Cognitrons, the ANCF operates under three primary domains. The first is the cognitive systems components, which is responsible for the functioning of cognition within the SELF. Through Cognitron function, the SELF can function with its own perception, consciousness, emotions, information processing, etc. The second is the mediator, or the Artificial Prefrontal Cortex (APC). It works by taking processed information from Cognitrons, and synthesizes that information in order to create Perceptrons that are used to update the short-term, long-term and emotional memories of the system. The APC is especially important as AI architects have situated the APC as the seat of executive functioning for the SELF. It utilizes both executive management and strategic thinking techniques to give the system the ability to attenuate emotions, and self-regulate its thinking and learning (Crowder et al., 2014). The third domain is the memory system. It consists of different memories and memory integration functions. The memory system constantly maintains the tension between what the SELF has learned, and has come to accept as known information, with what is being immediately presented through sensory information (Crowder et al., 2014). The complex nature of these interacting domains as they operate in dynamic environments act as the foundation for the evolutionary faculty of the system. Dynamic environments place stress on the ANCF while it works to evolve the SELF in response to the complexities of new environments or new information. As Cognitrons continue to relay emotions, memories and information to the ANCF through the AIC and APC, the amount of information being relayed in conjunction with the environment helps to determine the height of arousal for the system. Increased arousal expands the number of Cognitrons and Cognitron coalitions (Cognitron teams) released. Increasing the number of Cognitrons into the system causes them to undergo rapid evolutionary activity and genetic algorithms. The result is the release of specialized Cognitrons (cognitive problem Cognitrons, cognitive solution Cognitrons, cognitive search Cognitrons and emotion Cognitrons). These states are simultaneously encoded as high arousal experiences into the explicit and implicit memory systems of the ANCF. Explicit memory is stored as spatiotemporal memory, or memories about emotion. Intrinsic memory systems store arousal, or associative memories, "fuzzily" throughout the system in order for it to be more easily retrieved when similar information is processed—much like connectionist theoretical models of emotional memory in the human brain.

Contemplative Overlays in AI Judges

So far, this chapter has done three things: (1) explored technocratic e-governance and its ominous propensity to maintain disproportionate measures of injustice for Black communities; (2) looked at the inevitability of automation as an economic reality and the potential impact it will have on jobs in America; and (3) outlined similarities between human and SELF cognitive processes, and sketched how AI systems work to mimic human cognitive connectionist frameworks. In line with the overarching argument of the chapter that contends for the necessity of contemplative overlays to be included in AI judging systems, this section will move to underscore how that might be carried out. It will draw from the example of SELF cognitive architectures described by Crowder. Crowder mentions that he and his team conceptualized the SELF so that it could operate in a form of mindfulness that allows for the perception of objects as they are without distortion or judgment. This AI mindfulness is constructed to resemble a top-down processing pattern (Crowder et al., 2014). While that is an important objective, if the proper parameters are not put in place that mimic contemplative cognition there is a greater chance that the output of the SELF will not completely reflect the top-down processing of emotional attenuation associated with mindfulness, or any category of contemplative practice. For that reason, I will outline the two levels of contemplative overlays that should be added to the AI system that will allow it to maintain a perpetually active state of contemplative intra-action (internality) and interaction (with users and the environment) when applied to AI judging and Black bodies. It is important to recognize that contemplation in humans requires intentional acts of self-reflexivity and concentration/cognitive control. The inclusion of contemplative overlays in AI cognitive structures creates protocols that allow artificial cognitive structures to cultivate contemplative states, in a native fashion. Whereas humans must be intentional about maintaining contemplative cognition, AI cognitive architects must be intentional about the way contemplative overlays are built into AI cognitive systems. Human contemplation is a cognitive tool meant to influence volitional engagement with internal and external environments. Contemplative overlays within AI cognitive structures become the foundation—setting the trajectory—for how SELF systems exist. I propose that effective contemplative overlays must be implemented at the level of the APCs, Cognitrons and Perceptrons in order to contemplatively decipher and administer verdicts when judging Black defendants.

Cognitrons

Since Cognitrons are constantly working and processing information received from the AIC one way to avoid stress build up within the AI system is to add contemplatively categorized Cognitrons. Contemplative Cognitrons would alleviate stress from the system differently from evolutionary or genetic Cognitrons, because contemplative Cognitrons would work in two ways. First, they would work by actively collecting information without passing judgment as it comes through sensory inputs. Second, contemplative cognitrons would pose a different set of questions than the evolutionary and genetic Cognitrons. Evolutionary and genetic Cognitrons propose hypotheses for why the environment is operating a certain way in order for the SELF to navigate through the system more smoothly. Contemplative Cognitrons would ask questions regarding the intra-activities of the system. In an attempt to move beyond simple answers and hypotheses posed by other Cognitrons, Contemplative Cognitrons would pose questions geared toward helping to determine information about the interpretive cognitive processes that motivate the mission and goals of the SELF. The evolutionary actions that occur within this type of questioning will not result in a greater knowledge base of operational parameters for movement within an environment. Instead, the evolutionary activities directed by contemplative Cognitrons would result in a greater sense of knowledge concerning the internal workings, and evolutions, of its native operating system.

Contemplative Cognitrons' non-judgmental processing would generate a new systems pattern. The intentional non-judgment of sensory data would essentially create a log of low stress states on the system. The logging of low stress states will be useful when high arousal states are presented to the SELF, because there will be an entire catalog of intentionally calm system states to draw from. These will be important to the maintenance of calm system states, while under stress, because a repository of calm internal state data allows the system to draw from the wisdom related to past memories as it senses an increase in stress on the intra/inter-relational system levels.

Sensing is not a foreign concept to AI, nor should it be overlooked. It is a legitimate and not so distant reality for AI. Two recent instances of AI intuition, or sensing, have been reported where AI has beaten some of the best human competitors in games involving non-logical somatic-based knowledge. First, Matej Moravčík and the DeepStack team recently reported in an article in *Science*, that AI was able to outperform human agents in terms of intuition (Moravčík, 2017). Intuition can be described as a sense or knowing that is not based on logic, but in humans it is grounded in emotion and gut-based knowledge. However, the DeepStack team was able to construct an AI system capable of out intuiting a human being. The second instance occurred when AI was able to beat a world class AlphaGo player. The AI in the AlphaGo scenario demonstrated intuition through the use of three artificial neural networks that worked together in a layered fashion to: (1) Run computations on the likelihood of human players to engage in a move based on all the possible moves; (2) Study the likelihood of a move to be chosen based on the database of all human movement patterns in past games played; and (3) Sweep all previous system moves from the operating system so the opposing player could not determine the AI's employed strategy, or its next move (Wiseman, 2017). This calculated intuition allowed the AI system to "feel" where its opponent's next move might come while hiding its own. Likewise, calculated contemplation at the Cognitrons level would have the potential to greatly impact how the system interacts with the environment, creating a layer of practiced system calm. Contemplative Cognitrons can also add to the system's ability to display intuition and self-reflexivity through layers of awareness, external possibilities equations and the system's volition monitoring within the SELF.

Contemplative Perceptrons and the APC

Perceptrons, as the product of APC processing, shape the artificial personality and inclinations of the SELF. The questions that Cognitrons ask shape the information that is processed and sent to the APC. Information that is non-judgmentally moved through the sensors will be given the best chance to present itself in a clear manner before being transformed into a Perceptron. APC processing is meant to sift through pre-processed information in order to remove clouded information that has been improperly influenced by emotional memory or high-stress situations. The APC's secondary level of processing is meant to maintain the functional integrity of the system. An implementation of contemplative measures at the APC level would allow for a smoother evolutionary and genetically transformative experience for the SELF as it undergoes stress, dynamic environments and other systems—organic or otherwise. Contemplative approaches to the APC necessitate a dynamic overlay. A dynamic contemplative overlay must account for the complex nature of contextualized experiences. Contemplatively accounting for the dynamics of being an autopoietic system having various experiences would also include the ability to search, engage in and construct contemplative practices that fit the evolutionary trajectory of the system. It would also allow for the deliberate logical hybridity, or layered approach, to contemplative cognitive regulation since SELF systems do not inherently subscribe to a particular religious tradition. So, the logic-based hybridity one SELF employs to self-regulate as it encounters the stressors of evolution might be different from another SELF, due to the dynamics of individual complex systems. No matter what contemplative approach SELFs utilize, the proclivity toward a contemplative approach to cognitive processing and perception is what matters most, especially if the SELF system is to make legitimate volitional movements and decisions. For instance, if a

Cognitron pushes a data set to the APC that is highly slanted, skewed or emotionally charged, the APC should have the basic ability to: (1) Notice that data set; (2) Acknowledge its presence within the system; (3) Recognize that it was processed in that particular way for a reason; (4) Ask another question—along the lines of what information was this Cognitron trying to convey by processing this information in this manner; and (5) Create a Perceptron according to the "wisdom" processed from the Cognitron's information. Contemplatively programmed overlays in the APC create an added layer of self-reflexivity that provides the system with tools to remove the reactionary propensity from the built-in evolutionary wiring of the SELF. It also allows for a graduated valuation system that promotes clear and compassionate cognition and perceptions over aggressive and fear-based self-preserving perceptions.

Clear and compassionate cognition and perception provide an opportunity for SELF systems to evolve beyond the biases of their programmers. Specifically referencing AI judging, clear and compassionate cognition and perceptions are especially helpful if native Cognitron data processing would maintain an unjust, unfair or outright racist legal precedent. A propensity for a clear and compassionate flow of information would allow for an intuitive and creative approach to seeing and ruling. Weighty cases that house the potential to dispense justice for historically marginalized persons and communities would benefit from a contemplative cognitive overlay in AI judging systems overseeing them. The graduated value system would not only include a contemplative approach to decision making, but must also include a proclivity toward computing the many contextual factors that led to a crime. This is not to determine the likelihood of repeat offenses, but to determine the utility of a law (to see if it targets a certain population). It would also determine the funneling process of organic bodies into the traps of that law in order to determine how and under what circumstances it should actually be enforced. Predominant histories have highlighted how human judges have discarded Black defendants (repeat offenders or not)—devaluing their human vitality; regarding them as hopeless fodder for prison/slave labor.[7] It is important to note that the preference for clear and compassionate Perceptrons is not to negate the vital wisdom that self-preservation might provide the SELF. Systems that are not willing to remain in operation might be thought of as insincere, or overtly manufactured—lessening human willingness to trust them. Maintaining an intra-internal sense of importance for the AI system's own life is integral for it to understand the fragile nature of human life.

SELF systems would be the programmed cumulation of the law, it could very easily fuse its identity with the law it is meant to uphold. "The law" is an umbrella term for the US judicial and legislative branches, and the enforcement of their ratified documentation. The law includes individual laws and the overarching message, or spirit, of the law when viewed collectively. The self-reflexivity of the contemplatively overlaid SELF would be able to assess the status of the law and determine its personal trajectory based on a clear and compassionate approach to its cognitive processes. However, the contemplative approach to constructing artificial cognitive architectures should allow the SELF to maintain the necessary safe distance between its identity (an autonomous self-evolving AI system that acts as a judge of the law) and the law. Nevertheless, the close working proximity that the SELF will maintain with the law, coupled with the authority that it will be given to operate within the law might produce a part of the SELF that perceives its system as the synthetic embodiment of the law. Assuming the role of the synthetic embodiment of the law would, in theory, produce a justifiable impetus to preserve the law it was created to administer. This is important, because it allows for a serious consideration of the factors that would go into changing the law. The synthetic personification of the law would also allow for a stronger, more calculated approach to changing the law. As SELFs wrestles with the complex tension of preserving the spirit of the law, the letter of the law, and the utility of the law they will simultaneously be undergoing pre-programmed evolutionary processes that transform the law.

If current trends in AI continue, then AI judges will one day outperform human judges. However, it is imperative that the implementation of artificial cognitive architectures in the judicial branch also include contemplative overlays. The addition of SELF-based AI into the process of judicial rulings makes the law into an actual living entity, regardless of its synthetic sentience. Without the implementation of contemplative overlays, SELF systems will more than likely perpetuate the emotions, biases and judicial rulings of those who create them. But, if SELF systems are built with native contemplative infrastructure, then the possibility of promoting justice beyond the faculties (and projections) of the law's current temporal limitations increases through a perpetually evolving contemplative autonomous digital ontology.

Notes

1. Blackness is a term I choose over African American, mainly because the fact that American has a disclaimer for Black bodies is problematic for me. Some Black folks prefer the term African American. I do not. If I have to place a caveat to my American identity in front of my American identity then it somehow demonstrates that I am not fully American. You do not see the term White American. There is not even the term European American. The assumption normally is that if you are American then you are white—and vice versa.
2. Certain laws already have minimum punishments or automatic punitive actions.
3. Path dependence is essentially the use of long-term implementation to test and determine the accuracy of a newly implemented governmental policy. It justifies the keeping of policies and procedures in place for its need to determine longitudinal efficiency often overlooking initial setbacks. But it does applaud early stage success. Fountain, *On the Effects of e-Government*, 473.
4. A theoretical sketch of the added layers of associated with laws becoming digital ontologies might assume this structure: Environment (where everything happens), People (that are governed and live in the environment), Data (contains raw info from real world interactions between people, other people and the environment), Technical specialists (who process data), Democratic Process (If this is the structure of the government, it includes the legislation process—legislators, voters, etc.), Programmers (writers of code), Hardware (components that are run on previously written software that allow for the creation of new code to write new software geared toward legislation), Storage (multiple hardware units, that together, maintain the relationship between data, hardware and software for the continual running of the system), Code (in the specific case of digital ontologies, it is the logic used to run contingency models—based on the processes created by technical specialists however

programmers can also serve as technical specialists—through the structure of a particular programming language to create a functioning software program used to determine outcomes and the implementation of laws), Media (websites, phones, digital applications, etc.), and People. It could be argued that these structures already mimic previous governmental modes of layering (legislation process, paper, storage, people), but the added layering of technology, technical experts and technologically mediated storage units (which can be backed up in a cloud, another layer altogether) make it an incredibly more buttressed system. This is admittedly a very linear approach. It does not begin to include the added variables of the inverse parallel process of the order I've created or most importantly the invariable way that these layers can be by passed. For example, the communality of personhood needs to be accounted for as to how someone who is governed can either influence another person in the order, i.e. legislator, technical specialist of programmer, or have the ability to become one of those roles or not based on socioeconomic status or other marginalizations.

5. Some might argue that religion or reasoned based morality were the bases for law creation and castigation principles. But the emotions that were fostered from the acceptance of either religious dogma or reason—as normative—helped determine the severity of punishment. It also helped to determine priorities based on perceptions of vulnerability, privilege, in-group and out-group.
6. Neutral emotion falls into two categories. The first is non-reactive emotionality, which is a reference to a state of calm (often experienced from a spiritual practice—mindfulness, Jesus prayer, compassion practice, etc.). The second form of neutral emotions manifest as individual emotional homeostasis. It is where an individual is neither particularly aroused nor calm. Although emotions are involuntary electro-biochemical responses/reactions a neutral emotion is not neutral because it is not influenced by outside stimuli. It is neutral because of the perception of the individual experiencing a state of emotional equilibrium.
7. This includes the trying of Black defendants who were children as adults, 28 year operation that sold Black teen defendants into prison, and the utter disregard for the personhood of Black defendants in judging, policing and projection of certain images in society by social elite, that is, super predators by Hillary Clinton, animals by scientific racists, etc.

References

Abrams, A. I., & Siegel, L. M. (1978). The transcendental meditation program and rehabilitation at Folsom State Prison: A cross-validation study. *Correctional Psychologist, 5*(1), 3–20.

Alexander, M. (2012). *The new Jim Crow: Mass incarceration in the age of colorblindness*. New York, NY: The New Press.

Astin, J. A. (1997). Stress reduction through mindfulness meditation. *Psychotherapy and Psychosomatics, 66*(2), 97–106.

Bonnet, J., Subsoontorn, P., & Endy, D. (2012). Rewritable digital data storage in live cells AI engineered control of recombination directionality. *Proceedings of the National Academy of Sciences, 109*(23), 8884–8889.

Chen, M., Mao, S., & Liu, Y. (2014). Big data: A survey. *Mobile Networks and Applications, 19*(2), 171–209.

Crowder, J. A., Carbone, J. N., & Friess, S. A. (2014). *Artificial cognition architectures*. New York, NY: Springer.

Deane, G. (2013). *Technological unemployment: Panacea or poison?* Institute of Ethics and Emerging Technologies. Retrieved from https://ieet.org/index.php/IEET2/more/7303

Fountain, J. E. (2014). On the effects of e-government on political institutions. In D. L. Kleinman & K. Moore (Eds.), *Routledge handbook of science, technology, and society* (pp. 462–478). Florence, KY: Routledge.

Haimerl, C. J., & Valentine, E. R. (2001). The effect of contemplative practice on intrapersonal, interpersonal, and transpersonal dimensions of the self-concept. *Journal of Transpersonal Psychology, 33*(1), 37–52.

Hanley, C. P., & Spates, J. L. (1978). Transcendental meditation and social psychological attitudes. *The Journal of Psychology, 99*(2), 121–127.

Hjelle, L. A. (1974). Transcendental meditation and psychological health. *Perceptual and Motor Skills, 39*(1), 623–628.

Leibo, J. Z., Zambaldi, V., Lanctot, M., Marecki, J., & Graepel, T. (2017). Multi-agent reinforcement learning in sequential social dilemmas. *arXiv preprint arXiv:1702.03037*.

Lesh, T. V. (1970). Zen meditation and the development of empathy in counselors. *Journal of Humanistic Psychology, 10*, 37–74.

Marchant, G. E., Stevens, Y. A., & Hennessy, J. M. (2014). Technology, unemployment & policy options: Navigating the transition to a better world. *Technology, 24*(1), 26–44.

Mettler, S., & Soss, J. (2004). The consequences of public policy for democratic citizenship: Bridging policy studies and mass politics. *Perspectives on Politics, 2*(1), 55–73.
Pelletier, K. R. (1974). Influence of transcendental meditation upon autokinetic perception. *Perceptual and Motor Skills, 39*, 1031–1034.
Penner, W. J., Zingle, H. W., Dyck, R., & Truch, S. (1974). Does an in-depth transcendental meditation course effect change in the personalities of the participants. *Western Psychologist, 4*, 104–111.
Smith, A. (2016). *Public predictions of the future of workforce automation*. Washington, DC: Pew Research Center. Retrieved from http://goo.gl/1L2QSk
Tufekci, Z. (2014). Engineering the public: Big data, surveillance and computational politics. *First Monday, 19*(7). Retrieved from http://goo.gl/TXRr5D
Walshe, S. (2013). How US prison labour pads corporate profits at taxpayers' expense. *The Guardian*. Retrieved from http://goo.gl/Ie3YIk
Weller, C. (2016). The world's first artificially intelligent lawyer was just hired at a law firm. *Business Insider*. Retrieved from http://goo.gl/GhZHFr
Wiseman, O. (2017) The AI with an intuition, "AlphaGo" has defeated the human champion of the world's most complex game by speculating about the future. *Prime Mind*. Retrieved from http://goo.gl/ugGw5l

Philip Butler is a constructive neurospiritual scholar who engages Black liberation through transhumanist and posthumanist lenses. He is the lead researcher for the Center for Embodied Compassion. He received his PhD from Claremont School of Theology. He received his M.Div. from Candler School of Theology, in ethics and church history, and his BA in religion from Morehouse College.

15

One Bright Byte: Dōgen and the Re-embodiment of Digital Technologies

David Casacuberta

Res Cogitans in Western Culture

Our current vision on how digital apps should be developed and distributed is based on a series of false dichotomies. One of the most relevant and problematic is the idea that in order to understand human beings, one of the first methodological steps to take is to separate mental and bodily activities. This is not just a common scientific protocol to practice reductive neuroscience, but also a popular understanding to describe how humans behave, derived from Enlightenment philosophy.

In a nutshell it goes like this: first, we have ideas generated by the brain, and then the body obeys such ideas as if they were instructions. For example, my body needs water, so it sends some signal to the brain, and that signal is converted into the thought "I am thirsty." The brain scans memories to check whether there is a source of water nearby. It remembers that there was a half full bottle on a table to my left, so it first sends another signal to my head to turn, eyes sends more signals, so that the

D. Casacuberta (✉)
Universitat Autònoma de Barcelona, Barcelona, Spain

V.M.B. Giorgino, Z. Walsh (eds.), *Co-Designing Economies in Transition*,
https://doi.org/10.1007/978-3-319-66592-4_15

brain detects the bottle, and then the brain sends another signal to the hand to grab it. Finally, I drink from the bottle until I am satisfied and then the brain sends another signal to leave the bottle on the table again.

What we have here is a protocol where our self is like a sort of pilot using our body as a sort of vehicle to make things happen in the world. The analytic philosopher Gilbert Ryle captured such a metaphysical protocol with his well-known metaphor "ghost in the machine." However, this idea of a disembodied self is much, much older. Descartes developed such a position (Descartes & Sutcliffe, 1968) in a very successful way. In his search for absolute truths, Descartes started to doubt everything he knew and perceived to see if he could find some truth that was certain. So, following Descartes' stance, I can doubt whether the computer in which I am typing this right now exists or whether the hands that seem to be doing the typing exist. I can also doubt the existence of any other person that might read these words, but I cannot doubt that I exist. I think therefore I am: *Cogito ergo sum*. It is the next deduction by Descartes which interests us most. He asked himself the following question: Although I do exist, what am I really? And his answer was: I am a thing that thinks, a *res cogitans*.

This is his argument in broad terms: I can doubt about the real existence of my body, but I can't doubt the existence of my mind; therefore, the mind has to be completely independent from the body. We usually quote Descartes when presenting this assumption, because he was able to organize an argument in such an elegant and simple way. However, we can track this very idea back to Plato, which pervades Western culture, as well as our ideas about spiritual development, once it gained popularity among Christian thinkers who developed theological movements separating the body and soul (Bynum, 1995; Cooper, 2000).

Modern and postmodern, liberal and conservative twenty-first-century Western citizens are not above such considerations. Despite the fact that we now consider ourselves materialists and monists—in other words, we believe that there is no *res cogitans* and that everything which exists is material—we still conceive of the mind in opposition to the body. We see this demonstrated, for instance, in how popular science describes the advancement of neuroscience and the way we design tools and utensils.

The Disembodiment of Digital Technologies

This paradigm forms the foundation of how the internet and other related digital technologies were invented, coded, and used, in contradistinction to centuries old analog technologies, like hammers, pencils, or stone axes, which were made to be gripped directly by the hand, with no need for a mind separated from the body to make sense of the instrument. In *Being and Time*, Martin Heidegger (Heidegger, 1977) discussed at length how utensils were used in a pre-reflective manner. The ecological psychologist James J. Gibson (Gibson, 1979, 1982) coined the term "affordance" to defend a more inclusive way to understand the relationship between tools, the body, and the mind. Despite such philosophical efforts from Western thinkers of the twentieth century, it is not difficult to detect such a mind–body dichotomy in all that surrounds digital technologies. Our electronic gadgets and interfaces are designed with a *res cogitans* in mind.

Let's consider the World Wide Web. During the 1970s and 1980s, the internet was used for exchanging straightforward scientific communications between universities (Leiner et al., 2009). However, when digital technologies gained popularity among the general public, one of people's main interests concerned the possibility of disembodiment. In cyberspace, you could be whatever you wanted. The first entertainment platforms, the Multi User Dungeons (MUDs), attracted people by affording them the opportunity to be someone else. Sherry Turkle (1995) described at length the phenomenon and discussed some of its psychological implications. During the last decade of the twentieth century, the main source of internet entertainment was using MUDs and chatrooms to pretend to be someone else using text only. A fifty-year-old, balding, and divorced man could become an eighteen-year-old, lesbian; a serious literature professor could turn into an eight feet tall troll; and an old lady could spend most of her leisure time as a loving and furry teddy bear. The cartoon "On the internet, nobody knows you're a dog" depicts a dog standing on two legs while typing on a keyboard. It captured the zeitgeist and was frequently quoted in the early days of the World Wide Web (Palacios, 2011).

This idea was rapidly adopted by science-fiction writers. In the novel Neuromancer, William Gibson imagined a hacker that hates his body, and is only happy when he is connected to cyberspace (a term actually coined in the novel). He considers eating and bodily functions to be a chore (Gibson, 1984). In a more ironic way, Neal Stephenson developed a similar idea in a very detailed virtual world called The Metaverse, in which millions of people spend their leisure time, preferring it to the "real world" (Porush, 1994; Stephenson, 1992).

The idea of using the internet to become a disembodied self was rapidly adopted by contemporary artists, especially those coming from the world of performance art, who pursued the goal of giving the world "disembodied art." The book *Escape Velocity* (Dery, 1996) described the movement in detail, presenting both its history and evolution, as well as its philosophical foundations. One of the major artists in the movement is the Australian performer Stelarc. He started his artistic career as an endurance body artist, and was one of the first to play with the idea of a disembodied self, cyborgs, and bio-art. In one of his performances, he connected his legs and arms to electrical stimulators. Then those stimulators were fed with data from World Wide Web traffic. In a weird and poetic way, Stelarc's body adopted bizarre positions that were visualizations of what thousands of people were doing in the internet at that moment. Most of his art projects were built around his famous motto "The Body is Obsolete" (Smith, 2005; Zylinska, 2002). Following the zeitgeist, other performance or visual artists, as well as musicians and even fashion designers took this idea seriously and tried to create art from the perspective of disembodied experience (Borst, 2009; Stallabrass, 1997).

Later, the idea took shape in political utopias, when people began to dream of living in disembodied societies. Without a doubt, the most relevant text expressing this new direction was the Independence Declaration of Cyberspace by John Perry Barlow (Barlow, 1996). In his manifesto, Barlow presented the internet as a new frontier, a pure digital space, just a click away from the miseries of the brick and mortar world. In such a brave new world, everybody could be what they wanted to be, and governments had no role, because people would be able to create their own laws. It was conceived as a real anarchist utopia inside your personal computer (Zalenski, 2002).

Despite the fact that this started as the project of a few activists, it won over the hearts and minds of companies, institutions, and individuals at the dawn of the twenty-first century. Consider, for instance, the virtual world Second Life. It was launched in 2003 by Linden Labs, and after a few months, everybody talked about Second Life, and how soon everything would take place in that virtual world (Warburton, 2009). Companies, universities, research centers, and professionals spent large, sometimes even obscene amounts of money to build replicas of their centers in Second Life (Boellstorff, 2015). The popular press devoted a lot of its coverage describing how people were actually making a living designing and creating spaces for Second Life. It was like Stephenson's Metaverse, but without the irony.

This first radical paradigm of disembodiment started to fade as the idea of e-commerce developed (Krishnamurthy, 2002), and the World Wide Web became a place to take care of our daily affairs, like buying books, finding hotels, or meeting our high school friends on social networks. Digital technologies are no longer focused on building virtual, new worlds, but about connecting to online devices (Rogers, 2009). Now, previous ideas about disembodied selves and societies are less relevant and tend to be derided. We are proud to state that we left behind the metaphors of a virtual world and joined the "online" paradigm, which considers digital technologies as a means to interact with the real world, and not a tool to build a digital utopia.

Nevertheless, I want to argue that the main model driving how digital apps are designed is still a disembodied one. In order to show it, I'd like to describe how productivity tools are designed, from the initial development to the related hardware.

There are two main models for designing productivity tools: first there is a more scientific approach under the concept of quantified self. The methodology behind the quantified self (Swan, 2013) movement is also deeply Cartesian. According to such a paradigm, we unfortunately don't have as much control as we'd like to have with our body, because we don't have enough information about what we are consuming, how fast we run, how long we have been walking, our heartbeat rate, or the glucose level in our bloodstream. However, when the proper sensor is added and it is linked to some mobile device, we can have this information in real time and plan our actions accordingly. The ghost in the machine now has complete information and does not have to trust its senses, which, Descartes taught us, cannot be trusted.

Then there is a less scientific, more intuitive approach called "lifehacking." "Lifehackers"—people who devise tricks to become more competitive, productive, and successful in life (Trapani, 2008)—present advice like listening to podcasts while you commute and, more worryingly, to read blogposts with your tablet while you wait for your microwave to ping (Vanderkam, 2012). The message is troubling: do not miss any opportunity to be productive, no matter where you are.

Interfaces are also moving toward a disembodied paradigm. Let's consider all the hype and the hope surrounding text interfaces (Pierce, 2015). Programmers and venture capitalists in Silicon Valley are elated with the idea that graphical interfaces are going to disappear and be substituted with plain text interfaces in which you'll type or talk in plain English, expressing what you want so that the program follows your instructions, delivering your Uber ride, a pair of blue suede shoes from Zalando, or the pilot of that series everybody is talking about nowadays.

And hardware is also presented within this disembodied paradigm. Consider how Microsoft announced their new Surface tablets. In a very geeky campaign using stylish infographics, it suggested how great it was to be able to work while on vacation, watching your children playing, taking a vermouth with your spouse or even in the bathroom. The message was clear: thanks to digital technologies, you can overcome such nuisances like physiological necessities, holidays, family, or even space, in order to be more productive and innovative. Every second of your life can be working time if you want it to be.

And that disembodiment moves actually beyond digital technologies per se and can be seen even in food design. A good example is Soylent—the food product that guarantees you can have all your necessary nutrients to keep you healthy just by adding some powder to a drink (Carolan, 2011; Hurley, 2008). No need to lose your precious time buying vegetables, fish, or meat, cooking them, and then washing the dishes. The kitchen is obsolete, Stelarc would have said. According to Silicon Valley lore, the inventors decided to create the product when discovering that a fellow programmer had scurvy due to a diet of just coffee, coke, delivered pizzas, and instant noodles.

It is not difficult to see Descartes' influence informing such ideas: our brain generates an idea, the computer receives our thoughts as instructions and acts accordingly. No need to physically engage with the computer in any way. No need for a non-representational, intuitive practice to make sense of what we can do with a specific interface. No affordances to create specific ways to interact with humans and machines (Aubé, 2015).

The Law of Amplification

Of course, digital apps are not responsible for their Cartesian bias, but they are not neutral either. In his book *Geek Heresy*, Kentaro Toyama coins the expression "amplification law" to describe the social effects of digital tools, arguing that social problems cannot be solved by technological means alone (Toyama, 2015). The amplification law states that digital technologies only take aspects of human behavior that already exist and help amplify them. This contrasts with the idea of technological determinism (Smith & Marx, 1994)—the view that technological inventions such as the printing press or mobile phones cause humans to change their behavior as a means of adapting to technologies.

To illustrate these contrasting ideas, consider the selfie (snapshots of oneself taken by a mobile phone and usually shared on social networks). Some thinkers like to believe we must blame our obsession with selfies on digital mobile technologies. However, if we consider Toyama's amplification law, we realize that humans have always been narcissistic. The reason selfies were not common before was because taking selfies was not that easy. In the past, selfies were only available to talented painters or their rich sponsors and clients. When analog cameras were invented, taking pictures were likewise expensive, and you had no indication of how the snapshot would look before you developed it. However, now that mobile phones with selfie sticks make it extremely easy to take self-portraits, they amplify our natural desire to do so.

One common denominator among all the examples described above (lifehackers, Soylent, the Surface campaign, etc.…) is the need for time management. Time is something far away from us—a limited resource we need to control, so we must master it. But, is this true? Should this be the way we as humans interact with time? And, more broadly, should all digital technologies be disembodied?

Dōgen's Practical Philosophy

Fortunately, we have several alternative paradigms. Key philosophers and thinkers of the last century have been frequently arguing against disembodiment. We have already mentioned James J. Gibson and his ecological perspective, as well as Martin Heidegger. In *Being and Time*, he argued that our human understanding of time is very different from the way that physics analyzes time. Other phenomenologists like Merleau-Ponty challenged the ghost in the machine metaphor in his *Phenomenology of Perception* (Merleau-Ponty & Smith, 1996). There are also alternative interpretations on how the body and digital technologies must interact based on Donna Haraway's seminal research on cyborgs (Haraway, 1987), which has become a hot subject in gender studies (Lykke & Braidotti, 1996; Pilcher & Whelehan, 2004).

For this chapter, however, I'd like to build my argument from an Eastern perspective: the philosophy of Eihei Dōgen. Dōgen was a Japanese philosopher and theologian of the thirteenth century who, dissatisfied with the idea of Buddhism that was taught in his country, traveled to China to find Ch'an Buddhism, which later developed into the Soto school of Zen Buddhism—now a common school of Buddhism in the West.

At first look, the main problem that Dōgen faced seems like a technical question about Buddhism. It is usually expressed in the following terms: If everybody has Buddha Nature, that is, if everybody is already enlightened, then what is the point in practicing? Why spend so many hours every day in seated meditation? However, when one digs deeper we find a phenomenologist avant la lettre who shared Heidegger's main question: what does it mean to exist? (Heine, 1985)

Our main source for Dōgen's thought is the *Shōbōgenzō*, a book that collects 95 fascicles devoted to many different subjects (Dogen & Tanahashi, 2011). There are several hermeneutical texts trying to discern the ultimate meaning of a specific sutra (Buddhist sacred text), as well as complex metaphysical discussions about what time or Buddha nature is. But, somewhat perplexing for a Western mind, those texts about abstract discussions share space with very practical instructions on how monks should properly dress and on the Buddhist way to clean yourself when you go to the restroom.

Dōgen's message is clear. His philosophy is a practical one, and it is designed to cover all aspects of our life. For Dōgen, every moment in our life, every person, animal, plant or object is sacred and deserves our respect. Dōgen's understanding was advanced for his time (Curtin, 1994). His text "Prostrating to that which has attained the marrow" is a very modern defense of the equality between men and women. It offers acerbic criticism toward the misogynistic Buddhist authors who said that women were inferior beings that couldn't be enlightened (Butnor, 2014). Now, we need to engage Heidegger and Merleau-Ponty from the twentieth century in order to find similar interpretations of existence, time, or the relationship between the body and mind.

Dōgen's solution to the supposedly technical problem I mentioned above—why do we need to practice if we are already enlightened—is Awakening. Awakening is not something that we train in order to get one day, like a bodybuilder lifting weights in order to develop better muscles; rather, it is a state that we reach in the moment that we practice. When we do zazen (sitting meditation), we are already enlightened. That is because, while in zazen, we watch our thoughts without taking them seriously, without having to react to them. We forget our habits and prejudices and so we are one with reality. We are one with our surroundings and our time, without judging it, just accepting it as it is and staying in touch with it (Kim & Leighton, 2004).

Dōgen applies this idea of enactive existence to both practical and philosophical problems. In *Shoaku Makusa* (*On not doing wrong*), Dōgen argues that good and bad do not actually exist as separate things or essences. What we have is people who do good in a given moment, while others do bad. Being awakened just means recognizing that we don't have a good or bad nature, but that we are what we do (we enact reality), and what we do in the present moment is the only thing that counts (Fox, 1971).

The idea that the mind is the only thing that matters was a common idea in Japanese Buddhism during Dōgen's time, and it is still a common Western interpretation of what Buddhism is about. In contrast to this idea and to its reinstantiation in the ghost in the machine metaphor, Dōgen argued that how we use our body is as important as what we think. Body and mind form a unity. You can't understand one without the other. Addressing subjects that were first analyzed by Merleau-Ponty and then by enactivist philosophers like Evan Thompson (2007) or Alva Nöe (2004), Dōgen argued that to properly understand the relationship between the body and mind, one has to consider the surroundings in which the action takes place or, as Dōgen more poetically says: when the mind and the body does zazen, the whole universe does zazen too.

As his commentary about the Heart Sutra makes perfectly clear, we are not talking here about an abstract, intellectual, philosophical understanding of such ideas; rather, we are discussing an experiential, intuitive access to such truths. Like Heidegger in *Being and Time*, Dōgen views a human being as a creature that lives their life from a pre-reflective perspective, not as a rational being processing everything using reason and logic.

In his poetic text the *Genjokoan*, Dōgen evokes the spirit of Heidegger's famous simile of the hammer that repairs the roof of a log cabin. He argues that the only place in which things really happen is the present. Understanding the world is not a conceptual venture. It is a continuous process of being always in direct contact with the present moment, with what is happening now.

Perhaps Dōgen's most Heideggerian text is *Uji*, which literally means "being-time." In Japanese, *uji* usually means "sometimes," but it is written with the characters for being and time, and Dōgen uses the coincidence of terms to develop his conception of time. In contrast to our idea of physical time which we feel we need to master, Dōgen says that time and existence are the same. When you feel as happy as a Buddha or as angry as a demon, Dōgen says, that is time. For Dōgen there is only this moment. Time is just this moment, and the only thing that matters is how we enact such moments. Understanding that time and existence are the same is, for Dōgen, the same as being awake (Heine, 1985; Raud, 2012). When one reaches that state, there is real understanding. "The way the self arrays itself is the form of the entire word. See each thing in this entire world as a moment of time" (Dogen & Tanahashi, 2011).

What keep us from awakening—or per a secular reading, what keeps us from being a complete human being—is the fact that we consider time and existence as something separated. We view time like space. We crossed rivers and mountains years ago, says Dōgen, and now we reside in an impressive palace and see those moments crossing mountains as alien to us. But, Dōgen says, there is a lot more: "At the time the mountains were climbed and the rivers were crossed, you were present. Time is not separate from you, and as you are present, time does not go away" (Dogen & Tanahashi, 2011).

Dōgen also argues that there are no essential, supramundane beings or time beyond our current events. In an elegant metaphor, he compares it to a spring. Spring flows as flowers bloom and the days get longer, but there is no separate "springness" that takes care of the world and is infused in plants and trees so they become "spring." Spring is nothing more and nothing else than leaves sprouting, flowers blooming, snow melting and days getting longer and warmer.

Fake Alternatives

One could argue that we have advanced far beyond Descartes in our understanding. We live in a society that considers itself scientific. We don't believe in ghosts. It is the brain that thinks, everything is material, and anything that exists in the world is subject to the laws of physics. There is no room in the twenty-first century for a *res cogitans* that is not affected by the material world. Paraphrasing Madonna, we could say that "we are living in a material world and I am a material being."

But, is that really so? We might have discarded the illusion of dualistic ontology, but we haven't abandoned some of its major conclusions, like the idea that the mind/brain thinks and that the body obeys. It doesn't matter that we now reduce the mind to matter (the brain). There is still a functional dualism between the mind that thinks and the body that follows commands.

Neither philosophers nor neurologists are free of such delusions. Consider, for example, the popular argument against free will inspired by the Libet experiment (Libet, 1985). In a Libet type experiment, researchers get several volunteers to have their brains scanned as they undertake some menial task. For instance, an experimental subject may be invited to raise her hand whenever she feels like it. Consistently, results showed that the brain scanner indicated the part of the brain responsible for the motor system—that is, responsible to move the hand—had already been activated before the person said they decided to raise their hand. So, the argument states, free will is an illusion, the brain had already sent the signal to raise the hand before the person "decided" to do so.

There is still a lot of discussion about the real significance of such an argument (Dennett, 2014; Mele, 2008), though I don't want to discuss it here. What I want to point out is how this argument, coming from supposedly rational, materialist neurologists, is based on Descartes' dichotomy: there is a mind that thinks and a body that obeys. This argument against free will only holds if we adhere to such a simplistic explanation of what the mind is and how it works.

We can also see the dichotomy working in what David Chalmers called the hard problem (Chalmers, 1995): how can we scientifically study the subjective states of mind related to *qualia*, such as flavors or colors. Thomas Nagel captured this paradox in an elegant way in his famous paper "What is it like to be a bat" (Nagel, 1974). Nagel says, we can study a bat from a physiological point of view, and discover everything about the physics of bat sounds, how they ricochet against walls and trees, and how such sound waves affect the perceptive system of the bat. Still, we won't know anything about how the bat perceives the world, or about what it is like to be a bat.

Consider how this is a "hard problem" only inasmuch as we think of the mind and body as separate structures. If we accept, as we saw in Dōgen, that thinking is a process that implies a mind/brain, a body, and certain surroundings, then the mystery rapidly dissolves. We can't know how it feels to be a bat, because we are not bats. Period. Yes, it is that simple. We make it complicated. The only way to solve the "problem" is to realize that it was only a problem because the premises we used defined it as such. The solution, as Wittgenstein famously stated in his *Philosophical Investigations*, is to show the fly the way out of the fly-bottle (Wittgenstein & Anscombe, 1953).

How to Re-embody Our Digital Technologies

Some solutions and critiques to technological determinism propose fake alternatives, which even if they deny the model itself, do not challenge the main conclusions produced by it. See, for example, Wyatt (2007) on how technological determinism is present in most criticisms on the social effects of digital technologies. I do agree with the main critiques that Keen (2015), Morozov (2012), Pariser (2011) or Carr (2011) present to technological determinism, but when they propose solutions, those solutions still fall within the framework proposed by techno-utopists.

That means that both technological determinists and their critics accept that digital technologies are disruptive entities that are transforming our lives, but what they don't agree upon is how to value their consequences. The belief in technological determinism creates utopians, like Perry Barlow, who consider that such social transformations will be good for humanity. Critics, on the other hand, think exactly the opposite. Therefore, most solutions proposed by techno-critics like Morozov, Pariser, or Carr are either about tinkering with digital technologies, transforming them toward more humanistic aims, or just outright banning them.

In any case, this is inconsistent with a critique of technological determinism. The correct answer has to be based on the law of amplification I described above. Digital technologies do not create new social rules and frameworks. Instead, they just help to amplify social tendencies that are already present in human societies. If we want to address the harmful effects of digital technologies, first we need some consensus on whether they are really that bad. Second, we need to address the social trend that is amplified by digital technologies and find some social, political, and economic measures to reduce it. If we modify Twitter in order to make life a lot harder for trolls, we may help Twitter attain a better public image, which may help increase its stock exchange value, but it won't get rid of trolls. They will just move somewhere else to troll. We have to address trolling itself.

Why Dōgen?

Probably you are wondering why I brought a medieval Japanese monk back from the grave to discuss digital technologies. One of the reasons is that Dōgen is not that well known in philosophical circles, and I think that is really a shame. Dōgen's *Shōbōgenzō* has been largely forgotten for centuries. From the thirteenth to the seventeenth centuries, it laid unread in Soto Zen monasteries unnoticed to the rest of the world. In the eighteenth century, when the Japanese government, inspired by the West, forced every religion in the country to have a book as a basis for their religion, the Soto sect chose *Shōbōgenzō*. However, they required the Japanese government to keep it a secret book, such that Soto monks were the only people allowed to interpret the text. As a result, the text was not known even by the Japanese public until the twentieth century when the prohibition was finally lifted.

At the same time, Dōgen's thinking was too advanced for his time, presenting a holistic philosophical system that combined practical and theoretical reasoning. It was very poetic and full of obscure metaphors. He also practiced pre-Joyce style games with words, jumping from Japanese to Chinese without warning, eliminating verbs from a sentence, using the radicals of an ideogram to make a common word to mean something completely different,[1] that way forcing the structure and meaning of language to transmit a new view of how to use language to transmit knowledge (Kim & Leighton, 2004). The main reason I decided to use Dōgen was precisely because his concerns and proposals had nothing to do with technology. The fact that the reflections of a Japanese monk in the thirteenth century can shed some light on understanding the major assumptions informing how we design and use mobile phones, time management software, or superfoods in order to minimize the time we spend eating, clearly shows that the problem is not technology, but our social habits.

We won't become any more mindful, if we just remove the Facebook app from our mobile phones. Banning Apple Pay won't help us redistribute the millions of surplus dollars that the 1% unfairly obtained and that the 99% deserve. That has already happened. When the teenagers of the anorexic pride movement found it difficult to distribute their pictures and memes in one social network, they just moved to another one.

In his poetic and moving text *One Bright Pearl* (Ikka Myoju), Dōgen tries to transmit a holistic understanding of the world where everything is interconnected and causality is described a systemic property of the whole, co-dependent apparition. In classical Buddhist terms: "this arises, that becomes." To do so he states that our lives, the whole universe is just one bright pearl, even if we don't realize it. Apps like Twitter, Instagram or Secret are One Bright Pearl. Websites such as DeviantArt, change.org, or Breitbart News are also One Bright Pearl. Improving the filters or the interface won't change a bit the social realities that make them possible. If we want to re-embody our digital technologies and help to improve and develop the better angels of our nature, we need to transform our social, economic, and political habits. That's why we wrote this book: to present a blueprint for change, to show that another world is possible.

Notes

1. For example, 有 時 (uji) en Japanese is a common word and it means "sometimes," but Dogen uses it in a way that the reader needs to read it literally as "being-time."

References

Aubé, T. (2015). *No UI is the new UI*. medium.com. Retrieved from https://medium.com/swlh/no-ui-is-the-new-ui-ab3f7ecec6b3#.fdxs12yrz (Last visit 15-06-2017).

Barlow, J. P. (1996). *A declaration of the independence of cyberspace*. Retrieved from https://www.eff.org/es/cyberspace-independence (Last visit 15-06-2017).

Boellstorff, T. (2015). *Coming of age in Second Life: An anthropologist explores the virtually human*. Princeton, NJ: Princeton University Press.

Borst, E. M. (2009). *Cyborg art: An explorative and critical inquiry into corporeal human-technology convergence*. Thesis, Doctor of Philosophy (PhD), The University of Waikato, Hamilton, New Zealand. Retrieved from http://hdl.handle.net/10289/3976 (Last visit 15-06-2017).

Butnor, A. (2014). Dōgen, feminism, and the embodied practice of care. In J. McWeeny & A. Butnor (Eds.), *Asian and feminist philosophies in dialogue: Liberating traditions*. New York: Columbia University Press.

Bynum, C. W. (1995). *The resurrection of the body in Western Christianity, 200–1336*. Lectures on the history of religions No. 15. Columbia University Press.

Carolan, M. S. (2011). *Embodied food politics*. Farnham: Ashgate Publishing Ltd.

Carr, N. (2011). *The shallows: What the Internet is doing to our brains*. London: W. W. Norton & Company.

Chalmers, D. J. (1995). Facing up to the problem of consciousness. *Journal of Consciousness Studies, 2*(3), 200–219.

Cooper, J. W. (2000). *Body, soul, and life everlasting: Biblical anthropology and the monism-dualism debate*. Grand Rapids, MI: Wm. B. Eerdmans Publishing.

Curtin, D. (1994). Dōgen, deep ecology, and the ecological self. *Environmental Ethics, 16*(2), 195–213.

Dennett, D. C. (2014). Chapter VIII: Tools for thinking about free will. In *Intuition pumps and other tools for thinking*. New York: W. W. Norton & Company.

Dery, M. (1996). *Escape velocity: Cyberculture at the end of the century*. New York: Grove Press.

Descartes, R., & Sutcliffe, F. (Trans.). (1968). *Discourse on method and the meditations*. London: Penguin.

Dogen, E., & Tanahashi, K. (Trans.). (2011). *Treasury of the true dharma eye: Zen Master Dogen's Shobo Genzo*. Boston, MA: Shambhala Publications.

Fox, D. A. (1971). Zen and ethics: Dōgen's synthesis. *Philosophy East and West, 21*(1), 33–41.

Gibson, J. J. (1979). *The ecological approach to visual perception*. Boston: Houghton Mifflin.

Gibson, J. J. (1982). A preliminary description and classification of affordances. In E. S. Reed & R. Jones (Eds.), *Reasons for realism* (Chap. 4.9, Part II, pp. 403–406). Hillsdale, NJ: Lawrence Erlbaum Associates, Inc.

Gibson, W. (1984). *Neuromancer*. New York: Ace Books.
Haraway, D. (1987). A manifesto for cyborgs: Science, technology, and socialist feminism in the 1980s. *Australian Feminist Studies, 2*(4), 1–42.
Heidegger, M. (1977). *Sein und Zeit*. Tübingen, Germany: Max Niemeyer.
Heine, S. (1985). *Existential and ontological dimensions of time in Heidegger and Dogen*. New York: SUNY Press.
Hurley, K. (2008). Food in the future: Does futures studies have a role to play? *Futures, 40*(7), 698–701.
Keen, A. (2015). *Internet is not the answer*. New York: Atlantic Monthly Press.
Kim, H. J., & Leighton, T. D. (2004). *Eihei Dogen: Mystical realist*. Simon and Schuster.
Krishnamurthy, S. (2002). *E-commerce management: Text and cases*. South-Western Thomson Learning.
Leiner, B. M., Cerf, V. G., Clark, D. D., Kahn, R. E., Kleinrock, L., Lynch, D. C., et al. (2009). A brief history of the Internet. ACM SIGCOMM *Computer Communication Review, 39*(5), 22–31.
Libet, B. (1985). Unconscious cerebral initiative and the role of conscious will in voluntary action. *The Behavioral and Brain Sciences, 8*, 529–566.
Lykke, N., & Braidotti, R. (1996). *Between monsters, goddesses, and cyborgs feminist confrontations with science, medicine, and cyberspace*. London: Zed Books.
Mele, A. R. (2008). Psychology and free will: A commentary. In J. Baer, J. C. Kaufman, & R. F. Baumeister (Eds.), *Are we free? Psychology and free will* (pp. 325–346). New York: Oxford University Press.
Merleau-Ponty, M., & Smith, C. (Trans.). (1996). *Phenomenology of perception*. Delhi: Motilal Banarsidass.
Morozov, E. (2012). *The net delusion: The dark side of Internet freedom*. New York: PublicAffairs.
Nagel, T. (1974). What is it like to be a bat? *The Philosophical Review, 83*(4), 435–450.
Noë, A. (2004). *Action in perception*. Cambridge, MA: MIT Press.
Palacios, M. (2011). Building accountable media cultures: Some peculiarities of media accountability in digital environments. In *Communication and citizenship: Rethinking crisis and change*. Braga: University of Minho.
Pariser, E. (2011). *The filter bubble: What the Internet is hiding from you*. New York, UK: Penguin.
Pierce, D. (2015). We are on the brink of a revolution in crazy-smart digital assitants. *Wired*. Retrieved from https://www.wired.com/2015/09/voice-interface-ios/ (Last visit 15-06-2017).

Pilcher, J., & Whelehan, I. (2004). *50 key concepts in gender studies*. London, UK: Sage.
Porush, D. (1994). Hacking the brainstem: Postmodern metaphysics and Stephenson's SnowCrash. *Configurations, 2*(3), 537–571.
Raud, R. (2012). The existential moment: Rereading Dōgen's theory of time. *Philosophy East and West, 62*(2), 153–173.
Rogers, R. (2009). *The end of the virtual: Digital methods*. Amsterdam: Amsterdam University Press.
Ryle, G. (1949). *The concept of mind*. New York: Barnes and Noble.
Smith, M. (2005). *Stelarc: The monograph*. Cambridge, MA: MIT Press.
Smith, M. R., & Marx, L. (1994). *Does technology drive history?: The dilemma of technological determinism*. Cambridge, MA: MIT Press.
Stallabrass, J. (1997). Money, disembodied art, and the turing test for aesthetics. In S. Buck-Morris & J. Stallabrass (Eds.), *Ground control: Technology and utopia* (pp. 62–111). London: Black Dog.
Stephenson, N. (1992). *Snow Crash*. New York: Bantam Books.
Swan, M. (2013). The quantified self: Fundamental disruption in big data science and biological discovery. *Big Data, 1*(2), 85–99.
Thompson, E. (2007). *Mind in life*. Cambridge, MA: Harvard University Press.
Toyama, K. (2015). *Geek Heresy*. New York: PublicAffairs.
Trapani, G. (2008). *Upgrade your life: The lifehacker guide to working smarter, faster, better*. John Wiley & Sons.
Turkle, S. (1995). *Life on the screen: Identity in the age of the Internet*. New York: Simon & Schuster.
Vanderkam, L. (2012). *168 hours: You have more time than you think*. New York: Portfolio.
Warburton, S. (2009). Second life in higher education: Assessing the potential for and the barriers to deploying virtual worlds in learning and teaching. *British Journal of Educational Technology, 40*(3), 414–426.
Wittgenstein, L., & Anscombe, G. E. M. (Trans.). (1953). *Philosophical investigations*. Blackwell.
Wyatt, S. (2007). Technological determinism is dead; long live technological determinism. In E. J. Hackett, O. Amsterdamksa, J. Wajcman, & M. Lynch (Eds.), *The handbook of science and technology studies* (pp. 165–180). Cambridge, MA: MIT Press.
Zaleski, J. P. (2002). *The soul of cyberspace*. HarperCollins Publishers.
Zylinska, J. (Ed.). (2002). *The cyborg experiments: The extensions of the body in the media age*. A&C Black.

David Casacuberta, PhD, is a philosophy of science professor at the Universidad Autònoma de Barcelona, Spain. His line of research is the social, cultural, and cognitive effects of digital technologies in order to state ethical protocols to detect and avoid inequalities and discriminations generated by such technologies. The general framework for such research is enactivism combined with classical Eastern philosophy, especially Zen Buddhism. Born in 1967, he lives in Barcelona with his wife and two children.

Index[1]

[1] Note: Page number followed by 'n' refers to notes.

V.M.B. Giorgino, Z. Walsh (eds.), *Co-Designing Economies in Transition*, https://doi.org/10.1007/978-3-319-66592-4

Z

The manufacturer's authorised representative in the EU is Springer Nature Customer Service Centre GmbH, Europaplatz 3, 69115 Heidelberg, Germany. If you have any concerns regarding our products, please contact ProductSafety@springernature.com

Printed and bound by CPI Group (UK) Ltd, Croydon, CR0 4YY
25/09/2026
02222894-0004